ON THE ROCKETSHIP

ON THE ROCKETSHIP

How Top Charter Schools Are Pushing the Envelope

RICHARD WHITMIRE

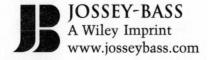
JOSSEY-BASS
A Wiley Imprint
www.josseybass.com

Copyright © 2014 by Richard Whitmire. All rights reserved.
Published by Jossey-Bass
A Wiley Brand
One Montgomery Street, Suite 1200, San Francisco, CA 94104-4594
www.josseybass.com

Library of Congress Cataloging-in-Publication Data

Whitmire, Richard.
  On the rocketship : how top charter schools are pushing the envelope/Richard Whitmire. —
First edition.
     pages cm
  Includes bibliographical references and index.
  ISBN 978-1-118-60764-0 (hardback) — ISBN 978-1-118-61126-5 (pdf) —
ISBN 978-1-118-61133-3 (epub)
  1. Charter schools—United States.   2. Charter schools—Wisconsin—Milwaukee—Case
studies.   I. Title.
  LB2806.36.W545 2014
  371.050973—dc23

                                                                              2014006767

Printed in the United States of America
FIRST EDITION
HB Printing   10   9   8   7   6   5   4   3   2   1

To the true disruptors: Rocketship parents pressing for better middle schools and high schools

CONTENTS

PART IV: THE PUSH TO EXPAND OUTSIDE SAN JOSE

PART V: THE FUTURE FOR ROCKETSHIP AND OTHER HIGH PERFORMERS

Introduction

The "Fibonacci sequence" certainly sounds intriguing, possibly because of the mystery-cracking role it played in *The Da Vinci Code*. In truth, it is more math trick than mystery. Named after an Italian mathematician who wrote about it in a book published in 1202, the Fibonacci sequence presents young students with a fun exercise. You start with 0, then 1, and then add up the two numbers before it. Here's how it plays out: 0, 1, 1, 2, 3, 5, 8, 13, 21, 34, 55, 89, 144, 233, 377, 610 (and so on). Watching the numbers soar is what surprises students.

John Danner, forty-six,[1] a Stanford-educated electrical engineer who cofounded NetGravity, an early pioneer in Internet advertising, raised the Fibonacci sequence in our first meeting as a way of explaining the exponential growth he planned for his Rocketship charter elementary schools. A steady launch cycle of adding new cities every year, with each city sprouting at least eight Rocketship schools, meant that within thirty years it should be possible to launch 2,500 Rocketship schools around the country. Why 2,500? Because by Danner's math (he calculates there are roughly thirteen thousand schools that fall in the "failing" category), it would take that many Rocketship schools educating a million students to make a dent in reducing the nation's steep achievement gaps between have and have-not students.

Few startup guys (and I use "guy" throughout the book as a mindset, not a gender designation) have failed to read the gospel-like *The Innovator's Dilemma*.[2] Author Clayton Christensen lays out the harsh rules of "disruptive innovation" that led to the shockingly fast decline of once-dominant computer maker Digital Equipment Corporation (DEC). Similar tales unfold about Sears, Xerox, and Bucyrus Erie, maker of cable-driven earth excavators that got buried by hydraulic excavators. These companies were overwhelmed by disruptive innovations that wiped out their once-profitable business lines. An updated list would include Kodak and Myspace.

When startup guys such as Danner look at public schools they see an enterprise far less nimble and well run than Bucyrus Erie or DEC. It's hard to argue with their logic, especially considering that most schools appear to be frozen in time, using the same school hours, classroom design, and instructional methods they have for decades. Most school curriculum is still built around the instructional units prescribed in 1906 by the Carnegie Foundation for the Advancement of Teaching. It's not as though schools are doing well despite their endearingly familiar but antiquated structure: about a third of the 2013 high school graduates who took the ACT tests, nearly all of them students planning to go to college, were not prepared for college-level writing, biology, algebra, or social studies, reported the testing company. The College Board reported even more dismal findings from the SAT: 57 percent were not prepared for college. Many white suburban parents appear to believe that the problem lies with only poor and minority students in the cities, but international test comparisons say that's false: the PISA[3] tests released in December 2013 showed that since 2009 teenagers in the United States fell from twenty-fifth to thirty-first in math, from twentieth to twenty-fourth in science, and from eleventh to twenty-first in reading. In that comparison, our wealthy students from families in the top quartile fell behind similarly well-off students in other countries. You might as well list public schools as the first entry in *Wikipedia* to define "smokestack" industry: one ripe for disruption. And yet, that has not happened. By comparison with public schools, Bucyrus Erie's cable-driven excavators look like Ferraris.

Where, the startup guys ask, are the disruptive innovations that should have toppled outdated school models long ago? The smart money in Silicon Valley bets on charter schools, which are publicly funded and independently run, as that disruptive innovation. But if the 6,500 charters now educating 2.5 million children are to be that disruption they are off to a sloppy start. Careless charter authorizers gave green lights to hundreds of charters that never had a chance to succeed. Lack of financing, poor academic vision, financial scandals—it's a long list. And then, those same authorizers balked at shutting down many of their own struggling creations. Okay, I agree, those are the bottom-feeder charter schools. But even the high-performing charters, the proven disruptors, the stars you read about posting great academic records in the worst neighborhoods (let's say the top 15 percent, the charters I will write about in this book) have until recently posted snail-like expansion track records, hobbled by the overwhelming need to raise fresh funding, an underwhelming supply of superbly talented school leaders, and a dearth of facilities to use. (Did you really expect struggling urban school districts to willingly turn over unused school buildings to charter schools that might eat their lunch?) Not exactly the stuff of which disruptive innovations are made.

Into this debate steps Danner with his vow to shrink achievement gaps by providing one million high-quality school seats. It is hard to know which of those goals was more over-the-top—launching 2,500 charter schools for those one million students or believing he could reduce the nation's achievement gaps. There are only a couple dozen elite charter group operators in the country, most of them bigger than Rocketship, and you don't hear their leaders making Dannerlike claims. As for leveling the nation's achievement gaps, that's a goal that has eluded government solutions ranging from the massive Head Start program to Title 1, programs that have pumped billions of extra federal dollars into schools serving poor kids. Why would Danner succeed when far bigger players with far deeper pockets have failed?

In this book I will tell the story of Rocketship, one high-performing charter group launched in San Jose and styled as a Silicon Valley startup, trying to do it all. Spoiler alert: they run into major turbulence and probably can't do it alone. Second spoiler alert: despite Rocketship's considerable headwinds, it is clear that Rocketship, when joined with the other high-performing charters—especially the blended learning charters that personalize learning by combining online learning with regular teacher-led instruction—have a decent shot at making Danner's dream come true. It may not play out quite the way Danner planned but in some cities it's beginning to happen. Later in the book I will visit a few of the places where these high-performing charter networks are being given opportunities to become Fibonacci schools, a term I will use for quick-growing, high-performing charter schools. As I tell the Rocketship story I'll drop in short, datelined inserts (in italics) that trace the key events in the growth of these special charter school networks, the schools that have proven they can slice deeply into the nation's education achievement gaps.[4] This phenomenon, giving the Fibonacci schools access to far more students, may be our best chance to save tens of thousands of inner city students from academic privation. And that's what the book is really about.

Notes

1. As of June 2014. Other ages in the book are pegged to the time line.
2. Boston: Harvard Business Review Press, 1997.
3. Program for International Student Assessment.
4. Other examples of high-performing charter groups that enroll high-poverty students include Aspire Public Schools, KIPP, Uncommon Schools, Achievement First, YES Prep Public Schools, Green Dot Public Schools, Mastery Charter Schools, IDEA Public Schools, Noble Network of Charter Schools, Harlem Village Academies, Brighter Choice Charter Schools, Success Academy Charter Schools, High Tech High, Synergy Academies, Alliance College-Ready Public Schools, BASIS Charter Schools, Touchstone Education, Match Education, STRIVE Preparatory Schools, and the schools run by the Denver School of Science and Technology. Here in Washington, DC, where Rocketship will open eight schools, other high-performing charters include schools such as D.C. Prep, E. L. Haynes, Achievement Preparatory Academy, Washington Latin, Two Rivers, and others. The school portfolio listings at the Charter School Growth Fund and NewSchools Venture Fund are good sources for identifying the high performers.

PART I

THE PLAYERS

ROCKETSHIP FINALLY LAUNCHES OUTSIDE CALIFORNIA

August 2013: Milwaukee, Wisconsin

This Thursday morning marks day four of the opening week for Southside Prep, Rocketship Education's first school in Milwaukee and the charter group's first launch outside its California base. A lot hinges on the success of this school, which may explain why founding principal Brittany Kinser is nervous as she prepares for her first morning coffee with parents. About forty parents, almost all of them Latinos who took a chance by enrolling their children in a little-known school, await her arrival in the cafeteria. Southside Prep opened with 270 students, a little more than 200 students short of the goal. Kinser's job this morning is to keep these parents happy and convince them to recruit their friends and relatives to switch schools and send their children here. She's about to ask the parents what they like and don't like about Rocketship's first week. It's that second question that makes her nervous.

The contrast between these Latino parents and the young, nearly all-white staff at Southside Prep, all graduates of top colleges, is stark. Kinser may be thirty-six but she looks at least a decade younger. Her quick body language and trim figure suggest that she is not just a runner, but a serious runner. Just minutes earlier at the "launch," a Rocketship tradition in which the entire school gathers each morning to chant the school's aspirational creed, hand out awards, and dance crazily to some really, really loud music, everyone gyrated to Katy Perry's "Firework," not exactly traditional school music. In tradition-bound Milwaukee, this is something different: a shot of hip California arrived in, of all places, South Side Milwaukee, a neighborhood that in just a decade flipped from Polish to Latino. And now this change, a Silicon Valley startup school located in a refurbished party props warehouse. How weird is that? Would these parents accept or reject Rocketship? Getting the Milwaukee launch off smoothly means every-thing to Rocketship. Stumble here and the stumble reverberates across the county. No wonder Kinser is nervous.

Getting to know why Kinser is nervous requires learning the Rocket-ship story, which means getting to know the founders.

JOHN DANNER

If you had to pick just two events that shaped John Danner, the first would be the day in 1978 when his father bought him an Apple II. A seventh-grader at the time, Danner was a boy who up to that point had shown a muted interest in either school or sports. Take it or leave it. All that changed when this Steve Wozniak–designed miracle appeared in his room. The Apple II, which set Apple on the pathway to becoming what it is today, was a complete package: two floppy disk drives, a monitor, integrated keyboard, sound, and eight internal expansion slots. But Danner didn't care about the bells and whistles on the outside; he cared about the guts. Immediately, he tore it apart, figuring out how to crack the copy protection code. The point was not to pirate games, although that was a bonus. The point was to prove you could do it. Soon, he was writing his own code. Danner began showing up at Silicon Valley computer clubs where he ran into early Apple pioneers. "When people ask me about middle school or high school I don't remember much. It was all about that Apple II. That was super valuable because I got immersed in how things worked at a deep level. It made me want to be a computer science major."

Understanding the second major event in Danner's life, which occurred in July 1995, requires some context. The really honest Silicon Valley entrepreneurs will tell you that although talent counts what really matters is being in the right place at the right time with the right experience—and the ability to think big. Or, to put it into the vernacular favored by venture capitalists, what really matters is having the right product-market fit quarterbacked by an entrepreneur capable of thinking big, really big. That sweet spot is just where Danner found himself in fall 1994 when Netscape released the first public version of its browser. Danner was in an ideal position to understand just how revolutionary Netscape would be. At the time, he was a software engineer at Silicon Graphics, which was founded by former Stanford professor James Clark. When Clark left Silicon Graphics to team up with Marc Andreessen, the team that produced Netscape, he took much of Danner's team with him. "Those were my colleagues working there, and I'd hear daily what was going on. I had a front row seat on Netscape."

Soon after Netscape got released, Danner knew that Internet businesses would become his future; he just didn't know how. He was twenty-seven years old, had worked for six years as a software engineer, had limited management experience, but somehow he knew the time was right to go big. So, to clear his head he quit Silicon Graphics and went on a three-month journey through Australia and New Zealand. On returning, he settled on one big thing: the Internet "subscription" model wasn't working. Nobody wanted to pay money to view the websites. New sites would pop up, become instantly popular, and then the instant they put up a pay wall their hits plummeted. Selling ads, not subscriptions, was the future, he concluded. Only it was hard to get clients to believe that this young engineer, whose most recent experience had been walking about New Zealand and Australia, had the chops to build that ad software.

In July 1995 all that changed when Danner walked into a meeting with the Yahoo! founders. He wasn't expecting much from the meeting, held in Yahoo!'s odd, secluded Mountain View office park location. At that point, NetGravity was more of a concept than a real company. There were no clients, no funding. Danner's cofounder wrote a demonstration for Yahoo! execs only the night before. Yahoo! already had millions of active users. Why would they need Danner and his phantom software company? But that's not how it turned out. "I told them that I had the idea that maybe sites could make money on advertising, and I walked them through it. They told me they had just had a board meeting with Sequoia Capital [a venture capital firm in nearby Menlo Park] and everyone had decided that advertising has to be our primary revenue source." Their question to Danner: "We need a product to do that today. Can you get in here right now? Where are your guys? Let's go!"

It was an entrepreneur's dream meeting. Immediately, Danner rounded up both "guys" to join him and got $500,000 in immediate "angel" funding. When told Yahoo! would be the first big client, startup money was easy to find. Within four months he secured $4 million in venture capital money. By the end of its first year, NetGravity had one hundred sites as customers, including most of the biggest. That Yahoo! meeting literally made NetGravity. Soon, investors would love NetGravity so much that the company achieved crazy-high valuations (crazy because, in truth, the company was barely profitable). But NetGravity had something its biggest competitor, DoubleClick, wanted badly, which was NetGravity's popular sites such as CNN and *USA Today*. Seize those sites and DoubleClick would become the industry standard. This is exactly what happened in October 1999. Although the sale of NetGravity was reported at a value of $530 million on the day it was announced, that value grew far higher, to $750 million, when the deal actually closed. And three months later, when the transaction was "unblocked," and NetGravity shareholders were able to cash in, the value grew even more, to $1 billion. Danner's share: somewhere north of $100 million.

That July day, Danner had found himself in the right place at the right time with the right talent. He did what most first-time startup entrepreneurs aspire to do: he got a win. He proved he could do it. At this point, a typical startup guy would start scheming about the next business venture. Problem was, Danner's heart wasn't into it. He wanted to do something important in his life, something big, and launching another advertising startup wasn't it. "There are few things in life less mission-driven than advertising companies," said Danner with a laugh. "For someone who wants a mission, it was not fulfilling in any way."

With his quick smile and affable manner, Danner can come across as very un-Silicon Valley. Almost Midwestern. If you just met Danner and he told you he was a Chevy dealer from suburban Cleveland, you would believe him. Over two thousand charter schools in thirty years? How naive can this guy be? Initial impressions of Danner fade quickly. Somehow, Danner moves through life a little differently than most people. His e-mails, a study in the word *frugality* and a source of amusement among his friends, suggest a monklike perspective on the world. Why write a three-word response when two words could suffice? His oral answers, however, couldn't be more different. Some people speak in phrases or maybe even complete sentences. The really good speakers manage to utter seamless paragraphs. In answering questions about either technology or schools, Danner answers in measured tapestries, starting with the fundamental, underlying philosophy and then narrowing the bandwidth until arriving at the precise point that was raised. And he does it all succinctly.

One coworker described Danner, without a trace of sarcasm or raised eyebrows, as a savant.

But possessing a gift for living in the future doesn't mean that Danner's next creation, Rocketship, will succeed. In fact, conventional wisdom suggests Danner's dream will fail. Most top-performing charter schools start slow, with a grade or two, perhaps kindergarten and first grade, and then expand a grade per year, taking five years to flesh out an elementary school of six hundred students. That deliberate pacing usually pays off. It takes that long to build a school culture, to settle on the right school leaders, to recruit and retain the right teachers. And that explains why high-performing charters, at least until now, remain minor players in the school reform movement. They lack the ability to scale quickly; they lack the right stuff to become Fibonacci schools.

Could Rocketship break through that scalability ceiling? Again, the odds don't favor that, but it is possible. Consider Rocketship Mosaic in San Jose, which got launched by startup principal Adam Nadeau in the 2011–2012 school year. Prior to joining Rocketship, Nadeau was a founding teacher at a KIPP school in Nashville. KIPP (which stands for Knowledge is Power Program but now just goes by KIPP), is probably the most recognized name among high-performing charter schools. "In Nashville, we opened the school with eighty fifth-graders, and every year we added eighty more fifth-graders. So, after four years of hard, game-changing work, we were serving 320 kids. Here, at Mosaic, we served 426 kids that first year, kindergartners through fifth-graders, on the first day of school."

If you think like a Rocketship leader, that the urgent mission is to prevent the achievement gap from even forming, then you have no choice but to go big fast. What's the point of adding just one grade a year? The point of going slowly, many charter groups would argue, is to maintain exacting quality, a valid point. But what if you came up with a charter school concept that could open a school serving 426 kids in multiple grades and at the end of the very first school year produce an outstanding test score average? That happened at Mosaic.[1] In Mosaic's second year, the school population soared to capacity, 640 kids. Suddenly, the Fibonacci sequence doesn't seem so crazy. Mosaic, which at the end of the 2013 school year had a waiting list of four hundred students, appears to be a test case for that controversial Rocketship philosophical challenge: plant a high-performing school in the midst of low-performing schools and let parents decide on the best way to fix an ailing school.

Suddenly, the idea of Fibonacci schools doesn't seem so crazy. Long odds, yes. But not a crazy idea. At least not entirely.

NOTE

1. Mosaic scored 872 on California's Academic Performance Index (API). The API ranks schools from 200 to 1,000. If you are educating poor kids, a score above 800 is great news.

PRESTON SMITH

One Rocketship leader once referred to John Danner as "the story" and wondered out loud to me, what would happen when "the story" left Rocketship (which happened in 2013)? Would Rocketship lose focus, funding, and momentum? But Preston Smith, the person Danner chose as a cofounder and designated successor, has his own story to tell. His story may not involve riches reaped from startup stocks, but it's a story more relevant to carrying Rocketship into the next decade, when we all discover whether Rocketship has Fibonacci potential.

Smith, thirty-five,[1] grew up in Rialto, California, which is just outside San Bernardino. With the smog blowing east from Los Angeles, Rialto is not anyone's idea of paradise. When Smith was in school the mostly blue-collar Rialto was undergoing rapid white flight. "In kindergarten a lot of my friends moved out." But the schools, Smith recalls, seemed good at the time. As a top student there, Smith applied to UCLA with confidence. He got turned down. He applied to Berkeley and got wait-listed. "I was shocked. I was student body president, had done mock trial, and had a great résumé. It just didn't make sense." The only non–Advanced Placement class he took there was econ and he still recalls all the track and football players coming to econ bragging about their UCLA acceptances. Devastated, Smith called the admissions dean at UCLA with one question: "Why?" The dean was honest. "We know about your school," answered the dean. "Your grades are inflated. If the biggest thing you have going for there are grades and leadership, that's not good enough. We take athletes, not scholars, from your school."

It was an "aha" moment for Smith that resonates today as he runs charter schools in high-poverty neighborhoods: zip codes matter.

Smith ended up graduating from the University of North Carolina, Chapel Hill, with an eye on going to law school. Then one day Smith attended a job fair and saw a table for Teach For America. He went over to the table mostly to make fun of them. "Bunch of do-gooders who want to get their hands dirty experiencing the community, but not too dirty." But they convinced him, so he signed up. "I really wanted to go to Chicago. I wanted to see the Midwest. I had already seen the West and South. I knew Chicago was full of African American students being failed. I felt like that was ground zero. I should dig in and figure it out." Chicago, however, was not to be. "They assigned me to San Jose, my fourth choice." And so teaching first grade at Clyde Arbuckle Elementary School, part of the Alum Rock district in San Jose, became Smith's new home. And teaching became his passion. He was pretty good at teaching first grade, good enough to become a finalist during his second year for one of Teach For America's best-teacher-in-the-nation honors. That made him one of the top six TFAers that year. Smith's classroom became a must-stop for anyone who wanted to see a crack teacher experiencing success with high-poverty students.

All that success led to an invitation from the San Jose community organizing group PACT (People Acting in Community Together): please, help us open a new school. On the table was a chance to become a founding principal at a "small autonomous school," a concession granted under pressure by the Alum Rock school district, which serves a large Latino community in San Jose. Thus was born LUCHA, which stands for Learning in an Urban Community with High Achievement. The school got launched as an anomaly, with ultra-progressive community activists carving out their ideal school serving high-poverty students.[2] By all accounts, Smith made a success of LUCHA, which probably led to his departure. He still recalls being called in by the interim superintendent and told, "Word on the street is you're a maverick. Well, we're going to have a corral and you're coming in. Get on the team." The school's success was a bit of an embarrassment to the district, says Smith, which led the district to pounce when Smith did something unthinkable: he fired an ineffective teacher.

Anyone who watched *Waiting for "Superman"* knows something about the "dance of the lemons." That's when principals who lack true firing authority dump their bad teachers on unsuspecting principals in other schools. Smith, being a new principal, bit on the lemon gambit and that bite hurt. This particular lemon teacher, it turned out, was in a "testing" grade, the grade in which a school's test scores get judged. Preliminary test scores in her classroom quickly went south. With only eight teachers in the entire school, one lemon sours the entire school. In the real world, the private sector world most of us know, that person gets fired. If you can't keep up with your work at Google or the production line at Subway, you get fired. In the school world, things don't work that way. You're supposed to live with the lemon, quietly, and plot to stick the lemon with another unsuspecting principal. But Smith wasn't playing the game. "The kids in her class were actually regressing. I don't get paid to see kids go backwards." So he wrote up her many shortcomings and tried to fire her. Problem was, she had tenure and that year was a contract-negotiating year for the district. The union "grieved" the attempt to fire her, which is not what any superintendent wants to deal with in a negotiating year. "I got called into the superintendent's office and told I had messed up."

Things only got worse. Smith says the district "suppressed" a report showing academic achievements there. "They wanted the story to be that we were skimming kids." Then, a new superintendent arrived in Alum Rock and called all the district leaders into a meeting to discuss the district's new "vision." At one point she looked directly at Smith and said, "And we don't need any more LUCHAs, right, Preston?" Just as Smith was asking himself, "What am I doing here?" he got introduced to Danner, who by this time had settled on charter schools as his next startup project. After teaching for three years in Nashville and helping launch a new KIPP school, Danner had returned to the Bay Area determined to build a new kind of charter network. He needed a principal and everyone he contacted (more details in "Did the Butterfly Effect Give Wings to Rocketship?") told him, "You have to meet Preston."

It was September 2006 when Smith and Danner first met. The scene: a plastic bench on LUCHA's playground. Recalls Danner: "I was fortyish at the time, and here was this twenty-six-year-old, who really looked young back then. I remember thinking, 'Who was this kid? Why am I here?' But within five or ten minutes Preston delivered an incredibly clear view of how things needed to work. So even though he was a young kid with slicked-back hair I thought, 'That's about how old I was when I started my first company.'" Smith recalls telling Danner about all the antagonism directed at him by district officials and hearing Danner say, "Wow, Preston, what are you doing here? Do you like punishment?" Smith told Danner he wasn't quite ready to leave. "This school is my baby." Danner was surprised by Smith's loyalty. "Here was someone who had started a high-performing school for low-income students. You would think he would be applauded, but the district was doing everything they could to undermine him."

Smith was intrigued enough to sign on as a consultant. Every day he would leave LUCHA by 6 p.m. and go work for Rocketship to help Danner ready the first school for launch. And the day that first school opened the principal was Preston Smith, who became Rocketship's cofounder. Alum Rock got rid of its maverick principal and Rocketship got a leader. But the bad blood between Rocketship and Alum Rock would soon resurface.

NOTES

1. As of June 2014.

2. The irony here is that in most cities' highly "progressive" citizen groups would fight charters or schools such as LUCHA, believing they drain resources from regular schools.

DANNER'S BIG PIVOT

1999–2000: Aspen, Colorado

After NetGravity was sold to DoubleClick, word got out that a tech entrepreneur blessed with the ability to think well into the future was looking for his next big thing. Just the kind of person Keith Berwick, who then oversaw the Aspen Crown fellows, searches for. So in 1999 Danner got tapped to join twenty other Crown fellows for a yearlong search for what Berwick describes as their "inflection points." In geometry, that's where a charted curve goes from negative to positive. In life planning, that's a turning point when the skills that got you that initial success are leveraged in a new direction. To find that new direction, the fellows agree to take the time to read materials provided by Aspen and then meet four times over two years, with each meeting lasting between four and five days. Also part of the fellowship program is a community project, which for some meant a chance to give that inflection point an important trial run.

Danner accepted the fellowship, but he was skeptical. "I think I was a pain-in-the-ass fellow," recalls Danner. "I had a lot of that young engineer-CEO-founder stuff in my head, and I was generally distrustful of all organizations. This one [the Crown Fellowship], in particular, was abstract. I was wondering what we were doing there and thinking about how I would organize the fellowship differently." It was startup world meeting think tank world. Slowly, however, the effect of being surrounded by twenty other successful people also challenged to search for inflection points changed his view of the fellowship. "One thing Berwick did well," said Danner, "was figuring out how to put the right twenty people in a room."

It didn't take Danner long to figure out his community project. The day after the news of the NetGravity sale broke Danner, who graduated from the elite Jesuit-run high school in the area, Bellarmine Prep, got a fund-raising call from the Jesuits. "If you are successful they are good at finding you." When Danner said he wasn't interested in contributing to a wealthy private school the conversation quickly shifted to the help the Jesuits needed in launching a new school in one of San Jose's poorest neighborhoods. Suddenly, he was interested. That was a phone call that would change his life.

For Danner's community project he chose to step in to help Father Peter Pabst launch Sacred Heart Nativity School, a middle school located in a Latino neighborhood in San Jose only a few blocks from where the first Rocketship elementary school would open seven years later, a neighborhood where only 10 percent of the residents have high school diplomas. One of Pabst's goals was to give low-income students from the neighborhood an education so solid that they could qualify for Bellarmine Prep. It was a swing for the fences, just the kind of project that appealed to Danner.

Danner's sudden switch from software startups to school reform was not intuitive. At Bellarmine Danner was hardly the social conscience of his class. Playing tennis, academics, and computers were his passions. But the Jesuits appeared to have reached him in some way during his high school years, an impact that lay dormant through his Stanford and startup years and reemerged after the sale to DoubleClick. "The Jesuits do a pretty good job of making you think about the world even as you're trying to ignore them." Danner's mother, who was active in nonprofits in Saratoga, California, where he grew up, was another influence. "My mother did a good job of convincing me social good was a good thing." Danner's wife, Allison, pointed to another influence: being part of a family caring for a severely disabled child, John's sister, who is only a year younger than John. "He grew up in a compassionate environment."

Pabst was grateful for the help. "In the seminary they don't teach you how to open a business or school," said Pabst, "so I was trying to meet as many people as I could." Danner was the perfect guy to meet. "There are a lot of similarities between startup businesses and startup schools," said Pabst. "John and I would meet once a week and he'd come up with a to-do list: set up a bank account, get book donations, find a company going out of business to give us computers on the cheap. John got bit by the bug. He saw it was so unfair that some kids don't have the educational opportunities others have. He saw the bleak area here, the terrifically low high school graduation rates."

Working to launch that school nudged Danner's startup instincts in a new direction, says Pabst. "Being entrepreneurial means taking risks.

We're taking risks with the kids we accepted as to whether or not they can succeed. This was a startup. It was something no one had ever done in San Jose. The last time a Catholic school opened in this area it was in an affluent area. Opening a school like this in a poor area is very different." At the end of the "project," Pabst was so grateful for the work Danner did that he named him a school cofounder.

Soon, Danner would head to Nashville where Allison joined the Vanderbilt law faculty. For Danner, Nashville would become the formal startup of his education career, a career that would lead to Rocketship and beyond. In 2010 Danner would win Aspen's $100,000 John P. McNulty award for his work founding Rocketship. Berwick acknowledges that Danner started out as a skeptical fellow. But that changed. "He turned into one of the most remarkable Crown fellows." As Danner began drawing up his Rocketship plans he heard some words of caution from one Aspen moderator. People like you, the advisor told him, are trying to do good and they assume people will applaud them for it. "But there are times that will not happen, times when people will hate you. It's not good enough to do good. Sometimes you have to fight evil." In the coming years Danner had reason to recall that advice.

PART II

THE STARTUP YEARS

A Charter Fund Designed to Nurture Top CMOs

April 2002: San Francisco, California

The NewSchools Venture Fund launches its Charter Accelerator Fund with $10 million, the first national effort to grow the high-performing charter management organizations (CMOs). One of the early contributors was Eli Broad from the Broad Foundation. Said Broad, "I believe that charters, choice, and competition create important forces that help us to better serve children in our nation's neediest communities." That original fund, which would grow to over $48 million, targeted charter groups in Oakland; Los Angeles; New York City; Philadelphia; Washington, DC; and Chicago. It supported thirteen new CMOs, three charter school facilities developers, and two charter support organizations. At the conclusion of the fund, the NewSchools CMOs operated charter schools with an aggregate enrollment of thirteen thousand students per year.

DID THE BUTTERFLY EFFECT GIVE WINGS TO ROCKETSHIP?

June 2002: San Jose, California

It is not impossible that the night Celia Gonzales stepped forward to give testimony about the "frustration, pain, and injustices" she experienced trying to find a decent education for her daughter was a trigger that years later would produce Rocketship. The butterfly effect, part of chaos theory that has dipped into popular culture, holds that a hurricane could have its source in a single butterfly that weeks ago flapped its wings in a land far away. That's the theory, anyway. In this case, the causal connection is not that theoretical.

The meeting that night was organized by the church-based PACT, People Acting in Community Together. Through months of community interviewing and organizing in East San Jose, PACT organizers had identified inadequate schools as the deepest of all concerns. Not only were the schools filthy, especially the bathrooms, but they were often staffed by seemingly permanent substitute teachers. For the most part, outcomes for the students in the Alum Rock schools were just flat out awful. Before calling this "action" at St. John Vianney Church, PACT and the parents had done their homework, including traveling to visit some small, autonomous schools in Oakland and New York City that parent leaders had helped create. That's what they wanted in East San Jose, but first they had to pressure Alum Rock school board members to do what few school districts do willingly: set up schools that are only partly under the control of the school administration and union. Testifying that night, Gonzales cried as she explained how her daughter had gotten lost in the Alum Rock system.

Also attending that night was an editorial writer from the *San Jose Mercury News*, who wrote this editorial about the dilemma:

> The problem is not that individual children are falling through
> the cracks. There is no floor; Alum Rock has become an abyss of

mismanagement and turmoil, where floundering students post among the lowest test scores and a discouraged staff the highest turnover rate in the county.[1]

At that time, John Danner was teaching in Nashville, unaware the meeting was even taking place. Preston Smith, then a very young Teach For America teacher in Alum Rock, also knew nothing about the meeting. But Matt Hammer, then-director of PACT, and Jose Arenas, a PACT community organizer, knew something about Smith. Arenas had a cousin whose son was having an amazing year at school, all because of an outstanding teacher: Preston Smith. When Alum Rock yielded on creating small, autonomous schools, Hammer and Arenas tracked down Smith and asked him to become a founding principal. At first, Smith hesitated. In his mind, he was still a newbie teacher, someone who knew nothing about founding a new school. But soon, Smith changed his mind.

Wait, the butterfly effect gets better. When Danner returned to the Bay Area determined to start his own charter schools he arranged a meeting with Hammer and other PACT leaders.[2] Quickly, the advice given to Danner was to get together with Preston Smith. According to Danner, "As Preston tells it, this guy literally picked up his cell phone during the meeting and called Preston and said, 'This is what you need to do next.' He encouraged Preston to reach out to me."

It is possible that even if PACT organizers had not called their action, even if Celia Gonzales had not been brave enough to testify, and even if the Alum Rock school officials had not yielded to pressure and agreed to start these new schools, that Danner and Smith would have met and launched Rocketship anyway. Possible, but not likely.

Notes

1. "'The Pain and Injustice' of Alum Rock Schools," by the editorial board, June 6, 2002.
2. Hammer, the son of former San Jose mayor Susan Hammer, was someone who knew his way around the power corridors of San Jose.

Hurricane Katrina

*T*he devastating hurricane damaged or destroyed more than 100 of the city's 128 school buildings, forcing about sixty-five thousand students to leave the city. Katrina opened up a rare opportunity to completely redo education in the city, a system regarded as one of the lowest performers in the country. Using the already-created Recovery School District, thousands of students were enrolled in charter schools. Suddenly, charter schools had an opportunity— available facilities, an official blessing, and adequate funding—to carry out an unprecedented experiment. If judged by test scores, the experiment has been an undisputed success, with test scores and college-readiness indicators rising.[1] A major player in boosting charter quality was New Schools for New Orleans, which since 2007 supported the launch or expansion of twenty-eight schools and make up a quarter of the open-enrollment charter schools there. The New Orleans reforms continue to play an influential national role, with other cities sprouting their own versions of the recovery district (see "Fibonacci Charters Summoned to Memphis").

NOTE

1. If judged by criteria other than test scores, the charter approach remains controversial in New Orleans. Too many former New Orleans teachers never got hired by the charters, say critics, raising issues of cultural conflict and economic impact. Also at issue is sustainability: can the charters there maintain momentum without the continued infusion of outside talent and money? Plus, parents continue to be confused about how to find a good school for their children and resentful of "outsiders" taking over their schools.

Startup Meets Smokestack

2005: Nashville, Tennessee; Palo Alto, California

In their book *The Startup of You,* Reid Hoffman and Ben Casnocha describe the roundabout route leading to cofounding LinkedIn, the networking site for professionals, a path that required persistent reinvention.[1] And they also cite numerous examples of other Silicon Valley startup people doing the same. Ever heard of the online game called "Neverending"? Probably not. That's the combo game–social space that rolled out in 2002. When founders Caterina Fake and Stewart Butterfield added a photo-sharing feature to their game (a feature that took only eight weeks to develop), they noticed the photo sharing quickly became more popular than the game itself. Immediately, they shifted strategies and launched a photo-sharing platform called Flickr, which in 2005 was acquired by Yahoo!

In Silicon Valley, there's nothing extraordinary in the stories about how LinkedIn and Flickr got launched. That's just how business is done in the valley—quick bursts of adaptations as business models get revamped to fit the needs of consumers. In the startup world, employees get a number, depending on when they signed up. In successful companies, low employee numbers often lead to high cash-outs. Those startup stories only seem extraordinary when compared to the rarely changing ways schools operate. On a hypothetical scale placing the industrial age on one end and the information age on the other, schools remain on the industrial side of the ledger. Only a slight touch of hyperbole is required to describe them as smokestack industries. In the smokestack world, nobody numbers their employees. What's the point?

Danner's story is that of a startup guy incubated in the famously fluid style of Silicon Valley suddenly getting dunked into the famously viscous world of K–12 schools. One quick example: after Danner created and sold his startup business he departed for Nashville to teach for a couple of years

31

at a Nashville elementary school. By all accounts, Danner acquitted himself well. On his own, he figured out not only that individualized education was the way to go but also came up with a way to deliver personalized learning to every child in his class. Danner felt confident about his teaching success and wanted to try school leadership, so one day he sat down with his principal and informed her of that. Keep in mind, at this point Danner was steeped in leadership experience, having previously been the CEO of a publicly traded company. Well, the principal replied, here's how it works around here: keep doing what you're doing as a classroom teacher for several years and maybe, just maybe, you'll have a shot at a leadership position.

When telling this story, Danner erupts into knowing laughter. Really, he insists, this is actually how that scene played out. This is how education *actually works* in this country. For startup guys, this kind of stuff is *unfathomable.* It's right out of a *Saturday Night Live* skit. Guys like Danner can't imagine promoting their software engineers based on how long they've sat in their chairs. You're kidding, right? They are baffled that educators seem to base their instruction on unscientific methodology, such as the ever-shifting "best practices" that get passed along from district to district. That's how the "whole language" debacle unfolded, as a best practice (Who needs phonics?) incubated in California that got passed along to the rest of the country like a virus. Only in recent years has the US Department of Education sponsored medical-style randomized trials of popular education programs. To their shock, researchers discovered that roughly nine of ten education programs that appeared to be promising in small, unscientific studies had either no effect on student achievement or caused a dip in achievement.[2] Belief systems in practice. What startup company thrives on belief systems rather than science? Tech entrepreneurs are even puzzled by the school reform movement. Why would high-performing charter schools expand by only one grade a year? A promising startup company crawling along at that pace would get burned by the competition.

Not surprisingly, startup guys howl at schools' use of technology. Who put generally tech-klutzy school superintendents in charge of guiding technology purchases? That's how you end up with showy interactive whiteboards that pass for innovation. That's how you end up with stacks of desktop and laptop computers that, in the end, get used only by the nerdy kids during recess. That's how you end up with digitized textbooks touted as pathways into the digital world. Putting superintendents in charge of technology violates a fundamental rule of Silicon Valley: build systems that fill an exact need for consumers. In school districts, superintendents aren't the true consumers. That would be the teachers, students, and parents.

I am not arguing that hip, talented, and moneyed startup guys should be put in charge of schools. As a group, they are arrogant, elitist, myopic, and willfully naive about the realities of maintaining important institutions such as public schools. And that's just the beginning of the downside list. Years of school reform campaigns led or backed by a moneyed elite have spawned an effective pushback movement among educators against the "billionaires club"—school reform critic Diane Ravitch's term for philanthropists supporting education reform—that wants to force business practices on schools. Sure, most of those practices are commonsense and inevitable, but in truth a lot of educators got pretty comfortable with the unbusinesslike benefits offered by smokestack culture. Teachers and district leaders, not to mention students, prefer the summers-off school schedule. A teacher compensation and rewards system based on seat time may sound like something lifted out of a frayed Soviet handbook, but teachers don't have to stress about the teacher next door earning more money; they can bank on every-year raises and their pay won't be based on student test results, a reform that makes them cringe. The turn-of-the-century Carnegie instructional units feel familiar to educators. Why change? These educators want "disruptive" change about as much as they want a food fight in the cafeteria. So when wealthy reformers stumble while trying to modernize schooling, veteran educators can laugh about the naiveté of startup guys who have never faced down a classroom of unruly eighth-graders. Let's be honest: they have a point.

This is where the Danner story gets interesting. Almost alone among the startup guys tackling education, Danner has walked the walk. He taught for three difficult years in Nashville public schools and then helped launch a KIPP charter *before* he even tried to design his own charter school. So when Danner tries to bring startup principles into the smokestack world, the clash between the two worlds gets a little more interesting, a little more reality based. It's not that Danner is right and traditional educators are wrong. It's more that he's a tech guy who has actually spent time in the traditional education system and yet launched new schools based on startup culture. Hence, Rocketship's design merits attention.

Understanding Danner's approach to building Rocketship requires understanding something about him. He's definitely a startup guy, but unlike a mercurial startup guy such as Steve Jobs or an imperious startup guy such as Larry Ellison or a wonder child such as Bill Gates, Danner is a bit of a rarity—a careful, one-step-at-a-time startup guy. He didn't bolt from Stanford to launch a startup. He waited until he got a master's degree. He didn't immediately launch his own company. Rather, he worked for several years at some of the iconic companies in Silicon Valley. At Oracle, as a young engineer, he saw the famous and infamous Larry Ellison in full attack mode. A competitor database provider had just spent a fortune buying software to compete with Oracle, an act that left Ellison fuming. "We're going to cut off their oxygen," Danner recalls Ellison saying. "They just paid a billion dollars for that company. We're going to make that (software) free and blow them up." And, over the next nine months that's exactly what Ellison did. To Danner, watching Ellison was watching leadership in action. "Larry had a lot of issues that are well documented, but he was both incredibly insightful on the market and sure of where it was going to go. It was amazing. . . . Execution is not always pretty, but it doesn't matter if everything you're doing is making people feel good all the time. What matters is you want to show your people they can be successful and win. That's what makes great companies. If you create that culture, people will deal with large amounts of crap. Oracle was a testament to that."[3] Making teachers and principals feel like winners, and therefore more likely to put up with long hours and constant change, became an early Rocketship hallmark.

When running NetGravity, Danner at times showed the same kind of brashness and arrogance seen in most young startup guys. But two traits tempered the arrogance. Unlike a lot of startup guys more than willing to pave over their mistakes, Danner seemed painfully aware of all the management mistakes he made along the way. There's a reason DoubleClick bought NetGravity, rather than the other way around. "At NetGravity, John was a CEO at the age of twenty-eight," said Jill Wear, a human resources specialist who has followed Danner through all his startups. "He learned every one of the lessons he was about to learn the hard way." John

Krystynak, who worked with Danner at Silicon Graphics and then became the first engineer at NetGravity, recalls running into Danner on the street after the business was sold and asked him about the turmoil at the end. "I did so many things wrong," answered Danner. "It would be easier to list the things I did right." Humility, says Krystynak, is something you rarely see in a startup guy. Danner was determined to avoid similar mistakes in his next startup, which was in fact Rocketship.

And so Danner arrived in the education world. Better put, the charter school world. He tried hard to keep at least an arm's length from Silicon Valley excess, driving a Prius rather than a Porsche. After leaving Rocketship, he hoped to move his family to India for a year, partly for business reasons but also to get his kids away from the wealthier-than-thou zeitgeist of elite Palo Alto. Maybe in Mumbai there will be issues more compelling than acquiring the latest Apple gizmo. The hubris from his startup days got honed into a low-wattage determination. Danner wasn't assuming he knew everything about building high-performing schools, but he definitely wasn't backing down when challenged by superintendents he thought were shortchanging poor Latino kids. He was friendly but private. He joined the Rotary Club in San Jose and stayed for five years—but just long enough to meet the political biggies. He resigned when he left Rocketship.

Both professionally and personally, Danner appeared to be embracing the Pareto principle. Named after an Italian economist, the principle holds that 80 percent of the effects come from 20 percent of the causes. To startup guys working in the valley, that means maintaining a rigid focus on the few things, or just one thing, your software does that's unique and indispensable to consumers. Lose that focus and you lose your customers. Translated into school design terms, that means that most of what makes a school succeed or fail hinges on just a few factors. Keep it simple. What emerged was an interesting demeanor, part startup-influenced, part Jesuit-influenced. In some ways, Danner comes off as an ascetic, beginning with his Haiku-like e-mails. It's a personality stripped down to do battle at the prime of his life, a time when all the previously learned skills would be marshaled for one purpose: narrowing the racial-ethnic achievement gap. Although Danner initially comes across as an everyman, you quickly discover he's an everyman who lives five years in the future (for better or worse . . . that would at times prove to be problematic). And then you glimpse flashes of his "no-hands" style of management. Krystynak, who worked with Danner at Silicon Graphics, tells the story about playing golf with Danner. At first, Danner comes across as a nonattentive golfer, unworried about not playing a great game. "He's happy-go-lucky, loves to laugh, and doesn't take things too seriously." But in golf, as in other sports, there always comes a moment when focus matters, perhaps when the group makes a bet on a particular putt. That's when Danner comes alive, concentrates, and often wins the bet—despite his previous sloppy play. "That's his CEO mode. You can only care about so many things, but he has the ability to see what's key, what to care about."

So what kind of school model emerges from this startup personality? To build his model, Danner pinpointed the one area he lacked expertise—school leadership—and convinced Preston Smith to join him as cofounder. Although Smith had no Silicon Valley experience, he agreed with Danner's startuplike strategies. Between the two of them, a charter model emerged that was designed to successfully educate low-income minorities and scale quickly. That meant focusing on just three things:

1. Inventing new ways to find and retain talent. In a school, 80 percent of the costs come from paying teacher salaries and benefits. He knew it was important to have great teachers, which meant paying them more. But paying them more means ballooning the budget, which means relying on philanthropy to make up the difference. For one or two schools, you might find philanthropists willing to kick in $500,000 to make up the difference—for a year or two. But that money-losing strategy would never work during a rapid expansion to one thousand schools, which was Danner's goal. The more schools you start, the more money you lose. To solve the talent dilemma, Danner leaned on the second leg of his Pareto strategy: technology.

2. Changing the way schools use technology. Prior to Rocketship, schools used technology as a possible booster tool, as though teachers using whiteboards during lectures or loading homework onto laptops would help students learn better. For the most part, the technology added little value in improved student learning. But that's not how Danner viewed the technology question. What if technology could be used to make schools more efficient? What if, Danner asked, you could find, or invent, learning software that was truly personalized for each student, software that by tracking what students are getting right or wrong could figure out how that student learned and therefore determine how to loop back and reteach missed material? In education technology terms, that's called *adaptive* software. In theory, adaptive software could teach the basics of math and literacy in Rocketship Learning Labs while teachers focused on character building and "higher-order" learning skills.

Students rotating into Learning Labs meant employing fewer teachers. Thus, a school such as Rocketship Mosaic could successfully serve 630 students with only sixteen teachers (plus aides). A traditional elementary school with that many students would employ at least twenty-one teachers, probably more. In theory, Rocketship teachers would earn more and spend less time on repetitive basic skills. And if promoted quickly they were more likely to stay in the teaching profession. Establishing the rotational system also meant making each teacher a specialist, either in reading or math, rather than a generalist, which is how the traditional elementary school down the street operated. Specialists, he reasoned, would always trump generalists.

3. Making Latino parents into education activists. This is probably Rocketship's biggest innovation and yet the one most people never grasp, probably because at most schools "getting parents more involved" rarely goes beyond sloganeering. With help from PACT and Preston Smith, someone trained by PACT who happened to be preternaturally gifted in the art of community organizing, Rocketship set out to achieve two goals traditional educators consider near impossible. First, they wanted to make most of the Latino parents in their schools into highly involved parents, with their own children and at school. And then, on a higher level, they set out to discover parents with hidden organizational talents and develop them into rock-the-boat activists. Before Rocketship came along, conventional wisdom held that Latino parents, with their limited language skills, their need to work multiple jobs, and their deferential attitude toward authorities, especially school principals, would never be fully engaged with school and certainly could not emerge as highly visible policy activists. Rocketship set out to upend conventional wisdom. As I will explain in later chapters, success here would prove to be big, even more important than innovating with teacher quality and blended learning.

Originally, charters were designed to be testing grounds, regulation-light environments where entrepreneurial educators could experiment with education practices that regular districts would then adopt. Danner never saw the point to that. Districts were never going to treat charters as anything but competitors, he calculated. From the beginning Danner ignored the intent of the California charter law and set out to create his own charter district, first within San Jose, then nationally. After all, the Rocketship goal was to make a sizable dent in the nation's achievement gap by the year 2030. Thus was born the Rocketship model: fewer, higher-paid teachers who specialized in what they taught with the Learning Labs taking care of basics such as addition and subtraction, freeing up teachers to focus on more sophisticated skills. That model could operate on California's skimpy $7,500-a-student funding. In fact, it should prove efficient enough, at least in theory, for each school to throw off an extra $500,000 a year (more a revenue goal than a revenue reality) to supply school services and fuel an office busy tooling up for national expansion.

The Rocketship model would be top-down directed, just the opposite of KIPP, where schools are essentially locally run groups. KIPP leaders all get the same training, but at the local level there's a lot of autonomy. Not at Rocketship, where local school principals are expected to implement every new twist in instructional methodology pioneered at the national office. On the surface, that would seem to violate all known rules about educators needing to cooperate, collaborate, and come to a consensus before making changes. Maybe, but that's not how startup guys operate. Did Steve Jobs strike you as someone hesitant to lead without reaching consensus?

The Pareto principle of schooling. Focus on the few things that determine 80 percent of the outcome. That's the Rocketship model. But would anyone buy it?

NOTES

1. New York: Crown Publishing, 2012.

2. Gina Kolata, "Guesses and Hype Give Way to Data in Study of Education," *New York Times* (September 2, 2013).

3. In 2013, as Danner left Rocketship, those words would seem prophetic. As will be explained in later chapters, that damn-the-torpedoes stance would bring Rocketship to a major crisis point. Not everyone wanted to run Rocketship Larry Ellison–style.

SCI-FI-INSPIRED SOFTWARE

February 2005: Bellevue, Washington

On Ben Slivka's LinkedIn page you see a swarm of startups, the fruit of his labors as a talented software writer, all of it rooted in his training at Northwestern University as a mathematician and computer scientist. His biggest fame and fortune came from his fourteen years at Microsoft, where he worked on every big project, including starting the Internet Explorer team in 1994. But by 1999 Slivka became convinced that Microsoft had been taken over by "politicians" determined to ride out the Microsoft gravy train, choosing Windows over the web. Not the place for a software engineer of his ambition who believed in the future of the web. So he stepped off the train.

For a time—nine months to be exact—Slivka tried out Amazon. But he left in June 2000 for reasons that only a software purist can understand. Something about Jeff Bezos "being a good human being but his hearing isn't so good." In short, Slivka did not share Bezos's vision. Slivka's stock options from Microsoft had expired several years earlier, meaning he became wealthy, extremely wealthy, to the point where asking about his Microsoft cash-out (which I did) is considered "rude." Point accepted.

What does someone in Slivka's unique position do? He's not a yacht kind of guy. Definitely wary of spoiling his kids with premature wealth. He and wife became, in his words, "accidental philanthropists." But as Slivka worked his way through this new world one pathway became clear: education. So Slivka decided to launch a new company partly inspired on long-ago science fiction reading, such as *Enders Game* by Orson Scott Card and *The Diamond Age* by Neal Stephenson—books that weave futuristic education tools into the narrative. In *The Diamond Age,* a powerful interactive book lands in the hands of Nell, a street urchin, who then leads a revolution. The theme in short: interactive education tools can change the world.

Slivka agreed with school reformers who believe we are trapped in a century-old industrial model in which children are treated as widgets— light years away from what is possible in education. Traditional school reform didn't seem to be touching that outdated model. But what if digital creations could leapfrog that system? "What if," Slivka asked himself, "you could build this massively multiplayer online game—but instead of shooting things, you were mastering all of K–12 education—that would motivate kids and allow them to learn at their own pace and their own way?"

Such a powerful online system, Slivka believed, could transform education, reaching hundreds of millions and eventually billions of kids, far more than even the best teachers in the world could possibly reach. The software would track every move a student made in the program. When a child failed to learn a concept, the software would lead the child to a different place where the concept was presented in a way most suited to that child. It would be the ultimate in personalized education, enabling children to learn exactly what they needed to learn at exactly the ideal pace. It would be a real-world version of "the Primer," the nanotechnology device that starred in Stephenson's book.

What Slivka began thinking about in winter 2005 became an actual company the following winter, a startup that eventually became DreamBox. Not surprisingly, any gifted software engineer dedicated to personalized learning would, at some point in the future, come across John Danner, someone who as the result of learning a few big lessons from his year teaching in Nashville shared the same dream of personalized learning.

Joel Klein Does the Unexpected

September 2005: New York City

*D*uring a visit to the Excellence Charter School of Bedford-Stuyvesant in Brooklyn, schools chancellor Joel Klein announces the city will pay up to two-thirds of the cost of constructing new schools for charters. Not just any charters, of course, but charters such as Excellence, part of Uncommon Schools, one of the most successful charter operators in the country. The charter operator would pay the balance, and then pay $1 a year for a ninety-nine-year lease from the city. The $1-a-year lease, combined with a drive to colocate top charters to existing school buildings, would end up defining Klein's legacy as chancellor. The positive academic results produced by the high-performing charters would make the procharter policy hard to reverse for future mayors, regardless of their stances on charters.[1] Said KIPP cofounder Dave Levin at the time, "When people ask us what the major impediments are to starting more schools like KIPP, it's the three F's—funding, facilities and freedom—and facilities are kind of the most prohibitive."[2]

NOTES

1. I'll make a personal prediction that Mayor Bill de Blasio will have a hard time scaling back charter schools that are succeeding with low-income minority students.
2. David Herszenhorn, "$250 Million Program to Promote Charter Schools," *New York Times* (September 10, 2005).

RECRUITING THE
KEY (OUTSIDE) PLAYERS

January 2006: Palo Alto, California

Don Shalvey . . . Joanne Weiss . . . Reed Hastings.

The founder of Aspire Public Schools, a partner and chief executive officer of NewSchools Venture Fund, and the Netflix CEO. With Aspire, Shalvey was a key early pioneer in charter schools, showing the nation how to take high-performing charter schools to scale. Joanne Weiss and NewSchools Venture Fund pioneered Silicon Valley–style methods for building out charter management organizations that enabled the best charters to expand quickly. And Hastings showed the nation he was willing to sponsor Netflix-like approaches to school reform.

John Danner managed to get all three on board to support Rocketship's launch.

DON SHALVEY

After selling his web advertising business and deciding to go into education, Danner looked around for school models he most admired. Immediately, he came across Don Shalvey and Aspire. "I think I literally cold-called him in 2001 and said, 'Here's who I am. I'm interested in your space.' He's very outgoing and so we got together in Oakland where he lived. It was that easy." The two stayed in touch when Danner left for Nashville to teach in the public schools and help launch a KIPP charter school there. As Danner began to design his own charter schools he examined Aspire's business plan and liked what he saw. "When I started writing my own business plan, I told Shalvey I was going to come back to the Bay Area and start Rocketship with a Learning Lab, and I wanted him on the board. He agreed, which surprised me."

Shalvey rarely attended board meetings, but that didn't matter to Danner. "Shalvey has always been a godfather of charter schools and he was nearby on the West Coast and willing to give me advice. Don is a connector personality; he's good at opening doors. His main role was allowing me to use his name as a calling card and reaching out to others. I don't think he had any major impact on our program. He's a somewhat traditional educator. He thought all the things we were doing were kind of insane. He called Learning Lab our Vietnam. I remember him saying, 'You're going to have all those kids in one room? It's going to be insane.' Many members of our first board were traditional educators, which was good for Preston and me. It made us prove ourselves more because these established people thought what we were doing was crazy."

Shalvey has a different memory of how they met. "It's very vivid in my mind, right out of the Silicon Valley playbook—'networking when you're not working'—a quote I always attribute to John Doerr. It was networking through Reed Hastings, who wrote me an e-mail saying there's this entrepreneur who wants to do a CMO [charter management organization]. Would you please spend some time with him? That was it, a standard Reed e-mail, not very long [akin to a Danner e-mail]. And now, after all these years, my family considers John family."

There were design differences between Rocketship and Aspire. "John had a really strong alliance with TFA and home-growing school leaders before opening new schools. His whole hub-and-spoke approach [growing fast to one thousand schools] . . . the first time I saw that I said, 'Oh my God, you're out of your mind.' That and the Learning Lab I would scratch my head at . . . for a long time I had this running joke with John: 'The best you can hope for is a Vietnam outcome. It is going to be a mess.'"

But Shalvey readily agrees that Rocketship didn't turn out to be a mess. "What I love about John is he'll listen to you and if he thinks you're full of shit he just keeps going. His plan was to be big, bold, and urgent. . . . My wife is a big John Danner fan. Every time she sees him she says he's just Reed [Hastings] with a little less experience." Like Reed Hastings, John Danner is impatient, eager to take urgent action. You never see traditional educators taking risks like Danner wanted to take, says Shalvey. "As an educator I could imagine all the places where it could go wrong, but John doesn't think that way. I would tell John he needed to build strong relationships, work with people who don't support you, work with the competition. But those things never mattered to him. He would just plop down another charter in front of someone else." From the beginning, Danner planned to take Rocketship national, an important strategic decision, says Shalvey. In California, charters are always going to be constrained by the cost of facilities. "But when you get into places such as New Orleans or Tennessee you can grow much faster."

JOANNE WEISS

It seems trite to say that in Silicon Valley business is conducted in very different ways, including philanthropy. But it's true, and an East Coaster writing about education doesn't fully realize that until experiencing something dubbed "venture philanthropy." The firm that defines venture philanthropy is NewSchools Venture Fund, which raises and invests money in a style that mimics the way business gets done in Menlo Park, Palo Alto, and Los Altos. Prior to becoming chief of staff to Education Secretary Arne Duncan, Joanne Weiss was a partner and chief operating officer at the Oakland-based NewSchools. The group was an early believer and investor in Rocketship-like ventures—charter school startups with the potential to go big with high-quality charters governed by CMOs. In late 2005 when John Danner arrived at NewSchools as "entrepreneur in residence," he struck Weiss as a different breed entirely.

"John was a really good entrepreneur, someone who thinks through his priorities and lets the little stuff slide, focusing instead on the big, game-changing issues. A lot of entrepreneurs don't know how to do that. Immediately, John honed in on two interrelated questions: scale and quality. John wanted to scale excellence—and the kind of scale he was talking about was creating one hundred new schools in a short period of time and in a number of different states, [which] brings with it a lot of issues and problems that don't matter if you're only trying to perfect a couple of charter schools. It's a different approach, much bolder—more arrogant Silicon Valley."

On one level, what Danner was proposing was kind of "nuts," Weiss concedes. "On the other hand, I really respected his out-of-box thinking. Nobody was thinking that way. If you are really going to solve problems you have to think about scale. Everyone else was attacking this as 'quality first and scale next.' John attacked it the other way around. He came at it from an entrepreneur's perspective, not an educator's perspective." To educators, launching a national charter school network from California, one of the worst funders of charter schools, would seem a nightmare. From Danner's perspective, California was an ideal launch pad. If Rocketship could thrive in California, imagine what it could do in Washington, DC, for example, where per-pupil funding was roughly double that.

Reed Hastings

In my job as an education reporter and author, when I interview a super-intendent of schools I'm accustomed to meeting the public relations person, getting a tour of the schools, and then sitting down with a formally attired superintendent who sits behind his or her desk while dishing out rehearsed lines. Interviewing Reed Hastings is, well, different. Sitting in the Netflix lobby, I look up to see CEO Hastings coming my way in jeans and a leather sport jacket, informally barbered in a goatee. He leads me into a soaring Netflix meeting room where Netflixers gather for quick business meetings (they all greet him by his first name). He guides me to the biggest coffee-prep area imaginable and offers to fix me a coffee concoction that would make Starbucks proud. And then we sit down to discuss unconventional education wisdom.

Hastings, who holds a master's in electrical engineering, is a serial startup guy. And similar to John Danner he's a startup guy with a considerable investment in education. That interest started when he joined the Peace Corps after college, teaching math in Swaziland from 1983 to 1986. "I came back to the US and got into computer science. Ten years later, after my first company (Pure Software) went public and I suddenly had money, I got back into education." Hastings enrolled in Stanford's Graduate School of Education, but before he finished a master's he plunged into politics, helping win a new pro-charter-school law in California. In 2000 Governor Gray Davis appointed Hastings to the state board of education and a year later he became board president. In 2005 Hastings got swept up in the controversy over how much English instruction and English-language testing was appropriate for non-English-speaking students. His advocacy for more English instruction prompted the state legislature to reject him as board president, which led to his resignation.

"My takeaway from all that is that there are great people in every district, and all through the state government, trying to serve kids better." Unlike a lot of entrepreneurs, Hastings does not blame unions for poor student achievement. "The leaders of the California Teachers Association are very thoughtful. They care about members' rights, but they also want a great public education system." Hastings even supports the right of unions to organize teachers in charter schools. "That's a good check and balance on quality management." Nor does Hastings embrace the usual school reform hot buttons—No Child Left Behind, teacher tenure reform, merit pay. "I don't think those things will work. Teachers are trying hard as is."

All that makes Hastings seem like a genuine education moderate. He's not. From his perspective, traditional public schools are the equivalent of Blockbuster's Video—a business destined to die. It was just a matter of when. District school systems may be chock-full of dedicated, hard-working teachers and administrators but they have a limited chance of success, he says. "They are trapped in a system that's impossible." Inevitably, school districts that make significant progress end up slipping back, he says, and if gains are not sustained what value do they have? The core of the problem lies with governance via school boards, he believes. "The bigger the school district, the more expensive the school board race. The only people who can win are those who have direct financial interests—union people, politically ambitious people. Their goal is to serve their constituents by making change. They shake things up because that's what they feel they were elected to do."

In that process of "change," the positive reforms under one school board inevitably become negative reforms under the next board, which was elected by the forces that resisted the original changes. The result: the once-promising district slips back into the rest of the pack. Hence, his attraction to charter schools, especially Rocketship. With its strict cost controls and near-rabid insistence on teacher quality, Rocketship has the startup qualities to achieve what other high-performing charter groups seemed incapable of achieving: going real big real fast.

Guaranteeing that positive changes remain positive requires replacing elected school boards with the kinds of boards used by nonprofits, says Hastings, where board members pick their successors. Board members who pioneered positive change have a strong interest in seeing that progress continue. "That way, they control their own destiny." The way out, Hastings believes, lies in growing high-quality charter school networks—networks such as KIPP, which is governed by board members who are dedicated to the long-term mission of improving education for less-advantaged students. That belief explains why, in 2005 when Hastings was introduced to John Danner, he immediately embraced Rocketship schools. To Hastings, Rocketship looked ideal: a strong mission and an incredibly ambitious growth plan—all guided by a nonprofit board. Best of all, the cofounder was a startup guy who shared his startup values. Yet another factor: although Danner and Hastings deny looking alike ("I've heard that plenty of times, but I don't see it at all," Danner says with a laugh. "I guess when you're you, you don't think you look like anybody else."), they both think alike and, in fact, do look very similar.

To Hastings, a prize-winning math major at Bowdoin College, the math on charter school networks such as KIPP and Rocketship is simple: the more high-performing charters that get built the more kids who end up going to college. Just because the rapid growth of the successful charter groups hasn't happened yet doesn't mean it won't happen. "It's going to happen gradually, but not overnight." Charter schools, Hastings argues, are the only education vehicles out there with the promise of transformative change. "This is the fastest change we've seen in fifty years. It's much bigger than the alternative schools we did in the 1970s. They are having a bigger impact than No Child Left Behind or state standards. In California we're adding over one hundred charters a year. In twenty years we'll have a completely transformative change."

Hastings became a key though somewhat unofficial player with Rocketship. He is listed on the Rocketship website as one of three members of the National Strategy Board, a "board" that undoubtedly has never met as a board. "When I first started Rocketship I literally bootstrapped it," said Danner. "I wasn't asking anyone for money. That first year, with 150 students, we were cash flow positive. I might have put in $20,000 of legal fees, but I wasn't looking for money. Hastings's importance, once that first school was up and running, was that he started to evangelize Rocketship among the school-reform community. He talked about us and what we were doing. And then he decided that he would give us money for each new school we opened, $250,000 for each of the first eight schools."

That money from Hastings turned out to be crucial for Rocketship's quick expansion in San Jose. "Every time you start a school you have to do real estate work eighteen months in advance, hire an officer manager a year in advance, get involved in recruiting, and order materials. You have legal costs. You have to build a building and order desks and chairs, but you don't get a penny from the state until the kids are in their seats." That $250,000, which Danner refers to as a "cash flow loan but in the form of a gift," was invaluable. When groups such as the Charter School Growth Fund saw the Netflix founder putting that kind of money into Rocketship it drew their attention and ultimately led to an investment: let's really get to know these guys. And that's why Reed Hastings earns that special place on the Rocketship web page.

THE HARD SELL
Pitching the First Rocketship

January 2006: Palo Alto, San Jose, California

Based on his teaching experiences in Nashville and then helping launch a KIPP charter school, John Danner knew he wanted to launch charter schools in California. It was only a matter of when and where. Danner's first instinct was to open a school in Oakland but Don Shalvey steered him toward San Jose, a city where there was great need and a paucity of charters. Next Danner set a target date for opening his school: fall 2007. That meant submitting a charter application to San Jose Unified Schools by spring 2006, which in turn meant Danner had to get cranking on the proposal. So January became what writers call BIC (butt-in-chair) time. Danner cleared half the furniture from their living room in Palo Alto and set up a large, flat desk. Danner's wife, Allison, a law professor at the time, didn't seem to mind. From time to time, she used the desk as well. And visitors to their home barely noticed. After all, this is Palo Alto, a short walk from Stanford University, an island of soaring real estate prices where entrepreneurs famously have no choice other than launching startups from their garages and living rooms.

Working eight hours a day on his laptop, Danner cranked out a three hundred-page proposal by March 1. Three hundred pages? Most charter applications run no longer than thirty pages. Danner wanted a document that would set the foundation not just for one charter school but a group of charters. "So I took the approach of saying more, not less. I wanted the transparency of saying what we wanted to do. Then, they could take shots at it and we could figure it all out." Danner, in his words, wanted to start a "discussion." As the coming years would reveal amid growing opposition to the expanding number of Rocketship charters, he succeeded in starting that discussion. Perhaps overly succeeded.

The Guts of the Rocketship Request

Danner's opus encapsulated everything he had been working on since selling NetGravity and deciding to take on the achievement gap as his next new thing. From his tough teaching experience in Nashville came an intense focus on personalized learning. From the teacher-retention problems he experienced while helping to launch a KIPP charter school in Nashville came his emphasis on delivering great professional development for teachers and rapidly promoting teachers into leadership roles. From his determination to solve the national achievement gap by the year 2030 came his slimmed down charter school model, a model designed to expand fast without the need for raising outside funding. From all those prior experiences came his special focus on blended learning, the glue that made it all possible.

One of the suggestions Danner made in that 2006 proposal—that teachers would be specialists in subjects such as math or reading and teach that single subject to all the students in a single grade at Rocketship—was, at least in hindsight, a sleeper. At the time, teacher specialization combined with the Learning Lab enabled Danner to launch a school with large classroom sizes and still win state bonus money for offering low teacher-student ratios. It was education sleight of hand: in truth, class sizes were "small" only because so many students were rotating out of the classroom and into the Learning Lab. But what may have started as a gambit to win extra funding would later prove to be a real winner for Rocketship.

It all sounded promising, and it was. And yet anyone reading that first application can see why it was headed into a buzz saw at San Jose Unified, where Danner hoped to win a charter approval. Danner's analysis of the strengths Rocketship would bring to San Jose made it pretty clear that he thought San Jose lacked those strengths. Anyone reading it would assume that many teachers in San Jose Unified had low expectations and that the district had no idea how to personalize learning. You would also assume that the best hope for Latino students in San Jose lay in signing up for a Rocketship school. It was not a let's-all-get-along approach. Clearly, Danner was headed for a confrontation.

Submitting the Application (from Danner's Perspective)

Filing the charter application in March was anticlimactic. Some office workers at school headquarters logged it in without comment.

That changed, however, when Danner first met with Don Iglesias, then-superintendent of San Jose Unified, at a downtown Starbucks. The meeting didn't go well. Nor did the subsequent meetings. To Danner, Iglesias was a remnant of a dying breed of superintendents, a blunt, command-and-control school leader who wanted complete domination over the district.[1] But Danner wasn't offering to open up a Rocketship *under* Iglesias's direct authority; he wanted Iglesias to grant an *independent* school within district boundaries. "He told me, 'You're not going to do this in San Jose. This is not what we need.' I asked him if he was familiar with the state charter law (where school districts must have substantial reasons to reject charters) and he said, 'This is my district, my responsibility is to the children and I don't think we have anything to talk about. Now go away.'" So much for the grand discussion at Starbucks.

Things only got more interesting when Danner appeared before the full San Jose School Board to seek approval. Danner came armed with slides of test data from No Child Left Behind to reveal the academic failings of specific elementary schools in the low-income Latino neighborhoods where Rocketship wanted to open. "When I showed board members the academic results for these schools Iglesias's face got redder and redder until he became visibly upset. He had awful frowns. I was thinking this was really bizarre. There was no format to say, 'Mr. Superintendent, can I help you?'" Only after the presentation did Danner learn from board members why Iglesias might be upset. Based on the questions asked by board members, it appeared the members had never seen those numbers before. Danner concluded that nobody had ever disaggregated the data for board members to look at their low-income schools separately. When high-income and low-income schools are averaged, test results don't look so bad. What Danner showed the board members was flat out bleak. Danner's slide showed five comparable elementary schools within a mile-and-a-half of where Rocketship wanted to start a school— schools that had more students below basic than at basic. "The board members should have been asking the district how their low-income schools were doing. I walked right into the middle of that without understanding that not only did the district not talk about [disaggregated data] they didn't have a plan for these high-poverty schools. They were like, 'Oh, everything is fine.'"[2]

Not surprisingly, Danner lost that vote.

APPEALING TO THE COUNTY BOARD

When it came to Danner and Iglesias, however, there was no bridgework. When Rocketship went before the Santa Clara County Board of Education in July to appeal the rejection, Iglesias was there to urge disapproval. And here's where things get much disputed. According to Danner, Iglesias went a bit overboard, first telling board members that Rocketship would be the "end of public education as we know it . . . He was ranting and raving." At the time, Danner thought Iglesias was making a tactical mistake. "Boards don't work on the facts as much as emotions and relationships, and the superintendent was just not composed."

Then, according to Danner, Iglesias really went too far. "He described in great detail why the families we wanted to serve didn't have the capacity to help their kids become high achievers. He said they didn't have time, they worked two jobs, and they're poorly educated. It was basically the Diane Ravitch argument that we have to get over the fact that we have poor people in this county we can't help, so we have to stop blaming the school system."[3] Danner said at this point he had to calm himself to prevent himself from overreacting to what Iglesias was saying. "If the guy running the school district thinks their children can't succeed it becomes self-fulfilling. As he was talking I was thinking that now it all made sense. If you're running this system, and you only have one way of doing things, then when children are not achieving you have to blame it on something else."

Danner was astonished Iglesias was saying this in public. Rocketship kept a cassette of the remarks and for several years used the comments as a recruiting tool. "When we would run information sessions for parents interested in Rocketship we would always have someone stand up and describe what the superintendent said that night. After hearing that, anyone not completely convinced they needed another school option would usually sign up. You could not have scripted a better way for Rocketship to get momentum in the community than for Iglesias to say that these kids are going to fail because their families are failures."

The county board gave Danner and Rocketship a green light, overriding a no vote from their own county superintendent, an extraordinary development. Rocketship was cleared for launch in fall 2007.

SUBMITTING THE APPLICATION (FROM IGLESIAS'S PERSPECTIVE)

In contrast with Danner, who grew up in a privileged family in nearby Saratoga, Iglesias grew up in San Francisco, the son of immigrant parents, neither of whom graduated from high school. His father, born in Guatemala, worked as an upholsterer, his mother as a secretary. Iglesias won acceptance to Lowell High School, an elite public magnet school, and went on to graduate from the University of California at Berkeley, later earning a master's in multicultural education from the University of Southern California. His teaching career was launched through the Teacher Corps, a Great Society program aimed at improving instruction in high-poverty schools. Iglesias was a principal for fourteen years before moving into central office management, eventually taking over as superintendent of San Jose Unified in 2003.

As superintendent, Iglesias says he devoted his efforts to overcoming minority achievement gaps. "Sometimes people believe that kids who speak a second language or come from poverty can't succeed. The goal was to change that." And Iglesias says he was making good progress on that goal. In 2006, when Danner pitched the first Rocketship, San Jose Unified was "not an unhealthy" school district, says Iglesias. "So when John said he wanted to develop twelve charter schools in the area my question to him was, 'Why San Jose Unified? I understand that there are [school districts] with tremendous difficulties, but San Jose Unified was not one of them. We were in [positive] motion.'"

Iglesias agrees the first meeting with Danner went badly (about the only point the two agree on). "Perhaps our initial encounter might have had a better outcome if John was more personable and less clinical in his discussion of his proposal. It would have been helpful if he was able to approach me with his personal passion for wanting to serve students and less technical in his description of students as 'data points.'"

To Iglesias, the state law allowed charter schools as small-scale experimental schools or schools designed to fit a particular niche demanded by parents. The charter law never intended charters to become mini-districts to compete with large districts such as San Jose Unified. In 2006, the area's economy was tanking and Iglesias already faced the unpleasant task of cutting millions from the budget. What Danner was proposing, a dozen charters with five hundred students apiece, was unthinkable. "That's thousands of kids; that would have a huge impact on our programs."

But the tension between Iglesias and Danner was about more than just budgets. To Iglesias, Danner was an arrogant startup guy trying to tell him, a son of immigrants who became a professional educator, how to do his job. "John is wealthy and he is politically connected through his family." (John's father was a prominent lawyer who became a judge; his mother ran nonprofits and sat on multiple boards). When Danner started telling the San Jose Unified School Board about "failing" downtown schools, he was indirectly calling Iglesias a failure. Who was this prep school kid to judge him? No wonder Iglesias slowly turned redder and redder. "John had the audacity to propose a dozen schools in our district and say that we were failing. I wasn't happy about that." Iglesias denies that personal animosities played a role in the district's decision. The Rocketship proposal got turned down because it was flawed, says Iglesias. "When we analyzed the curriculum we found it was weak and sketchy. . . . He wanted to hire non-credentialed teachers. The curriculum was weak; there was no ELL (English language learning) plan."

Iglesias said he raised the same objections at the county board meeting. And he angrily rejects Danner's assertion that he talked down about Latino parents. "If I didn't believe [Latino students] could get good academic gains, why would I be in that urban setting? That is absolutely not true. John has visions of grandeur and wants to set up a false history of people saying he couldn't succeed. I would never say that our kids couldn't succeed."[4]

WHO'S RIGHT, DANNER OR IGLESIAS?

Unfortunately, the recording of that county board meeting was destroyed; the board is obligated to keep those recordings for only five years. And the cassette Danner and Smith had of those remarks—the one they used to market Rocketship as a school system that truly believes Latino income children can succeed—has been tossed. We will never know exactly what Iglesias said. The question of whether Iglesias was right to say that San Jose schools in those high-poverty neighborhoods were making good progress, and therefore didn't need rescuing by John Danner, can be put into perspective. Several times during our interview, Iglesias referred to Washington Elementary as an example of a struggling school on the way up. "Washington is an amazing school. The parents are all over that school. They have programs where moms read to the kids in Spanish."

The fact that Iglesias singles out Washington Elementary is telling. Not only is Washington one of the five schools cited by Danner in his presentation as failing, but the first Rocketship school, Mateo Sheedy, would be established not far from Washington, allowing good apples-to-apples comparisons. (And in 2012 Washington Elementary become a key player in the fight between San Jose Unified and Rocketship over whether Rocketship could launch a third school within Washington's enrollment zone. That fight over the proposed Rocketship Tamien site is detailed in "The Pushback Gets Real: The Fight over Tamien.")

The "who's right?" answer reveals much about both Iglesias and Danner. At that time, Washington Elementary was, as Iglesias described, a school on the mend. Steady, upward progress on state reading and math scores ensured that Washington ducked No Child Left Behind accountability measures that singled out schools failing to make progress. To Iglesias, and most superintendents, that's progress, and they are correct. But when Danner looked at those same test scores he saw a different picture. In 2006, Washington scored a 654 (out of a possible 1,000) on the California state test. On that test, a score of 700 is considered "basic," which means, as an entire school, Washington Elementary scored below basic. Put another way, only 22 percent of Washington's students were rated as proficient in reading, 40 percent in math. (Just for the record, Washington Elementary, the school cited by Iglesias as fast improving, was one of the better performing "failing" schools cited by Danner. At Gardner Elementary, another school on Danner's list, only 16 percent of the students were proficient in reading that same year, 30 percent in math.)

Where Iglesias saw a school making significant year-to-year progress, Danner saw a school where many of the four hundred students stood little chance in a workforce that demands far more than below-basic skills. Professional educators place great value on incremental improvements, the kind of change they think is possible and lasting. Based on decades of school reform, they have a point. To startup guys, that kind of incremental improvement means something else, a sign of a flawed product doomed to fail in the marketplace. Or, in this case, children who will always be limited. Also a good point.

I asked Iglesias, who retired as superintendent in 2010 and now lives in Santa Cruz, what he thinks about how that first school, Mateo Sheedy, turned out. Iglesias said he was glad Rocketship was succeeding, at least on the surface, but raised questions about whether the success was sustainable as the Rocketship system expands. "When you do well at one school can you leverage that and do it at multiple schools?" And he took one more shot at Danner: "Honestly, I don't know John that well, but he came off as arrogant and rude, someone who wants to design not a school, but alternative school system in his image. That was never the intent of the charter law."

NOTES

1. Many who worked with Iglesias dispute this characterization. In fact, there is almost no common agreement about what happened at any of the Iglesias-Danner meetings and confrontations, which is why, in the end, I decided to separate the versions of what transpired.

2. Another disputed point. Iglesias says San Jose Unified was required to provide board members with disaggregated data. "We were one of the first school districts in California to use data to drive student learning and increase staff performance." Danner's comments on the board members are "disrespectful and ill-informed," Iglesias told me.

3. Ravitch, a prominent critic of both charter schools and the school reform movement, would undoubtedly dispute this characterization. She argues that schools receive too much blame for the ills caused by poverty. In recent years, the two opposing sides have moved slightly toward the middle, with the "no excuses" charter advocates conceding that poverty is a massive negative force and Ravitch and her allies saying they never meant to suggest that schools can't make a difference.

4. Agreeing is former school board member Leslie Reynolds, who attended the county meeting. "Don was merely pointing out the obvious, that students who come from poverty, that are non-English speakers and have non-educated parents who are often not available to participate with their child's education, all contribute to a harder but not impossible road to mastering the many necessary educational skills needed to succeed at school."

OPENING MATEO SHEEDY
Tough Times

August 2007: San Jose, California

Danner and Smith were ready to launch their first school with 160 students, but their new school building was a year in the future. That was a problem but the problem was solved, or so they thought, by renting for a year St. Paul's Methodist Church at the corner of Tenth and San Salvador. Seemed like a good idea, except for a few problems. Actually, more than a few. For starters, the church had no air conditioning and that San Jose summer turned out to be a wilter with classrooms feeling like they were in the upper nineties. Not only was there no AC, there were no fans. The electrical upgrades undertaken to open the school were devoted to powering laptops.

To alleviate the heat problem they brought in a lot of drinking water and an electrician to hook up ceiling fans. It didn't help much, in part because the "playground" was just a blacktop parking lot next to the kindergarten room, and the heat from that blacktop swirled up from the macadam and poured into the classroom. Smith worried the parents would pull the kids out of the school. "I remember putting this one little girl into her mother's car and she had long bangs, which were clamped to her forehead. She was totally wet. You just knew the kids had been sweating all day. I put her into the car thinking, 'Oh my god, her parent is going to pull away and say, "What are you doing to my daughter?"'" It didn't happen. Both parents and students endured the heat.

The heat, however, was just one of many trials faced by the Rocketship founders. Smith, who was in charge of running the school, had to endure multiple parking lot issues. For the most part the church staff didn't need the parking lot during school hours, but Rocketship couldn't just take over the parking lot, either. Occasionally, there was a midday community meeting and the churchgoers didn't want to be denied parking.

The solution: forty jumbo-sized traffic cones, almost four feet high, placed throughout the lot, to save parking spots for the church. Sounds logical, except the task of setting out the cones each morning and taking them down at night fell to Smith, who had to arrive at school every day by 6:30 a.m. to start setting out the infernal cones and then, before going home in the evening had to gather them up for storage. Total time consumed on cones: at least an hour a day. Leaving the cones out overnight was not an option. "If I left them out overnight they'd get scattered all over the neighborhood. For a drunken college student, what could be more fun than throwing around a bunch of cones?" Finally, Smith told Danner he would have to come up with enough money to pay the custodian staff to move the cones. "I will never move another goddamn cone in my life."

Cones weren't the only heavy maintenance chore. Every day all forty laptops had to be taken down, put on a cart, and rolled to the only secure location in the church. That also usually fell to Smith. And then, every Friday night the church dance team met in the only large room available, which served as Rocketship's Learning Lab. "Every Friday night we had to break down the Learning Lab, in its entirety, the computers, bookshelves, carpets, dividers, tables, and move everything into the corner. And then, Monday morning, we had to set everything back up. It was wearing; it was draining; it was hell."

The worst part of breaking down and building up the Learning Lab was knowing the entire lab was proving to be pretty much worthless. The servers failed often, in part because the students kept kicking out the plugs. "We had the big server machine sitting there under the table," said Danner. "A chord would get kicked and every kid's computer stopped running the program." Given Danner's previous Silicon Valley wizardry, the technical burps may seem odd, but even Danner couldn't make the unique student sign-on software—the system in which students are supposed to scan in and get led directly to the right program—work. It proved to be, in tech lingo, kludgy, a truly damning word to be uttered in Silicon Valley. A specially written program was supposed to allow students to sign on and then immediately send them to the digital learning program that a particular student most needed. A breakthrough in individualized learning. Only it wasn't. "It was done in a quirky haphazard way by a volunteer and it just never really worked very well, so it actually caused a lot more problems than it solved," said Danner. "It would just crash and send kids to the wrong place. By the end of the year we scrapped it."

Danner recalls the day an important California education reporter, John Fensterwald, came to visit the new school. "That day, all the computers were broken. Somebody tried to distract the reporter, but sure enough he wrote an article saying there were ninety-nine awesome things about Rocketship but the one bad thing was the technology. It was a bit rough for the Learning Lab that year."

For Smith and the teachers the startup was exhausting. One day Smith felt himself coming down with strep throat so he went to the emergency room and asked for a penicillin shot. Naturally, the doctor wanted to delay antibiotics until the throat swab proved positive. Smith was having none of that. "I tell him the situation at Rocketship Mateo Sheedy. I have to put the Learning Lab together Monday morning. Our teachers are on the ropes; they will quit if I don't show up, that I absolutely have to be there Monday morning, and I say, 'You are going to give me a penicillin shot, and if you won't, I will go to another doctor.'" Finally, the doctor succumbed and gave Smith the shot. Monday morning, Smith returned to school and discovered that fellow teacher Maricela Guerrero later visited the same doctor with the same symptoms and the same urgent message. This time the doctor didn't even argue; she got the shot immediately. Rocketship Mateo Sheedy was getting a reputation, at least in San Jose emergency rooms.

Not surprisingly, the difficult working conditions quickly led to teacher dissatisfaction. Smith started the year with seven teachers. By Thanksgiving, one quit. By January he had to fire one teacher. Within a week, the teacher hired to replace the teacher who quit also quit. True, working conditions were challenging but another factor was a flawed decision Smith made to hire traditional teachers for what amounted to startup jobs. Those teachers were used to a nice classroom, a school district with a professional human relations department. They were used to getting their needs met. They showed up to work for Rocketship and found far tougher conditions.

It was a tough startup, but something revealing played out that year. Smith gave up trying to find a traditional teacher to enter the startup charter world, so he took over math instruction for second and third grades. And the English teacher for those same kids was Guerrero, who the following year would take over the newly built Mateo Sheedy as Rocketship's flagship school and produce startling academic outcomes. In short, those second- and third-graders at the startup year, in that hot, crowded, chaotic school where nothing seemed to work, were being taught by an all-star cast, Smith and Guerrero. In that first year, those Rocketship Mateo Sheedy students emerged as winners, scoring an 891 on the California academic assessments. For a first-year school stocked with low-income minorities, that's just flat out great.

Good news, but what played out that first year didn't prove the Rocketship theory that superstar teachers weren't needed, especially with a tailwind provided by blended learning. In truth, superstar teachers ended up doing it all, with little or no help from the kludgy blended learning. Rocketship schools taking off in a Fibonacci manner was a long way off.

NewSchools Launches Charter Accelerator Fund II

January 2006: San Francisco, California

With the second fund, the strategy broadened a bit. This fund would pour more money into the existing successful CMOs to bring them to larger scale and find new CMOs to support and extend the CMO model by encouraging more charter groups to focus on turning around failing urban schools. Charter Accelerator Fund II concentrated on eight target cities: Boston; Chicago; Denver; Los Angeles; New York; Oakland; Washington, DC; and New Orleans. By 2012, the NewSchools' portfolio included thirty-one school management organizations operating more than 330 schools, serving over 130,000 students. Five of the thirty-one charter groups were involved in restarting low-performing district schools.

How to Build
a Fibonacci School

August 2007: San Jose, California

Nationally, Rocketship schools are known for pioneering new forms of blended learning instruction. So, the first things visitors look for in Rocketship schools are a lot of high-tech toys. They will be disappointed. There are computers in every classroom, but what classroom today lacks computers? In truth, Rocketship classrooms don't look that different. But when the visitors stop looking for digital toys they notice something different about the San Jose schools: there are a hell of a lot of kids crammed into a tiny space!

On average, a US elementary school sits on between six and eight acres. It has a library, playground, parking lot, and an outside playing field enjoyed on weekends by soccer and T-ball teams. In addition, each classroom is at least 960 square feet. In these schools, everything feels campuslike, plenty of room for kids to move around without banging into one another and creating, well, kid issues. Here's what you experience in a Rocketship school. Instead of eight acres, the school sits on just one acre. Instead of those comfortable, 960-square-foot classrooms, Rocketship classrooms are sized at between 600 and 640 square feet, just enough to fit thirty kids and still clear code requirements. As for the big parking lot, go look for neighborhood parking. And the sprawling playing fields full of weekend sports teams? Better go to a public park.

And the craziest thing about Rocketship schools: any little oasis of comfort, whether it be the principal's office, copy room, or faculty lounge, has a way of getting transformed into some kind of academic function involving students, not adults. When visiting Rocketship Discovery Prep I always knew that using the faculty bathroom meant slipping quietly into the back of a crowded classroom. Any teacher with an expansive view of personal space would probably be better off applying to traditional schools. Rocketship schools are not built for teacher comfort.[1] But here's the thing about those traditional schools in San Jose where Rocketship mini-campuses are springing up. The campuses often look a lot better than the student outcome data.

When Danner first visited Artik Art & Architecture, a San Jose design firm with considerable expertise in building schools, traditional and charter, architect Bill Gould could scarcely believe what he has hearing from Danner. Every time Gould explained the basics of school construction as it usually plays out in California, Danner stepped in to challenge: what do you mean? Why do I need this? Is this because code requires it? "John kept pushing and pushing," recalls Gould. "He wanted more money for the program, less for the facilities." At times, Danner pushed the limits so far that Gould thought he was coming off as "goofy." After that first meeting Gould immediately checked Danner out on Google. "What he wanted sounded so crazy to me I needed to know if he was for real or a crackpot." Gould read the history of NetGravity and quickly concluded that Danner was for real. What Danner wanted was what few other school builders ask for: a stripped down model that could expand nationally with only one purpose in mind: eliminate the learning gaps for poor and minority kids. He wanted Fibonacci schools. T-ball really wasn't on his mind.

Over the months that followed, Gould and his partner, Stephanie de Raynal, worked with Danner as he immersed himself in the technical details of school construction. The challenge was new to Danner, who again brought a startup mentality to the usually staid world of school construction. At times, that startup mind-set became infectious even when he was demanding the impossible. "What's amazing about John," said de Raynal, "is after sitting in a meeting with him you feel like you can do anything, even things that don't seem plausible. John challenges everything."

What they settled on was modular construction, where large chunks of the building are assembled offsite and then shipped to the school site for assembly. All the interior work gets done on the factory floor, including bathrooms and electrical. Not only does it cost less, but the turnaround time from start to finish is half that of a traditionally built school, a handy feature in the charter school world where legal challenges had to be anticipated. Rocketship's first school, Mateo Sheedy, was placed on a plot of land just over an acre. Factory assembly time took two-and-a-half months, on-site work another two-and-a-half months. The price per square foot, including the site work, was $180. A more traditional school would have taken at least a year and cost about $350 per square foot.

Over the next several years, new Rocketship schools kept going up in San Jose, most of them located on lots barely over an acre, all of them modular construction. Some of the schools were located in dicey neighborhoods. "I went to one [prospective] site," recalls Gould, "that was one of the toughest neighborhoods in all of San Jose and wondered what everyone would think about seeing this white guy with a camera hanging out there. There was a group of three or four guys who walked onto the site behind me. I thought, 'Oh shit.' This was clearly a gang area. So I walked right up to them and shook their hands. They asked me what I was doing and when I told them we were thinking of putting a school there, they asked a couple more questions and the tension just want away. All of a sudden they were happy I was looking at it as a school." One school was shoehorned into a spot so tight and inaccessible that the modular manufacturers had to use temporary access via a freeway on-ramp.

At one point Danner came to the architects and challenged them to come up with a model set on a mere quarter acre—a contingency in case Rocketship expanded rapidly in land-tight San Francisco. Why can't people park underground? Asked Danner. Why can't we put the playground on the roof? Why can't we have valet parking? "We went through some serious analyses to try to make that happen," said Gould. "Luckily we didn't have to. We had hit the limit of our skills and code requirements." Lucky only because San Francisco school leaders resisted Rocketship's entry into their domain.

Always, Danner immersed himself in every aspect of the construction. And always, the building contractors had the same reaction to Danner. Every person they introduced Danner to, says de Raynal, had the same reaction: is this guy for real? Is he crazy? "We'd always chuckle over that. John is this amazing visionary thinker, but he can be really frustrating."

NOTE

1. The Rocketship school in Milwaukee is more spacious and has a full gym, a concession to the reality of Milwaukee weather.

PART III

THE GROWTH YEARS

The Ideal Personnel
Department? Not within
Rocketship

January 2008: San Jose, California

Midway through the first year of Mateo Sheedy, Preston Smith real-ized he needed a new personnel strategy. For the most part the vet-eran teachers he had hired from traditional schools didn't pan out. The chaos of a first-year charter startup was too much to bear. Hard to blame them. It was hot, crowded, and teeming with extra teacher duties. But for a charter group with national expansion ambitions, this was a showstopper. "Clearly, I had hired wrong."

When starting up a new school there are advantages to hiring young teachers who never experienced the comforts of quiet faculty lounges or a constantly available janitorial staff. In short, not knowing what they didn't know would be a huge advantage. "And there was the whole tech thing," said Smith, "being willing to adapt and work on the model with us." To get all that and draw in the best potential teaching talent in the country there was only one place to turn: Teach For America, which recruits top college graduates for two-year teaching stints.

When Smith started talking to TFA the first big concern was that only one out of every three TFA teachers stuck around for the long term. For a fast-growing charter, that would not work—too much burn-through for the amount of professional development they planned to invest in each teacher. The second takeaway was more promising. Many TFA recruits stay in education for roles other than classroom teaching. Through a mix of hubris and hopefulness, Smith and Danner decided they could make it work. Their perhaps unrealistic goal was to keep two-thirds of those TFA hires within Rocketship.

Why did Rocketship believe it could beat the odds? First, Rocketship planned to pay their teachers roughly 30 percent more than district teachers. That had to help. Second, they planned to promote them quickly into leadership positions, hoping that laying out a career path would help them hang onto their talent longer. And finally, Smith and Danner were convinced that the mission-driven Rocketship would appeal to prospective young teachers. What other charter group was so brazen as to openly declare that its goal was eliminating the achievement gap by educating a million students by the year 2030? That's the kind of swagger that induces top college graduates to sign on the dotted line.

"I think there are two myths about TFA," said Danner. "The first myth is that first-year TFA teachers are a tax on academic results, that they can't be effective that first year. Our thinking is these are very smart, motivated people. Maybe the problem is in their development." To support the first-year recruits Rocketship created the position of academic dean at each school. "That worked well. Our brand new TFA teachers compare well to the teachers we brought in from the outside, including TFA alums. To me, that makes a ton of sense. I taught for three years in a district in Nashville, and the professional development there was perfunctory. There's no way you get better at teaching in a job where all you have to do is sign in and sign out every day."

The second myth, says Danner, is assuming most TFA teachers will leave once their two-year commitments are complete. Most school districts advise new teachers that it will take ten years of teaching to qualify for a leadership position; with Rocketship, that shrinks to two to four years. "If they are going to stay in education, they want to have as big an impact as possible. At Rocketship we found a fit between our needs for growth and what these twenty-two- and twenty-three-year-old TFAers want for their careers."

So Rocketship didn't just ink a deal with Teach For America. Smith and Danner went all in. Teach For America was far better equipped to tap into teaching talent than Rocketship, they reasoned. Why not make Teach For America Rocketship's de facto personnel department? In the early years nearly all Rocketship hires were either TFA-experienced teachers or TFA first-year recruits, right out college. Most school districts are more cautious about TFA, bringing in a handful each year. Hiring more than that would seem dicey—some first-year teachers are awful, including TFA recruits. Plus, that would upset the teachers union. But Rocketship had no union to worry about. And Smith was confident he could make TFA recruits into good teachers in just one year. Betting on a new strategy, and then doubling and tripling down, was quickly becoming part of Rocketship's DNA.

Drawing on advice from Don Shalvey, the experienced founder of Aspire charter schools ("You will need some adult leadership"), Smith and Danner created a formula that made sure every school had a mix of teachers. If a twelve-teacher school opened up, ideally the school would have four first-year TFA recruits, four teachers who had completed their two-year commitment with TFA in other places, and another four teachers from other Rocketship schools (nearly all of them, of course, would have TFA backgrounds as well). Staffing hasn't always worked out that precisely, but that was the rough goal.

Through the startup years of Rocketship, when promising teachers asked to teach at Rocketship they were directed to TFA. "Some of the best training and support is through TFA, so we encouraged them to go through TFA. We got them interviews. We bore the risk, and we vouched for them. But they still had to go through the TFA selection process." Although essentially turning over your personnel to TFA sounds like a cost savings, it actually cost Rocketship more. "TFA is more expensive than recruiting directly," said Smith. "We paid a finder's fee, and we paid for them to earn their credentials." When everything gets added up, those TFA teachers cost Rocketship between $8,000 and $10,000 extra per year. "It was absolutely worth it," said Smith. "TFA is an incredible recruiting and selection company. They find exemplary talent, and they have standardized the process; they are like a huge headhunter. You can make assumptions about the kind of talent they are going to get."

In 2009 Aylon Samouha was Teach For America's senior vice president of teacher prep support and development, a job that allowed him to travel the country visiting partner schools using TFA teachers. It was also a position that gave him some ideas about what was working and not working in those schools. Based on his previous experience with Kaplan Learning, a for-profit education services company where he used a very early version of online learning to correct learning deficiencies, Samouha began to formulate a plan for an ideal school, one that used blended learning to personalize instruction. When he discussed that with TFA founder Wendy Kopp, she dashed off an e-mail introduction to John Danner. When Samouha visited Rocketship, he was struck by what he saw. Not only was the school leading the way with blended learning but also Rocketship appeared to have come up with a formula for making first-year TFA recruits teach with the expertise of more experienced teachers. "From seeing so many classrooms run by corps members, I know what a typical first- or second-year corps classroom looks like. But in my random sample of ten classrooms, the corps members I saw were all in the top third (of teacher effectiveness). That should not be possible in a randomly selected sample. It was my sign that Rocketship was on to something. I told John and Preston that these were some of the best corps members I had ever seen."

Based on those observations Samouha joined Rocketship in 2010, taking on the key job of overseeing the academic model and teacher training.[1] From the beginning, Rocketship beat the TFA retention odds by a wide margin. Four TFA recruits that were hired for the first-year Mateo Sheedy opened in its new location in August 2008. Today, three of those four remain in Rocketship. Overall, through 2013, roughly two-thirds of all TFA hires stay within Rocketship.[2] That was the target.

In 2010 Rocketship made an unusual pitch to TFA: we will give you higher recruiting fees if you give us your list earlier and allow us to sort through the applicants based on who we think has school leadership potential—a direct outgrowth of Rocketship's grow-fast strategy. Yes, we need good teachers but we also need good teachers who will become great principals, especially startup principals willing to go to other regions of the country. TFA agreed, and Rocketship began paying an extra $2,000 per recruit for that privilege (an option TFA now extends to all its Bay Area partners). By using TFA as its recruiter, Rocketship clearly rolled the dice. And it worked, at least in the early years.

NOTES

1. In 2013, turbulence at the top of Rocketship's leadership would prompt several departures of key operatives, including Samouha.

2. Teach For America says the percentage of TFAers who choose to remain in the classroom after their two-year commitment is only slightly better at Rocketship than at other schools. But that doesn't count the number of TFAers who move into leadership roles such as academic deans, assistant principals, principals, or work with national expansion.

Alum Rock District Rejects Rocketship ... Is That a Bad Thing?

August 2008: Santa Clara County, California

Many of the low-income Latinos who live and work in the San Jose area live in the Alum Rock School District, which made it a place Rocketship wanted to be. Preston Smith knew the district well. He taught there with Teach For America and then colaunched an alternative school there, LUCHA, before leaving for Rocketship. But the Alum Rock School District leadership and school board wanted nothing to do with Rocketship, despite the academic success stories that emerged from Rocketship's Mateo Sheedy during its first year in San Jose. Rocketship was competition, pure and simple. Knowing their application to open a charter in the Alum Rock area was going nowhere, Smith and Danner didn't bother waging much of a campaign to win approval. Maybe twenty-five parents showed up at the school board meeting to witness the rejection—a step that had to be taken before Rocketship could apply to the overarching Santa Clara County Board of Education, the alternative authorizer, to open a charter in that area. That's exactly what Rocketship did.

The irony: the rejections by San Jose and Alum Rock made it easier for the county board to grant Rocketship multiple approvals. Said Smith: "I think they were like, 'Whoa, you guys keep getting rejected, what's going on here?'" In August 2009, with approval from the county, Rocketship opened Si Se Puede (Spanish for "Yes, It Is Possible," a phrase used by Cesar Chavez and the United Farm Workers) Academy in the Alum Rock School District.

ROCKETSHIP FINDS A FRIEND

November 2008: Santa Clara County, California

W hen Danner and Smith tried and failed to win a charter from San Jose Unified they appealed to the Santa Clara County Board of Education. That county board is a bit of an oddity. On the surface, it looks like a regular school board but in reality it's more of a niche provider of services to the thirty-one school districts: Head Start, foster care, special education, alternative schools for expelled or incarcerated students. Interestingly, the county board got handed one more authority: the power to grant charters. Most of the county's thirty-one school districts in its orbit see charter schools as unwanted intruders plotting to snatch their students.[1] The county board, by contrast, has no students to snatch. For anyone looking to start a charter school, this board is the safe harbor.

That first Rocketship school, Mateo Sheedy, got approved by the county board in fall 2006. But Danner and Smith had far larger plans. They calculated that there were fifteen thousand underperforming students in the region, most of them low-income Latinos. To make a dent in the regional achievement gap meant building thirty Rocketship schools. To Danner, Mateo Sheedy was a mere foot in the door. Rocketship needed a champion on the county board who would stand up to the inevitable heat that would come. In November 2008, an unlikely charter champion, Joseph DiSalvo, got elected to the board.

Some people are hard to read by appearance. Not Joseph DiSalvo. With his long hair and goatee, DiSalvo is exactly what he looks like: a 1960s lefty who, when it comes to kids, never left his leftyness behind. He laughs when I suggest he is a reconstituted sixties liberal. Of course! DiSalvo, a former teacher and principal in San Jose who once served as a union president for Santa Clara County teachers, watched as the California Teachers Association, at least from his perspective, veered into the politics of self-interest. He didn't follow. "It's crazy. We've become far too adult centric." His former colleagues became union-style liberals, reliably working to elect candidates on the Democratic ticket but just as reliably standing in the way of key reforms that might compromise work rules designed to benefit teachers over students. DiSalvo remained an old-school liberal, never hesitating to criticize either the union or his own schools for doing too little to trim achievement gaps. Wrote DiSalvo in his blog about approving more Rocketship schools:

> The status quo was unacceptable: 50 percent of San Jose's students scored below grade level proficiency on math and language arts on California Standards test, and there was an achievement gap of at least 30 percent.

> There is no doubt that the vast preponderance of teachers, principals and superintendents work tirelessly to see that all children succeed. However, they sometimes fall victim to a system that works in favor of the adults rather than the children. For 30 years, the results have not budged when it comes to the achievement of low-income students. The gap has only narrowed incrementally.

. . . .

> Rocketship's schools show that their blended learning model, use of Teach For America teachers (80 percent of the total full-time equivalent of teachers), and teacher home visits, matched with the aforementioned factors, produce extraordinary results for a mostly free or reduced lunch qualified population of learners. Hundreds of parents signed up for Rocketship's waiting list to win a lottery slot for their children to be enrolled.

DiSalvo grew up in San Jose, graduated from San Jose State University, and at the age of twenty-three took a job teaching incarcerated youth. "It was fascinating work." Then he taught at a county children's shelter, followed by a long stint as an administrator, followed by several school leader positions, including serving as a principal at a school in tony Palo Alto just off the Stanford University campus. DiSalvo retired at fifty-seven, and in 2008 ran for a seat on the county board. What DiSalvo saw within sprawling Santa Clara County was a proliferation of school boards stocked with members more concerned about protecting turf than reducing racial learning gaps. "These boards can be an impediment to innovation, creativity, and growth. They are too conservative at times on issues about children." At that point, DiSalvo had to reconcile his hesitations about moving away from the model favored by traditional liberals (charters not welcome) with his concern about racial learning gaps that weren't diminishing under that common school archetype.

Change, concluded DiSalvo, will only come about through disruptive forces. And with Rocketship DiSalvo found his disruptive force. If Rocketship could demonstrate that low-income Latino children can arrive at middle school performing at least at grade level, if not beyond, then why couldn't the traditional elementary schools do the same? Approving Rocketship schools will force those schools to compete by adopting Rocketship methods, he reasoned. DiSalvo, who soon would become board president, presided over multiple approval hearings for Rocketship schools. In the end, DiSalvo usually corralled enough votes for Rocketship to carry the day.

NOTE

1. An exception is the Franklin-McKinley School District, which adopted a charter-friendly strategy to educate its high-poverty students. In January 2014 the district won a $100,000 grant from the Gates Foundation to deepen the relationship between its traditional schools and charter schools, which includes Rocketship.

CHARTER SCHOOL GROWTH FUND PUTS ROCKETSHIP ON THE MAP

November 2008: San Jose, California

Usually, the Denver-based Charter School Growth Fund[1] requires three years of student progress data before stepping in to fund a promising charter school group. At this point, Rocketship barely had two years of data and a mere 320 students.[2] Not a typical candidate for funding. But Danner and Smith were determined to give it a try, so they flew to Denver to be interviewed. At one point the fund leaders asked each to leave the room so they could grill Danner and Smith separately. The same questions were asked of each—and Smith and Danner responded the same way. To the fund leaders, Smith and Danner looked like solid leaders who thought alike and were building a promising new charter school model. As a result, Rocketship won $2.3 million of expansion funding.

The grant came at a time when other foundations were taking a pass on Rocketship. To those other foundations, the new, blended learning model championed by Rocketship looked a little, well, too new. Let's wait and see. "Everyone else still thought we were insane," said Danner. But the fund (which today invests 20 percent of its national fund in blended learning) saw Rocketship's promise differently. It was Rocketship's first major grant. That money, says Danner, was critical mostly for the influence it had. "It was kind of a validator." If the Charter School Growth Fund found promise in Rocketship, then maybe others should as well.

And it certainly didn't hurt to have Reed Hastings, an early supporter of the fund, lobbying on your behalf, telling everyone at the fund that Rocketship was the future.

NOTES

1. A nonprofit funded by foundations and individual philanthropists.

2. To get a third year of data, they used test scores from LUCHA.

Slivka's Sci-Fi Software Gets Shipped
DreamBox

February 2009: Bellevue, Washington

When Ben Slivka decided to create his own interactive learning software in 2006, the online options for students, parents, and teachers were pretty bleak. For decades, the big textbook publishers had offered up catalog after catalog of new and updated textbooks that were plush and expensive, something akin to Microsoft's computer-based software. Nobody wants to walk away from cash cows like that. And so, for the same reason Microsoft delayed shifting to the web, the textbook publishers delayed going into online education. What made more sense to them was duplicating their textbooks on CDs or placing them online, thus making them digital cash cows.

But digital learning doesn't work that way. If it's not interactive and personalized for each student it might as well be a frayed old textbook. The few independently developed digital math programs were linear, asking students to proceed from one step to the next. And if you run into trouble? Raise your hand and ask the teacher for help. What was the point of that? Might as well return everyone to classroom lectures.

Slivka knew he had an opportunity to create something different, mostly because he and his team weren't educators. They were software writers, and good ones. Slivka says software engineers are not like journalists. A really good journalist might be twice as good, or twice as productive, as a lesser journalist but a software writer can be exponentially better. A talented software engineer on a roll can do in one night what a team of 150 engineers fail to do over the previous week. The reason DreamBox did what other online programs couldn't do, says Slivka, is simple: "We had better software engineers."

Slivka's team created a platform, essentially an engine with all the nuts and bolts hidden, with a programming language resting on top, a language that actual educators could use to write interactive lessons. The first teacher Slivka hired was Mickelle Weary, who had taught his son at a Seattle private school seven years earlier. "I must have made an impression on him [Slivka]," said Weary, who was a first-year teacher. "You know, first-year teachers often aren't great, but I tried really hard. I was trying to do individual learning, letting [Slivka's son] and another really smart kid to do things together." Succeeding at personalized learning made an impression on Slivka.

The best way to experience DreamBox is to sign on as a prospective parent and take a quick trip through the program. To entice the kids, the math programs might be constructed as treasure hunts displayed as elaborate maps. Students who successfully solve logistical problems along that pathway get a little closer to the treasure. The real treasure, of course, is the hidden mapping that sucks up every move made by your child and then uses that information to build a complete package of math skills. Personalized learning.

"Kids are not books, where one page follows the next," said Dan Kerns, DreamBox's chief architect. "They are all over the map. You might have one kid at the 'normal' and everyone else at different parts of the bell curve, with the hard-to-reach at one end and the bored at the other. Part of engagement and teaching is finding out what kids need to learn. We have deeply integrated assessment into learning. We're constantly asking, 'Does the kid really know the stuff we're teaching?' If the machine doubts that, it loops back and gives a refresher. . . . At the end of the day in a DreamBox classroom all the kids are doing something different. That's because it has measured and adapted."

And so, in February 2009 DreamBox was launched. On its own merits, DreamBox may have been as innovative as Dropbox, but the reception was vastly different. Whereas Dropbox soared, DreamBox sputtered. DreamBox was aimed at parents of young children, but how many of those parents were even aware their children needed a program such as DreamBox? That kind of awareness doesn't even develop until middle school when kids start bringing home lousy math grades.

As it turned out, Slivka had created a software model that was light years ahead of its business model. Few parents were interested in buying a product they didn't know they needed. Kids weren't finding it on their own. One interesting development surfaced early, however. The Dream-Box team noticed that "parents" listing their family size at between twenty and thirty children were buying DreamBox. As it turned out, these were teachers buying it for their classrooms. "They raved about it," said Kerns. "They told us it solved real problems they had." Soon, DreamBox reoriented itself to classroom sales but that wasn't an easy switch. How many tech-naive school superintendents are going to take a chance on a bunch of startup guys unknown in the education world? It was great that teachers liked DreamBox, but that didn't necessarily translate into a workable business model. Companies like DreamBox need lots of cash to keep innovating, but the company wasn't generating that cash and investors were getting hard to find. It wasn't at all clear that DreamBox, despite being one of the first truly adaptive learning programs to emerge, would make it.

ROCKETSHIP WINS FIVE
MORE CHARTERS

June 2009: Santa Clara County, California

Responding to the rejections of Rocketship in the San Jose and Alum Rock School Districts, the Santa Clara County Board of Education authorized five more Rocketship schools for the county, an action taken with little debate or dissension. In hindsight, both the board and Rocketship were newbies operating in a legal gray area. What's a countywide ask, anyway? In the charter school world, this was an entirely new beast, which probably explains why there was so little pushback from the surrounding school districts that would be affected by these blanket approvals. Those district superintendents remained a bit puzzled by Rocketship. "We were still small at the time," said Smith, "and a lot of people still didn't believe that we could build the facilities and actually get it done. They thought we were a lot of talk and no action."

The five-charter approval would be the last time Rocketship would slip by unnoticed. And if the many school districts within the county realized that the ask for five charters would soon be followed by an ask for twenty charters, they probably would have showed up to object to the five. "Asking for twenty," said Smith, "is like taking the hornet's nest, knocking it down, and jumping up and down on it."

FINDING KAREN MARTINEZ . . .
IT'S AN ART

September 2009: East San Jose, California

Anyone who doubts that great wealth begets great poverty needs to visit Silicon Valley. The fortunes made cashing in Apple, Google, and Facebook stocks spawned the construction of thousands of California-hip mansions, the purchase of untold numbers of luxury and sports cars, and millions of indulgences at famous-and-fabulous restaurants. All that, in turn, led to demand for thousands of low-wage workers to trim those ornately landscaped lawns, bus those dirty, fancy dishes, and detail those fabulous cars. That last group of workers, nearly all Latino, sees the wealth of Silicon Valley only at arm's length. They live in places such as East San Jose, with multiple generations grouped in one home. Don't even think about finding a parking spot on their street. For the most part, they send their kids to crappy schools that do little to prepare the next generation for a shot at getting into Stanford and sharing in some of that Silicon Valley wealth.

Why don't we hear them protesting their inadequate schools? White and Asian parents in high-income neighborhoods would never put up with that. Conventional wisdom holds that hobbled by language barriers and the need to work several jobs in irregular shifts these parents are kept busy and cowed. Surely, school authorities are the experts here; let them be experts. Then came PACT, People Acting in Community Together, whose community organizers concluded that the status quo didn't have to be destiny. It was PACT organizers working mostly out of churches who started a parent movement demanding something different from the usual Alum Rock schools that serve the children of East San Jose—charters and small, autonomous schools that resemble charters, the kind of schools they had seen work well in other urban areas. That gave birth to LUCHA, a small, autonomous public school cofounded by Preston Smith. That same parent movement gave Smith political support when the district and union pressed to trim back that experiment.

When Smith left for Rocketship he took that community organizing strategy with him. The strategy operates on two levels. Rocketship itself handled all the internal parent organizing, helping the parents become active supporters at the school and at home with their children. But there's another level to parent organizing, a higher level, in which parents with hidden leadership talents can be identified, nurtured, and trained to lobby publicly not just for more Rocketships but for better schools to send their children to after Rocketship. What was the point of building great K–5 schools if only crappy middle schools and high schools awaited in the later grades?

At Rocketship, that job was initially farmed out to PACT. Organizers such as Matt Hammer and Marie Moore approach a school of five hundred low-income Latino students knowing that among those parents are at least ten very special people who have no idea they are capable of running a large meeting or standing up to superintendents, school board presidents, and principals. But they are. Surrounding those special ten are another twenty parents who also have leadership capabilities. Together, those thirty parents can wield enormous political clout. Finding those thirty parents, however, especially those special ten, is an art. Matt Hammer has devoted his career to finding these leaders.

"You are looking for someone who's got some connection to the anger, sadness, and pain in their lives," said Hammer, "so a lot of times with these first conversations you're having with somebody you are trying to pull out these tough stories of anger, disappointment, pain, difficulty, and getting people to start to reflect on that. You are looking for somebody who's got that spark of energy that often comes out of this mixture of pain and difficulty. And then you are offering them the opportunity to do something that connects to their interest."

In September 2009, that kinetic energy sparked at Rocketship Si Se Puede, where Karen Martinez had just enrolled her daughter, Daniella. To date, Daniella's school story had not been a happy one. Although she attended a good school in a good neighborhood she was academically troubled, a third-grader reading at a first-grade level. Martinez repeatedly pressed her daughter's teacher and principal for answers but was put off. "They would say, 'Oh, she's special needs,' but they didn't have any reasons for it." So Martinez started looking for other options and followed up on a friend's suggestion to check out Rocketship. She liked what she saw and enrolled Daniella.

"The turning point was when I came to Si Se Puede to volunteer and saw the literature teacher hovering over my daughter, who seemed very happy. My daughter didn't speak then. She was not autistic but she was intimidated being in a new school and didn't speak at all. The teacher had her repeating three sentences: 'I am smart. I am able. I will read.' That was a true turning point. And it wasn't just the literature teacher; it was the math teacher as well. Our child wasn't anything special, but she was special to us and to see someone else care about her that way, well, that was the day I said to myself, 'This school is something special.'"

Martinez was determined to be a rock-solid Rocketship parent, so when she saw a notice inviting parents to a meeting about where parents might send their children to middle school she showed up. Martinez was not someone likely to be shocked by a presentation laying out the dismal middle school options facing parents in that neighborhood. She knew that from the ground up, starting with her own troubled childhood. She spoke no English until third grade, and at the age of sixteen became a mother, at one point living in a car with her son. Eventually, she got a GED. Later, she married a man with four children so the blended family included five boys and two girls. Not a single one of the boys did well in school; for a time the youngest ended up in the state juvenile justice system. Today, he works with her father, an eighteen-wheel truck driver. "All my boys struggled academically with math and reading."

So Martinez was determined that her girls would not suffer that same fate. And what she heard from PACT organizer Marie Moore that night infuriated her. Moore had all the student outcome data for the middle and high schools Daniella would attend and the prospects were not promising. To Martinez, it seemed clear that if she didn't seize the moment her daughters would suffer the same fate as her sons. Martinez had the entire package: anger, pain, disappointment, and a determination to do something about it. When Moore invited parents for a follow-up session, Martinez readily agreed. What followed were lots of one-on-one conversations with

Moore, pulling out the threads of her personal story and developing an action plan, starting with recruiting more parent leaders.

Martinez become one of the "special ten," organizing a PACT action in June 2011, where school officials were challenged to commit to San Jose 2020, a feel-good agreement made among politicians and school leaders to reduce the racial-ethnic learning gaps by that year. Was San Jose 2020 something more than feel good? Soon, Martinez evolved into a force. When visitors showed up at Rocketship schools and asked to meet parents, Martinez was often one of those parents. I observed several of those meetings and always felt the impact when Martinez led off with her story of anger, repentance, and resolve. It had a revival feeling. When Martinez spoke everyone sat up a little straighter and afterward asked, "Wait, who was that?"

Martinez was among the group of parent leaders who set out to lure a top-performing middle school charter school to San Jose. After a lot of research, PACT identified a promising candidate in Oakland, a school led by John Glover who, after a lot of convincing—community rallies organized by parent leaders such as Martinez—decided to site his next school in San Jose: Blanca Alvarado Middle School, part of Alpha Public Schools. It's where Martinez sent Daniella, who by this time had more than recovered academically. To make sure Alpha became a reality, Martinez and others spent hours going door to door soliciting parent interest. To convince the Alum Rock school leaders that a charter should be approved, advocates needed hundreds of names of parents willing to take a chance on a new school. Martinez wore out two pairs of shoes, and still has two scars on her knees from that effort, but they got the signatures. And then she and the other parent leaders lobbied hard to make sure the school won permission to rent Alum Rock facilities that weren't being used by the traditional schools.

At times, Martinez can get a little, well, too intense. That happened when she volunteered to set up a recruiting table outside Washington Elementary to recruit for Rocketship's new Tamien school, a site that would draw even more students from Washington (see "The Pushback Gets Real: The Fight over Tamien"). Principal Maria Evans didn't take kindly to the challenge and, according to Martinez, stormed out to the recruiting table, grabbed a flyer and told a Washington parent, "Do not listen to this crazy woman. She is lying to you!" At that point, Martinez recalls confronting Evans, saying, "Give us your lowest performing students and we're out of here. Until you can serve all your students, I'm going to be on the sidewalk every day." One thing led to another and at one point Martinez admits to venturing into the school's office to deliver a similar lecture to Evans, which prompted Evans to threaten to call the police. Preston Smith, who today laughs about that memory, says he advised Martinez to cool it a bit.

The point is not whether Martinez acted appropriately that day. Rather, the point is that someone who once lived in a car with her son, someone who barely earned a GED, someone who didn't speak any English until third grade, was now acting as an in-your-face parent leader. Anger harnessed, artfully. If it can happen here in East San Jose, it could happen anywhere. Conventional wisdom is suddenly not so conventional.

ACHIEVEMENT GAPS IN
FABULOUS SILICON VALLEY?

October 2009: Silicon Valley, California

For children whose parents work within the orbit of the famous icons of Silicon Valley—Stanford University, Apple, Netflix, Oracle, and Google—finding good public schools is not a challenge. But for the sizable army of work-a-day people who keep the region livable, the challenge is different, to the point of being flat-out depressing. In 2009 came an unusual acknowledgment that the problem was truly bad, and it was widespread. In a report called SJ2020, the Santa Clara County Office of Education laid out the reality in blunt terms: between forty and sixty thousand students, or more than 40 percent of San Jose's children, weren't at grade level. Not surprisingly, poorly educated Latino families bore most of the brunt. Although 85 percent of Asian American students were on grade level, only 41 percent of Hispanic students were, a striking gap of 44 percentage points.

SJ2020 refers to its goal: eliminating the achievement gap by the year 2020, a goal embraced by the "two Chucks" who quarterbacked the report, then-county schools superintendent Chuck Weis and San Jose mayor Chuck Reed. The goal turned out to be wishful thinking, but it did trigger two significant developments—radicalizing both Chuck Reed and the Santa Clara County Board of Education, which became determined to use its charter-authorizing power to achieve that goal. Starting in 2007 the board green-lighted multiple charter schools, giving Rocketship near carte blanche to open schools anywhere in the county—actions many of the superintendents in the thirty-one school districts in the county found reckless. But as of 2013 the board, supported at times by Mayor Reed, hadn't backed down. Their goal: fulfill the promises of SJ2020.

In May 2013, SJ2020 got lapped by an updated and even broader look at the achievement gap in Silicon Valley. This "Broken Promises" report by a new advocacy group, Innovate Public Schools (founded by Matt Hammer, formerly of PACT) found even starker achievement gaps. In the Sunnyvale Elementary School District, 82 percent of the Asian students were proficient in algebra compared to 10 percent of the Latino students. In San Mateo and Santa Clara counties, only 20 percent of Latinos and 22 percent of African Americans graduated from high school having passed all the courses needed to qualify for admission at the University of California and Cal State compared to 71 percent of Asians and 53 percent of whites.

Clearly, not much progress had been made since the SJ2020 report came out four years earlier. About the only "good" news in the report were profiles of the top three schools succeeding with low-income Latinos. Two of them were charter schools, including Rocketship Mateo Sheedy, a signal that the county board and Mayor Reed appeared to be on the right path.

This is not just a San Jose or California state issue. In 2013 the Lumina Foundation released a fresh college attainment report: among twenty-five- to twenty-nine-year-olds, 66 percent of Asians and 45 percent of whites hold at least an associates' degree compared to 25 percent of African Americans and 18 percent of Hispanics. The foundation's goal for Latinos is to boost college enrollment from 2.7 million in 2012 to 3.3 million by 2016. That big a boost doesn't happen without a major shake-up of business as usual. Reed was agreeable, as well as the county board. But the thirty-one school districts in the county? Not so much.

District-Charters
Compacts Launched

*I*t all started with an unusual set of roundtable discussions: thirteen carefully selected school superintendents from around the country matched with CEOs of high-performing charters gathered in Los Angeles courtesy of the Gates Foundation. Would they find common ground? The discussions were "lively," say those present, as the leaders sorted through the positive and negative perceptions of one another. But at the end of the discussions there was an unexpected high level of interest in pursuing collaborations. That's what Gates's new deputy director, Don Shalvey, was hoping for. Shalvey, the Aspire Public Schools cofounder who counseled Danner in starting Rocketship, had joined Gates the year before. Shalvey knew that without collaborations with traditional school districts, top charters would never have the impact their leaders hoped for.

By December 2010, the first "compact" agreements between districts and charters were signed: Baltimore, Denver, Hartford, Los Angeles, Minneapolis, Nashville, New Orleans, New York City, and Rochester.[1] In 2011, Boston, Central Falls (Rhode Island), Sacramento, Chicago, Philadelphia, and Spring Branch (Texas) joined. A year later, Austin (Texas) joined. In 2012 the foundation invested $25 million in seven of the compact cities to support "deepening" the relationship. By October 2013, sixteen cities had inked compact deals. Could traditional school districts boost their academic performance by aligning with higher-performing charters? (See "Houston's Spring Branch Schools: The Future?" and "Where's the Tipping Point?")

NOTE

1. Rochester later withdrew from the compact.

Danner (and Reed Hastings) Discover DreamBox

March 2010: Palo Alto, Los Altos, California; Bellevue, Washington

It's almost a cliché to say that business plays out differently in Silicon Valley than in, say, Philadelphia or Kansas City, but it's true, and the fate of DreamBox Learning illustrates the point. John Danner "discovers" DreamBox and mentions his discovery to his friend and Rocketship supporter, Netflix founder Reed Hastings. After Hastings sees DreamBox in action at a Rocketship school, he e-mails his friend Dan Kerns, DreamBox's chief architect (the two worked together several years earlier; in Silicon Valley, all the best software engineers know one another) to say, nice job. Kerns e-mails back saying, funny you should write now; we're out of money; nobody's been paid in a while, and we're going to have to close or get sold. So Hastings buys DreamBox. Just some startup good ole' boys who know other startup good ole' boys doing business quickly and cleanly.

That chain of events started with Danner's search for adaptive software to use in Rocketship schools. "We were looking for a very specific thing, a piece of software that would work for fifty or one hundred kids in a computer lab, so that when they got confused they didn't have to raise their hands and ask for help from an adult because with that many kids having an adult remediate all the problems just didn't work." But Danner couldn't find that software, anywhere. "The companies just didn't look at the world that way. They thought you needed an adult, that it was the job of the adult to get the kids back on track."

But that didn't make sense to Danner. This was 2009. Software writers could easily make their program adapt to the student so when the student got confused the program would loop back and address the weakness. Why was adaptive software so hard to find? Well, say the software salespeople, that's just not how we do it. We write our programs like linear textbooks: students do this lesson, then the next lesson, and if they get stuck they raise their hands. Danner was astonished, but he kept looking. "So we searched for around six months and then we found this company called DreamBox that was doing a math program the right way. When a student got stuck you'd see this thing pop up, ask a couple of questions, and then based on those answers the activities that student was getting would change. It was in tune with what the kid was struggling with. Our first thought was, 'Why are these the only guys who are doing this?'"

After visiting the DreamBox team in Seattle, Danner knew he had found his program. Rocketship started using DreamBox for its math program, which led to Hastings seeing the program, which led to Reed Hastings purchasing the company. Hastings didn't want to own the company, so he structured the purchase through a gift to the nonprofit Charter School Growth Fund, a transaction worth around $11 million. "I'm still active in California education politics," said Hastings. "I didn't want people to think I was doing this to make more money. If it's financially successful, the rewards don't go to me."

At this point, Ben Slivka bowed out of the company he had created. "It was clear we were not profitable all along. . . . the choice was to take the bird in the hand or try to stay independent and find more money. Reed made an offer and it was the best deal we had, so we took it." Taking over as CEO of Dream-Box was Jessie Woolley-Wilson, a former executive with Blackboard. "Within a year she turned the company around," said Danner, "and now they are selling millions of dollars of software . . . the core lesson here is having a great product while doing bad sales work will get you every time. This company would have died. One reason we were excited about working with them is we wanted to use DreamBox as kind of a script to get to the rest of the software industry and say, look, if these guys can do this type of adaptive software so can you."

Today, DreamBox has plenty of competitors. In fact, anyone visiting a Rocketship school will see that DreamBox isn't the only math program teachers like to use. ST Math, many of the teachers will tell you, is more visual and allows students to work with more independence. All this is light years away from what Danner found when he first started his search for adaptive software and found none. "We would ask the designers why they built their program around a teacher always standing there, and they would tell us the teachers are there anyway so they might as well help. That was kind of crazy."

Yet Another Boring Education Book? Not Exactly

April 2010: Albany, New York

When Doug Lemov's book, Teach Like a Champion: 49 Techniques That Put Students on the Path to College, *was published there was every expectation of modest sales. Not many people buy a book about teaching techniques. For decades, education professors churned these books out like cheesesteaks. Who really reads them? But this book was different. Lemov, from the top charter group Uncommon Schools, spent a lot of time documenting—filming with inexpensive video cameras—the exact techniques that great charter school teachers use to successfully engage hard-to-engage students from high-poverty neighborhoods. As it turns out, thousands of teachers were interested. The book became a publishing phenomenon: by 2013 it was on its way to selling a million copies and there are several follow-up books. These weren't just charter school teachers buying Lemov's book. Traditional public school teachers also wanted to know the secret. Teachers colleges folded it into their curriculum. This would prove to be an early example of education seepage, a way charter teachers could talk to traditional teachers. Perhaps most important, it was a signpost that competition—"what were those charter teachers doing that we need to know about?"—was becoming a factor.*

States Repeal Charter Restrictions
(Okay, a Bribe Was Involved)

July 2010: Washington, DC

Education Secretary Arne Duncan delivers his "Quiet Revolution" speech at the National Press Club, summing up the impact from his department's "Race to the Top" (RTT) initiative. RTT never involved that much money, only $5 billion, a pittance in federal spending, but the reforms it spawned in states and local school districts were striking. To compete for grants, school districts had to carry out simple tasks they should have done long ago, such as devising teacher evaluation systems (seventeen states came up with evaluation systems). Plus, states were encouraged to lift caps on charter schools. As a result, thirteen states lifted their caps: Connecticut, Delaware, Illinois, Indiana, Iowa, Louisiana, Massachusetts, Michigan, Mississippi, Rhode Island, Utah, New York, and Tennessee.

Fresh Charter Strategy from the Department of Education

August 2010: Washington, DC

*A*wards are announced for the Department of Education's first charter replication and expansion competition aimed at CMOs—further evidence of the department's emphasis on helping the high-performing charters scale up. A dozen CMOs shared $50 million in grants. Among the winners: KIPP Foundation, $14.5 million; Aspire Public Schools, $5.5 million; IDEA Public Schools, $8.7 million; Mastery Charter Schools, $5.1 million; Uncommon Schools, $2.6 million; YES Prep Public Schools, $2.7 million; Achievement First, $1.6 million.

Growing the High-Performing (and Blended) Charters

November 2010: Broomfield, Colorado

*T*he Charter School Growth Fund launches Fund II, a $155 million fund aimed at supporting the growth of high-performing charters nationwide. About $30 million of that fund will focus on "next-generation" blended learning charters similar to Rocketship. Eventually, the next-generation grants will lead to thirty thousand new seats in blended learning charters.

Fund I from the Growth Fund opened in October 2005. By September 2013, overall funding by the Charter School Growth Fund passed the $185 million mark in grants and loans to be distributed to charter schools, enough to create 260,000 more seats for low-income students. Unlike traditional schools, which don't have to worry about facilities, most charters need an extra boost to get launched.

Double Setbacks . . .
Rocketship Changes Course

February 2011: East Palo Alto, California

In the early years of Rocketship the mission was clear and evangelical: go where low-income, minority students need good schools the most. Anywhere. But Rocketship was just getting started. It was premature to open a school far from its home base. John Danner and Preston Smith needed a nearby "anywhere" to keep Rocketship expanding. From the geographic perspective of San Jose, where Rocketship had already launched several successful schools, it seemed clear where Rocketship should go next. Just up Highway 101 in the direction of San Francisco was the beleaguered Ravenswood School District serving the poor and minority children of East Palo Alto. Actually, not serving those children very well, at least based on test scores that ranged from bad to awful. In fact, the Ravenswood School District was famously bad, mostly because it was located just across 101 from wealthy Palo Alto, home to Stanford University.

To Rocketship, East Palo Alto was intriguing. The students there were a little more diverse than the nearly all–Latino students in San Jose; this would be Rocketship's first exposure to African American students. To date, the poor performance of the students in East Palo Alto had been blamed on poverty, which was mostly accurate. But could schools alone make a difference? Others had tried and failed, including some of Stanford University's most famous education faculty members, who in 2001 launched the Stanford New School there, a charter the Ravenswood City School Board closed in 2010 after its students continued to post dismal test scores.[1] But Smith and the Rocketship team were not deterred. After all, the high-poverty students at their flagship Mateo Sheedy were posting math scores every bit as high as the white and Asian students on the wealthy Palo Alto side of 101. We can do this, they all agreed. What could go wrong?

At first, all their hunches about Ravenswood being the right choice proved true. Gathering signatures from interested parents was a cakewalk. Parents seemed desperate for other education alternatives. "Within two weeks we had about one thousand signatures," said Smith. "It was impressive." At that time, says Smith, Ravenswood had five board members: two likely to vote against, two who could be persuaded to vote yes, and a swing vote. To Rocketship, it all seemed doable. So when Smith and other Rocketship leaders showed up to present their proposal to the board it looked like the education reform circus had come to town. More than two hundred people showed up for the first board meeting, a combination of existing Rocketship parents and prospective parents from East Palo Alto. The Ravenswood board was not happy with this outburst of reform enthusiasm. "They were literally kicking parents out of the hallways, telling them they were breaking fire codes and moving them to an adjacent room. They were rude and nasty to us and the parents. They appeared shocked by the turnout. But I thought it was great. I thought we could win." The rude reception and hostility from the superintendent should have given Smith a hint about where things were headed, but Smith remained optimistic. Rocketship had overcome political resistance before. Ravenswood was a tiny district chock-full of parents who wanted better schools. Again, what could go wrong?[2]

Thirty days later when the board reconvened to take an actual vote on whether to allow Rocketship to launch its schools, it became clear what could go wrong. During those thirty days the union and district officials had tag teamed to do some phenomenal outreach. Mailers and phone calls had gone out to parents saying Rocketship's arrival would lead to shuttered schools and fired teachers. Ravenswood parents who showed up to support Rocketship the first time had been called into principals' offices and told to shut up. "On the night of the meeting, when Rocketship supporters showed up they were told to take off their Rocketship T-shirts," said Smith. "They were literally throwing the T-shirts into the trash. At one point I ran into a girl who was maybe twelve who told me I was trying to fire her teachers, that Rocketship is evil. I mean, if a twelve-year-old girl is saying this, that means there was a campaign by teachers and principals talking to students." This time, there was an even bigger crowd at the board meeting, and 90 percent were opposed to Rocketship. "I mean, the district and union really did their jobs," said Smith in admiration. By a three to two vote, Rocketship lost.

The appeal of the denial to the San Mateo County Board of Education didn't fare any better. There, the Rocketship staff was informed that if it came into Ravenswood the school would get folded into a long-standing court order correcting special education services in the district, a result of not serving those children in earlier years. It was the school board equivalent of a poison pill to ward off takeover attempts. Rocketship would have to fall under their rules and regulations. That was a nonstarter; the rules would disrupt Rocketship's successful education formula. To Smith, it was also bizarre. "It's kind of like a divorce we weren't part of, and we're the new guy in the relationship but we have to pay alimony. We had nothing to do with it."

After losing a vote at the county board, Rocketship walked away. A legal challenge to appeal the mandatory inclusion would have burned up years and more than a million dollars in legal fees. "I felt awful," said Smith. "We had community support; parents wanted this school. I didn't know what to tell them. It pains me to know Rocketship could have had an impact." Danner sees it the same way. "You have to give them credit; it was a nice little poison pill they created. But it was screwing the kids in East Palo Alto."

A parallel effort to open schools in Oakland also got rejected. "We got our butts kicked there, and we deserved it," said Smith. "If you are going into a region like that you had better have funds and people on the ground eighteen months before applying for a charter. You need to build a relationship with the community and build a brand, to let them know you're not there to take down schools and jobs. We are here to make sure everyone gets a good education. You need resources to do that, and you need trust." Both Smith and Danner drew the same lesson from Ravenswood and Oakland. "It's not worth going where you aren't wanted," said Danner. "That process is expensive, takes a long time, and it's distracting. It can take six months to go through all the processes."

From the beginning, Danner hoped Rocketship would become more than just a group of high-performing charters. He wanted Rocketship to be a disruptive force, forcing change. In San Jose, for example, the disruptive force would be flooding the middle schools with "overqualified," poor Latino kids guided by parents who have learned the lesson of political activism. The same parents who tasted political success, demanding more Rocketship charters, would also demand better middle schools. But it's hard to be disruptive when local school boards make it difficult or impossible to open even one school, let alone expand quickly.

The big lesson learned from the setbacks: go not where you are most needed, but where you are needed and wanted. There were plenty of cities brimming with students forced to attend low-performing schools—cities that would embrace Rocketship's arrival. From that realization flowed a new expansion plan: New Orleans; Washington, DC; Memphis; Nashville; San Antonio; Indianapolis; and beyond. Plenty of places wanted Rocketship. Really wanted them.

Notes

1. That school was founded by professor Linda Darling-Hammond, who headed President Obama's education transition team. As a prominent critic of Teach For America, which provides nearly all the teachers to Rocketship, Darling-Hammond's setback in Ravenswood was a "moment" in the battle between edgy school reformers and softer reformers such as Darling-Hammond, who enjoy support from the unions.

2. The Ravenswood superintendent did not respond to requests for an interview.

A Corporate Jet Packed with Movers and Shakers Touches Down

March 2011: San Jose, California

With its cutting edge blended learning and impressive test scores, Rocketship was seen by many educators and reform-minded political leaders as a glimpse into education's future. As a result, John Danner and Preston Smith were accustomed to getting a barrage of requests to visit Rocketship schools, as many as one thousand visitors a year—so many that tours were limited to Tuesdays and Thursdays, from 8 to 10 a.m. But even by those standards this request was unusual. Pretty much the entire political and business leadership of the city of Milwaukee wanted to fly in and tour Rocketship schools. Danner and Smith weren't sure what to make of the request. Not only did the visitors want to stay for two full days but also they wanted to meet San Jose community members as well. At the time, Danner and Smith had an informal list of cities where they thought their charter group was most likely to first expand outside of California. Milwaukee wasn't even on that list. But when the mayor, the head of the chamber of commerce, and city council president want to come calling via a corporate jet loaned out by a Milwaukee industrialist (read, possible donor), you pay attention.

Danner and Smith may not have known a lot about Milwaukee, but the Milwaukee politicians, business leaders, and education experts aboard that plane knew a lot about Rocketship. Howard Fuller, a former Milwaukee Public Schools superintendent and now a school reformer with national influence, was married to Rocketship board member Deborah McGriff, a partner in NewSchools.[1] But this was not a case of Fuller cheerleading the others; they had done their research on Rocketship and liked what they saw, especially the Learning Lab and intense parental involvement. After seeing the Rocketship teachers in action in San Jose and listening to the parents, these Milwaukee insiders, including Mayor Tom Barrett, council president Willie Hines, and Timothy Sheehy, president of the Metropolitan Milwaukee Association of Commerce, didn't just want to add Milwaukee to the list of Rocketship expansion candidates. They wanted Rocketship to move Milwaukee to the top of the list, and they thought they had the chops to get that done.

On the surface, Milwaukee might seem like an odd candidate to execute a full court press to get Rocketship to come to their city. Milwaukee is home to the nation's oldest school reform movement, a voucher and school choice program that got approved twenty years earlier when vouchers were so new that partisans had to define them before they could debate them. State lawmakers, led by former governor Tommy Thompson, were convinced that a drenching school choice movement would empower parents and produce better schools. All they needed was a green light from the Wisconsin Supreme Court, which arrived in June 1998. The top two benefits they hoped for were that parents who were pleased with school choice would stay in the city rather than move to the suburbs when their children came of school age and the competition would force rapid school improvements.

In short, neither happened. White flight to the suburbs was as striking in Milwaukee as in any other big city, says Alan Borsuk, a former Milwaukee reporter and editor who now writes about schools from a position at the Marquette University Law School. Most surprising to school reformers, the schools didn't get any better, at least when measured by student achievement. With the benefit of hindsight, that should not have been unexpected. The school choice laws steered clear of setting up any vetting process to sort out good and bad schools. The assumption at the time was that vetting would occur naturally via market forces. Those school reforms may have made some parents happy, especially those getting state aid to pay for parochial and private school tuitions they most likely would have paid anyway. But they failed to accomplish the far more important goal of delivering "high-performing" school seats to Milwaukee students.

What went wrong? "When we got started on this in 1989 school quality was not the driving force," said Fuller as he was having breakfast with John Danner later on in Milwaukee. "The driving force was choice.

And what was also operating at the time—that we now know is not true—is that parent choice alone will drive quality. There was this notion that parents are going to choose really great schools, and if there are terrible schools, parents will leave them. In reality, it doesn't work that way." As it turns out, parents have all kinds of reasons for choosing schools. Maybe a school is closer to where a parent works. Maybe a school has a better basketball coach. Maybe a school switch could keep a son or daughter from flunking Spanish. Worse, when parents are given choice, not only do many pick schools for nonacademic reasons but also they move schools a lot. Not helpful, at least when it comes to academic achievement.

By 2010 it was becoming clear that the nation's oldest school reform movement was on its way to become the nation's least distinguished reform. But what to do? Education experts from nonprofits weren't the only ones who glimpsed a silver lining in the failures. A handful of charter schools, places such as Milwaukee College Prep, were providing those high-quality schools. Soon, a plan emerged from the nonprofits and charter leaders, a plan that was immediately embraced by influential business leaders such as Tim Sheehy: create twenty thousand "high-performing" school seats by the year 2020. Another think-big goal, the kind set by startup guys and philanthropists.

The 2020 plan rested on three legs: boost capacity at existing successful schools, bring good schools up to great, and recruit outside charter management organizations to bring successful charters to Milwaukee—the source of the push to bring Rocketship to Milwaukee. The appeal of recruiting Rocketship wasn't just that Rocketship could boost test scores; it was that Rocketship, the press darling of the charter school movement, would choose Milwaukee as its first expansion site. That would send a message that Milwaukee was once again a school reform player and that, in turn, would trigger other positive reforms. The two key players behind recruiting Rocketship were the well-connected Abby (Ramirez) Andrietsch, cofounder of Schools That Can Milwaukee, and the even better connected Sheehy, someone who had invested many very frustrating years in trying to make Milwaukee into a city that turned out students prepared to meet the international business challenges. After all, Milwaukee might qualify as a rustbelt city but it was still a relatively successful rustbelt city, home to Johnson Controls, Rockwell Automation, Harley-Davidson, and

Northwestern Mutual. The world was still buying what Milwaukee was making, but that depended on maintaining a skilled workforce.

It didn't take the Milwaukee delegation long to convince Danner and Smith that they could meet Rocketship's three threshold requirements: foundation money to set up the launch, political clout to get eight charters approved (Fuller, Hines, Barrett, and Sheehy more than filled that role), and a supportive school reform network (Schools That Can Milwaukee fit the bill, along with the Teach For America office in Milwaukee, which identified a promising teacher, Rodney Lynk, who was willing to move to San Jose for training as a Rocketship teacher and administrator-to-be).[2] And so, improbably, Milwaukee moved to the top of Rocketship's expansion list. As Danner and Smith had learned the hard and expensive way in Oakland, San Francisco, and East Palo Alto, the trick is to go where you are needed and *wanted*. Milwaukee had the want.

Of course, having the money and clout to win approval for a string of Rocketship schools in Milwaukee is not the same as ensuring that schools open at capacity and succeed. In theory, the Rocketship leaders understood the challenges in Milwaukee. In San Jose, everyone knows the Rocketship brand, especially in the poor Latino neighborhoods. In Milwaukee, the Rocketship brand means nothing. In San Jose, charter schools are a new phenomenon. In Milwaukee, two decades of barely successful school reform have dulled parents' education reform sensibilities. They've seen charter schools come and go. Why take a chance on the latest? In almost any other city in the country, financially challenged Catholic churches would be a fertile recruiting ground for Rocketship. Here, they had been thrown the voucher lifeline; they weren't about to give up their students to fill a competing Rocketship school.

The warning signs in Milwaukee were abundant. Lighthouse Academies, which got its start in Oakland, launched a Milwaukee school in 2012 and fell short of filling all the seats. The Milwaukee insiders who recruited Rocketship warned Danner and Smith that recruiting could get rocky. "We were up-front with Rocketship that they need to recruit, and it would not be easy," said Andrietsch. There were other warning signs, some that few could have anticipated at the time Rocketship *green-lighted* (their term) Milwaukee as the first launch outside their home state. Scott Walker's campaign to turn Wisconsin into a red state triggered an unexpected side effect in liberal Milwaukee. Walker personally called Danner to encourage him to bring Rocketship to Milwaukee. Democrats once open to school choice cringed at embracing any policy pushed by Walker, which dampened enthusiasm for school choice among liberals and African Americans.

But if Rocketship leaders were worried about choosing Milwaukee as their first launch outside California they didn't show it. They had bigger issues bubbling up in San Jose—issues that caused them to take their focus off the Milwaukee launch. That would prove to be problematic.

NOTES

1. NewSchools Venture Fund switched its name to NewSchools.
2. Lynk, an African American, also figured prominently into Rocketship's plan to open Rocketship's first school in an African American neighborhood, on Milwaukee's North Side.

Leaders of Top Charters Tapped as State Commissioners

April 2011: Nashville, Tennessee

*T*ennessee governor Bill Haslam appoints Kevin Huffman, a veteran administrator at Teach For America, to become the state commissioner of education. In May, John King, the founder of Roxbury Preparatory Charter School in Massachusetts and a managing director with Uncommon Schools—someone who helped found some of the highest-performing charter schools in New York—was appointed education commissioner in New York. In September, Stefan Pryor, a cofounder of the Amistad Academy charter school, was appointed state commissioner in Connecticut.

Top Charters to Get
Stiff Test

May 2011: Nashville, Tennessee

Newly appointed education commissioner Kevin Huffman appoints YES Prep founder Chris Barbic to take over the newly formed Achievement School District, which will run the state's lowest-performing schools, those where students test in the bottom 5 percent. The goal is to move those schools to the top 25 percent within five years (a goal most educators would consider next to impossible). There are thirteen YES Prep schools in Houston serving eight thousand high-poverty students YES Prep boasts of a 100 percent graduation rate, with 100 percent of its graduates accepted by a four-year college. Barbic will ask high-performing charters to stretch, in some cases taking over entire neighborhood schools without seeking "opt-in" agreements in which parents and students agree to the stiffer academic challenges (see "Fibonacci Charters Summoned to Memphis").

BLENDED LEARNING
ROCKETSHIP STYLE
This Stuff Works!

August 2011: San Jose, California

SRI International releases a study of Rocketship's blended learning math program, provided by DreamBox, and the news is good: using control groups of students who did and didn't use the program, SRI reports significant additional progress made by students using DreamBox. The report is encouraging to Rocketship and DreamBox. "This SRI study validates DreamBox Learning's core value proposition—that intelligent adaptive learning is a game changer in education," said Jessie Wooley-Wilson, CEO of DreamBox.[1] The study, funded by Rocketship, encourages Danner, Smith, and other Rocketship leaders to push harder on blended learning. They appear to be on the right track. At Rocketship Mateo Sheedy, student math scores soar to startling heights.

Over the next two years, however, some significant questions about blended learning will arise. Where's the limit on ratcheting up the amount of time students spend on blended learning? Is the signature Rocketship Learning Lab really the right way to administer those online programs? Are the blended learning literacy programs working anywhere near as well as the math programs? Rocketship is running into a familiar problem; it's a lot easier to boost math scores than reading scores.

NOTE

1. A federal study from the What Works Clearinghouse (WWC) released in December 2014 found DreamBox had no effect on learning. Responded DreamBox's Daniel Kerns, "DreamBox believes that the WWC report draws conclusions that are erroneous and

misleading. With hundreds of thousands of students using Dream-Box Learning Math in school districts nationwide and throughout Canada, DreamBox Learning, Inc. finds the WWC report to be both disappointing and irresponsible and believes it is a disservice to educators and students." But the story does not end there: in a surprise development the WWC considered new evidence about DreamBox and in March 2014 reversed its negative finding, concluding that the program has "potentially positive effects."

KIPP Opens Its
One-Hundredth School

August 2011: Atlanta, Georgia

*K*IPP *Atlanta Collegiate, located in an impoverished west Atlanta com-munity where the median household income is $19,000, opens as KIPP's one-hundredth school. Founded by Dave Howland, a teacher from another KIPP school in Atlanta, KIPP Atlanta Collegiate is Atlanta's first KIPP high school. It will grow a grade a year until it reaches grades 9–12.*

In 1994 KIPP started a program for forty-seven students in Houston. In 1995 founders Mike Feinberg and Dave Levin created the first two KIPP Academies in Houston and New York and they became fully grown 5–8 middle schools in 1999. KIPP first replicated the original two academies in 2001 as it expanded by three schools, KIPP DC KEY Academy in Washington, DC; KIPP 3D Academy in Houston; and KIPP Gaston College Prep in Gaston, North Carolina.

A Discovery That Would Lead to Big Changes (and Bigger Drama)

November 2011: San Jose, California

At Rocketship Discovery Prep third-grade teachers Bridget Keating and Amy Filsinger were known as the "kickout crew," the teachers the principal had to kick out every night because they were staying too long. But these two literacy teachers were staying late for a reason. Despite all their time and best efforts, their students weren't making the progress they thought they should. The evidence was clear, posted on a data wall in the school's copy room that day. The student growth figures showed their students were making respectable progress, equivalent to a year-and-a-half of growth in a single year, but for these two teachers, who were fully aware of how far behind these kids were when they arrived at Rocketship, that wasn't sufficient. On the surface, everything was clicking, says Filsinger. "Our classroom culture was strong, the parents were supportive, the homework was coming in—but we were not seeing the (outcome) data we wanted to see."

One problem was their classes were awkwardly balanced, with some students at grade level, or even ahead, and others behind by anywhere from two to five years. Therefore, any large-group instruction ended up missing half the class, either on the high or low end. It made sense to slice the class into fluctuating ability groups, but a single teacher has no time for small-group instruction clustered that way. But what about combining their classes? One teacher would specialize in catching up the slower readers and the other targeted a different group. This being Rocketship, there was no bureaucracy standing in the way. Soon, Keating and Filsinger carved out four reading lessons in a day, rather than one. "It allowed for flexible groupings and flexible time," said Keating. "This was especially effective with the lowest readers, who had had been riding on the coattails of the highest readers, slipping through the cracks during class discussions.

Bottom line: each student got nearly sixty extra minutes a week in carefully tailored, small-group sessions. "We were able to shift kids, based on their progress, which was nice. We shifted every day." At the end of every day, the two teachers gave their students "exit tickets," which were three-question quizzes to determine what they had learned and what they had missed. The next day, the results from the exit tickets guided what got taught to whom.

When Discovery Prep principal Joya Deutsch saw the first-year results from the combined classes, she was astonished. The academic predictions made at the beginning of the year based on early testing got turned upside down. In third grade, for example, two dozen kids predicted to fall into the basic or below-basic ended up scoring proficient or advanced. The same trend played out in fourth grade. Not only did the good readers get far better, the students who had been at the bottom rose quickly.

Deutsch told Smith about the results, but it wasn't clear anything would ever come from it. Just two teachers doing nice work. But their discovery would later have a huge impact on Rocketship.

Rocketship Bids Big
Give Us Twenty More Charters in Santa Clara County

November 2011: San Jose, California

Just sitting in the audience that evening at the Santa Clara County Board of Education you knew right away that this would be no ordinary school board meeting. What started as a steady trickle of Latino parents, many of them wearing Rocketship T-shirts and accompanied by children waving Rocketship banners, soon turned into a steady stream, then a torrent. First the huge, main meeting room filled up. Then all the adjoining rooms got packed. In all, roughly seven hundred people jammed in to watch a session that usually might draw no more than a handful of observers.

Especially striking was who showed up. In shiny Silicon Valley, these Latino parents are the ones tasked with keeping it that way. This was their night to demand something for themselves: schools that would give their kids a shot at the better life that surrounds them and yet still remained well out of economic reach. They wanted to see the Santa Clara County Board of Education grant another twenty Rocketship schools. That would triple the number of existing schools and eventually lead to something unprecedented, an independent school district of fifteen thousand students, drawn from the poorest neighborhoods in this sprawling county. If all went to plan—Rocketship's plan, that is—that district would finally shrink its considerable academic achievement gap.

That hope was expressed in the signs (Spanish on one side, English on the other) carried by the Rocketship students:

More Rocketships/More Kids to College
College Class of 2030
Everyone Deserves an 892 API School

One by one, parents accompanied by translators came forward to testify: "I don't have a lot of money," said one mother. "All I have is my encouragement that my kids go to college." Another mother: "A lot of families want to move their kids to Rocketship, but there is a long waiting list." A third mother of two girls: "Rocketship is giving us parents hope. They believe in our kids. You have the ability to be champions tonight."

On this night, the board would turn aside objections from the teachers union, from surrounding school superintendents—and from the board's own staff—and grant three more charters. The vote on the full twenty got postponed, but in December all of them got approved. At least on the surface, Rocketship appeared to be on a roll. Twenty more charters in the San Jose area with other charters approved for Milwaukee, Nashville, Memphis, the District of Columbia, Indianapolis, and New Orleans. School reformers in cities such as San Antonio appeared to be willing to do whatever it took to bump up their chances of landing a cluster of Rocketship schools. Hey, that worked for Milwaukee. To Danner and Smith, the world had to look pretty promising.

The optimism was not warranted. True, winning a countywide ask of twenty charters was unprecedented. Where else in the country had that happened? But the huge win also awakened the opposition. Board president Joseph DiSalvo wrote a blog about being "verbally attacked" by union members over that vote. The union, wrote DiSalvo in his blog, "wants to put up legal roadblocks against doing what is proper for our underserved children. CTA's (California Teachers Association) interest appears to be in keeping the status quo. The status quo has not done right by low-income children for decades."

Union resistance, however, would prove to be the least of Rocketship's worries. It was clear that opposition was growing among the powerful superintendents overseeing traditional school districts in Santa Clara County. To them, this county board charged with small-change educational tasks was punching far above its weight class. How dare they give Rocketship authority to insert charter schools a few blocks from their lowest-performing schools? That was anathema. To them, that would sap those schools of resources, turning struggling schools into failing schools. One of the opposing local school board members likened it to forcing homeowners to accept soldiers in their homes—soldiers who could take their money and food at will.

On the surface, what looked like a huge win for Rocketship was likely to turn into a problematic win because the opposing superintendents settled on a weapon for fighting back: zoning. Just because the county approved charters didn't mean the county board could force the zoning changes needed for new charters. Warned two school trustees from Los Altos: "Based on advice from our counsel, there is no legal basis for the county board to usurp the power from local school districts to issue exemptions from local zoning requirements." The local school boards were about to throw down the gauntlet. Enough of this arrogant startup calling itself Rocketship.

Granting authority to open twenty new schools would prove to be a world apart from actually opening twenty new schools.

SETTING UP ROCKETSHIP TO FAIL?

April 2012: San Jose, California

In spring 2012 Smith knew Rocketship was riding a potentially rogue wave. Yes, the Santa Clara County Board of Education had approved an additional twenty Rocketship charter schools, but building out a charter school network is never that easy. Anticipating a bumpy path, Smith budgeted regular meetings with Stephen McMahon, the president of the 1,700-strong San Jose Teachers Association, a square-jawed, plain-speaking kind of guy who gets education Realpolitik.

At one of those meetings, McMahon had an intriguing offer: how about taking over one of our troubled schools? From the beginning, it was clear this was as much a challenge as an offer. What McMahon was truly saying was this: if Rocketship thinks it has the answer to educating poor and minority students then take over one of our failing schools chock-full of those kids. To McMahon, that's what charter schools were supposed to be about. "The California charter law designed them to create pockets of innovation, so they have the freedom to try things and be different." What Rocketship was attempting, building a school-district size network of schools, subverted the intent of the law, he thought. McMahon had a point. So, if Rocketship truly had the chops to turn around a troubled school then demonstrate it! Show us the innovations! "If Rocketship can do that, then they should put us out of business."

McMahon wasn't bluffing. He was convinced that Rocketship's model was nothing special. Rather, their success flowed from "selection bias," attracting only students whose parents were willing to sign the Rocketship forms agreeing to the longer hours and school volunteer duties. McMahon didn't think San Jose Unified was at risk of being put out business. He had grown weary of seeing Rocketship collect accolades around the nation for posting great test scores of low-income Latino students. If denied selection bias, he assumed they would do no better than other San Jose Unified schools.

The traditional public schools in San Jose, as with all traditional schools across the country, lack that selection advantage, McMahon argued. "Public education is a societal mandate. It is compulsory for a reason. There are a large number of families who wouldn't be in school unless we force their hand. We know that if you're not educated that causes long-term detriment to society, so we're going to force you to go to school and learn." School systems such as San Jose Unified have entire departments tasked with chasing down truants who don't want to be in school. Just one or two of those defiant students can doom a classroom, says McMahon. Rocketship, by contrast, has no truant officers. It has few defiant students with uncooperative parents. All their children, and their parents, choose to be there.

"I have a big thing about the selection bias," said McMahon. "If we took our five hundred best kids, or kids who wanted to be there, and opened a new site with our best staff, we would beat Rocketship scores. We have enough knowledge to be competitive. They get a student population we don't get." McMahon's offer to turn over an entire school was dicey but real. "For us, it was a high-stakes challenge. I don't know of a single union local willing to give up a school."

In this book, the school's identity will remain confidential. McMahon didn't want a local school to know it was being offered up as takeover bait. But here is a brief description: this elementary school is a textbook example of a school that has drawn every imaginable local, state, and federal resource. The more it fails, the more money pours in to turn it around. Today, it occupies a beautiful campus but persists in its academic stuttering mode. Its student population mirrors the kinds of students served by Rocketship, but its 2012 test scores were a world below and going upward nowhere fast. At Rocketship Mateo Sheedy, 76 percent of the students tested at proficient and above in reading, 93 percent in math. At the school in question, only a third of the students were proficient in reading, half in math.

Immediately, Smith recognized it as a challenge and probably not a bluff. There was no way McMahon would make this offer without clearing it with San Jose Unified superintendent Vincent Matthews, Smith believed. Union presidents don't have the power to turn over an entire school to a charter operator.[1] (In January 2013, two months after I interviewed McMahon at his union headquarters, he left the union to work for San Jose Unified as chief business officer.) Smith also recognized the underlying motive. He assumed the offer was made only to prove that Rocketship would fail. When that failure became public, the Rocketship monkey would be off their backs. "At one point I drove him to the point where he actually said that it was a dare and he didn't think we would be successful. [McMahon denies saying this.] He said he wasn't rooting for Rocketship to be successful. I'm thinking, Why should I partner with someone who is out to undermine us and doesn't want us to be successful?"

In the end, the restart negotiations broke down for two reasons. In the first year of the restart, families should have a chance to opt out and attend a neighboring school, Smith insisted. That was fine with McMahon. And in subsequent years, all families would have to opt in to the Rocketship school. That was not fine with McMahon. To him, that amounted to giving Rocketship the selection bias he thought was solely responsible for their success. No deal. McMahon insisted that in year two the Rocketship school would accept any and all students the district sent their way. That pretty much ended the negotiations. Said Smith, "We want people come in, see the program, and sign up for it. Charters are about choice and doing things differently." McMahon remembers the failed negotiations differently. "They didn't do it because deep down they know their success does not come from the instructional model. . . . They know their system only works when people choose it."

"At some point we will do a restart," said Smith. But not now, not this offer.

NOTE

1. McMahon says there was no preapproval from the district. "I was not the typical union president and often acted on my own. At the same time, I know that if Rocketship had agreed, we could have pulled it off."

ROCKETSHIP DOUBLES DOWN
ON A REINVENTION

June 2012: Redwood City, California

Andy Stern, Rocketship's new chief financial officer, had only been on the job for a couple of months. Stern, fifty-seven at the time he joined Rocketship, spent twenty-five years in Silicon Valley as the CFO for many technology companies. In Rocketship's main headquarters in Redwood City, not far from San Francisco International Airport, the typical employee appears to be a twenty-something, which makes Stern look like somebody's father. But that's exactly what Preston Smith and John Danner wanted: a senior staffer who had the financial gravitas to scrub the numbers and lay out, in forceful terms, Rocketship's potential—or peril. On this day, as Stern met with Smith and Danner, he had peril on the agenda.

From the beginning, Rocketship had a simple model for growth: each school would throw off enough cash to generate money to be used to launch other schools. And with the first several schools, that worked nicely. Rocketship schools got built on tiny parcels of land using inexpensive modular construction. Compared to traditional schools, they operated with an exceedingly modest front office. And with the blended learning model, where students spent a good part of the day overseen by lower-paid teacher aides, Rocketship needed fewer teachers. Rocketship could operate a school with just sixteen teachers, compared to the twenty-one teachers needed in more traditional schools. It was a carefully honed financial model that was working—until 2012.

Here's how Danner recalls the warning words that day from Stern: "Hey, the numbers aren't adding up. The formula we used to finance schools one through eight won't work for schools eight through twenty." When Danner and Smith looked at Stern's numbers they realized he was right. Over the last five years, cash-strapped California had reduced its per-student funding by a fifth. Worse, the state was delaying its payments to schools by as much as six to nine months. All this was happening at the same time outside funding to launch new schools was disappearing. If Rocketship stood still and added no more schools, everything will be fine, says Stern. But if we continue to expand we will lose $1 million for each new school.

Here's how Stern recalls Danner's reaction: "Oh shit." To Danner and Smith it wasn't clear where additional savings could be found. Already, class sizes had been raised to the max. Ensuring the kind of cash flow they needed to expand would mean pushing class sizes to thirty-five or forty. "That would be horrendous," said Danner. The other option was delaying the pay raise promised to Rocketship teachers, raises that meant each teacher would earn roughly $10,000 a year more when they returned the following school year. The delayed raises, dubbed "the pause," were announced at the end of the school year. That announcement didn't go over well. When the teachers returned after the summer, Rocketship issued a "never mind": the raises would go through as scheduled.

There was only one way to dig out of this mess: a model change that would drive more savings.

Then the other shoe dropped. Just when Danner and Smith were digging into the model change dilemma they got more bad news in the form of surprising state test results on the California API from the previous year. There was good news in the report. Rocketship's flagship school, Mateo Sheedy, hit 925, which was almost unheard of in a school where 85 percent of the students qualified for free or reduced lunches and 68 percent spoke English as a second language. And Rocketship Mosaic, in just its first year, hit 872. In the world of school startups, that just doesn't happen.

But not all the news was welcome. Rocketship Discovery Prep almost failed to crack 800, ending up with an 805. Another school, Los Suenos, dipped forty-five points. Yet another, Si Se Puede, eked out a gain of only two points. For a charter school group accustomed to being cited as tops in the state for educating poor, minority students, that was startling and embarrassing. You can't make the case for rapid expansion if you don't have all your schools hitting academic home runs every year. This news was a lot to absorb. Especially surprising was the forty-five-point dip at Rocketship Los Suenos, down to 793. "We had a rough start there," said Smith, "because the Rocketship school culture never got set. There was a lot of bullying, kids being mean to each other, not behaving in class, not listening to the teachers. Not being good Rocketeers. It was a nasty campus. The kids were running the campus, not the teachers. Plus, the teachers were getting burned out."

When John and Preston looked deeper in the data they saw something even more alarming. Until now, there had been steady upward movement by the lower-performing Rocketship students, with the bottom quartile moving up each year to the middle or high-performing group. At the end of the year, no students got left in the lowest group. But this data showed kids who never moved up. Immediately, John and Preston realized they needed to regroup. Rocketship scaled back its next-year expansion plan by two schools. But that only gave them breathing room. Quick action was needed.

The real issue was how to take a high-poverty school in the 800 range and push it into the 900 range. To date, only Mateo Sheedy had achieved the ultimate Rocketship goal. The challenge is turning that corner with all schools, not just one. "Eight hundred [API] is doable," said Smith. "It's not easy, but it's doable. Nine hundred is real work. Can you take these kids from proficient to advanced? That's a huge shift in kids' abilities. It's not just basic skills. It involves critical thinking, a depth of understanding, and a heightened level of learning. At Rocketship we can get kids to an 820 or 860, but to get the consistently over 900? We haven't cracked that nut yet. . . . Like a lot of charter schools, we were doing a good job closing the achievement gap but not putting our kids where the affluent kids are. At least not yet."

For Danner and Smith, it was a one-two punch. According to their CFO, the Rocketship financial model was askew. According to state tests, the Rocketship academic model wasn't taking them into the 900 range. This is not the stuff of which Fibonacci schools are made. For Rocketship, this was an existential crisis. Here they were, poised to launch twenty schools in San Jose, plus their first out-of-California launch in Milwaukee, and the two key parts of the Rocketship model weren't working properly. "John and I are talking hard; we have to do something." But what? Pushing a thumb down hard on the financial model could push the academic model deeper into the red zone.

Already, Danner and Smith had a plan on the shelf that would solve part of the problem: push the Learning Lab–classroom time closer toward 50-50, which meant students spending far more time in the lab. That would help solve the financial model problem. Not only would they not have to rely on finding as many superstar teachers but also they could employ fewer teachers, relying more on the lower-paid coaches-tutors in the Learning Labs. "So around July of 2012 we go to the school leaders and say we're really serious about this 50-50 formula, and here's a new bell schedule," said Smith. "We're going to start making the shift this school year. Here are the academic results we want, and we want them by the 2013–2014 school year. If you have a better plan then rock on, let's do that plan." Mapping out that new model was Smith and other top Rocketship leaders, plus three key principals. Together, they were known officially as the redesign team. If these influential principals could pioneer a new model, the rest would go along.

One of the principals was Joya Deutsch, who ran Rocketship Discovery Prep. Smith knew she would be hard to convince that major change was needed. But he also knew the other principals were aware of that, so it was important to have her on board. Andrew Eliot-Chandler, a first-year principal at Si Se Puede Academy, who only one year previously was a teacher at that school, was the public intellectual of the group. "He loves to have his Rubik's cube with him and solve it ten different ways in one minute," said Smith. The last of the principals, Adam Nadeau, who executed a brilliant startup at Rocketship Mosaic, may have been the most important add. Considered a rising star within Rocketship, Nadeau has the kind of quiet charisma instantly felt in any gathering, a mix of skepticism, irreverence, and deadly seriousness.

One Tuesday night, while meeting at Rocketship Alma, the team had a mini-revolt that turned into a breakthrough. The principals hated the 50-50 idea. Although all Rocketship teachers believed in the power of adaptive online learning they had never been comfortable seeing their kids march off to Learning Lab every day. What happened in the Learning Lab may have been true learning, but it rarely lined up with their classroom work. One day in the future, perhaps, Rocketship would discover a technology system to make those two worlds seamless, but that day had not yet arrived. Losing their students for that time meant the special culture teachers worked so hard to establish got interrupted. Instead of sending the kids for more minutes in the Learning Lab, the principals argued, why not bring Learning Lab into the classroom? Made sense.

The next problem to solve was the weakness revealed from digging deep into the test results, with too many low performers not moving up and too few students at the proficient level moving up to advanced. Without solving that problem, Rocketship schools never had a chance to become 900-API schools. The answer, everyone agreed, required more small-group instruction with students in constantly shifting groups depending on their skill levels in different instruction. Sounds good, but a single teacher in a classroom of thirty kids never has that kind of time. But maybe there was an answer,

At this point, Deutsch brought up that experiment at her school, the class-combining work pioneered by Amy Filsinger and Bridget Keating. It was an "aha" moment. Combining classes to allow more small-group instruction and blended learning was not new; other charter schools were the pioneers here. But for Rocketship, it seemed the ideal path to take. Already, Rocketship schools knew more about blended learning and personalized instruction than almost any other schools in the country. Why not go all the way? The change had the twin potential of saving money and improving instruction—the exact solution Smith and Danner were searching for.

Soon after, Rocketship dove into the "model change," which meant bringing the computers into the classroom so that teachers could monitor what skills the students were learning online. It meant combining the grades (in some cases knocking down walls) so there were three teachers available to divide the students into small groups. It meant training teachers to become experts in differentiated instruction. It meant everyone tolerating initial chaos in the rapid rotations and larger classrooms. It meant explaining to parents that no, their children won't get lost in a class of 120 students.

On the surface, it was kind of crazy. Rocketship was launching a transformation that resembled the trendy "open classroom" experiment of the 1970s. Today, the open classroom movement is regarded with an eye roll as perhaps one of the most useless and embarrassing education innovations ever launched. Preston Smith is too young to have endured that debacle (the noise and general chaos quickly became intolerable). But he was aware of its reputation. Despite that, neither Smith nor the principals were deterred. It seemed right for Rocketship. In fact, Rocketship was willing to bet its franchise on making it work.

"When it comes to schools, most people say they want innovation and entrepreneurship," said Smith. "We talk about it a lot. But when you get too far out you're experimenting with kids, and that's something we want other people to do. But you have to be willing to take risk, learn fast, and get it out to see if it works." In the high tech world along Highway 101, that's conventional wisdom. In the education world, rushing out a 1.0 version that will get tweaked into a 2.0 version by how students react, well, that's nothing short of heresy. So here was Rocketship, about to commit education heresy.

Oh, and Danner wanted the model change completed in single year. That's how startup guys roll.

ONE MILLION ROCKETSHIP
STUDENTS BY 2030?
NOT HAPPENING

October 2012: Redwood City, California

At this point it was clear to everyone at Rocketship that the lofty goal of making a huge dent in the nation's racial-economic learning gaps by 2030 was unrealistic. In short: stuff happens. East Palo Alto rejects you. Oakland does the same, only more emphatically. San Francisco proved to be problematic on multiple levels, especially real estate. DC got pushed back a year due to the challenge of finding the right startup leader for Rocketship. Even in the Rocketship hometown of San Jose, the resistance was swelling, with San Jose Unified suing to block the power of the overarching charter-friendly Santa Clara County Board of Education to grant zoning exemptions that would allow for another twenty Rocketship schools in that county.

"That goal of 2030? It may have worked out on the back of an envelope at some time," said Kristoffer Haines, who oversees Rocketship's national expansion plans, "but given politics, leaders, facilities . . . It just wasn't happening. It would require faster growth than was happening." As Preston Smith put it, this is a compound interest problem. Every time a school launch gets delayed, every time Rocketship gets denied another launch city it gets progressively harder to make that one-million-student goal. Claiming that Rocketship was going to educate a million kids by 2030 was not only a near-impossible goal but it made Rocketship appear naive to other charter operators. And to traditional school districts where Rocketship hoped to win charter authorizations directly, it made Rocketship appear arrogant and threatening. "The more we talk about the one million kids, the more we agitate the resistance," said Smith.

Rocketship had to acknowledge a pullback from the one million goal. And so, at a meeting of the five-person Rocketship executive committee, the discussion turned to what was actually doable. Looking over the cities that wanted Rocketship, cities where foundations and local political figures could act as strong advocates and make it happen, what evolved was this: within five years, during the 2017–2018 school year, Rocketship would aim at serving twenty-five thousand students.

That goal was daunting—going from 3,800 to 25,000 students in five years—but achievable and believable. It was a goal that Rocketship teachers aspiring to be Rocketship principals in new cities could connect with: I see me in this role in this city in this year, and that's why I will stay. Sometimes, however, even downsized goals can become outsized.

ROCKETSHIP AND UNIONS
It's Complicated: A Rocketship Teacher Sits down with a Union Leader—Her Mother

November 2012: San Jose, California

In the Silicon Valley world of entrepreneurial risk takers, unions are often thought of as institutions from another era, something you know about more from textbooks or cinema than real life. Although many of these startup multimillionaires support union-friendly Democratic candidates, the notion that companies such as Apple and Google could have been built under union rules dictating that code writers should be paid based on how long they worked for the company rather their creativity and productivity is fantastical. So it should not come as a surprise that when startup guys tackle school reform they avoided the unionized, traditional school districts and chose, instead, the mostly nonunion charter schools. John Danner was no exception.

"Look, the union contract in San Jose Unified is 452 pages long," Danner told me. "We're a startup. The whole point of a startup is to be flexible. The job changes every day." That's especially true at Rocketship, which in 2013 decided to reinvent itself virtually overnight, tearing down school walls to combine grades and dismantle its unique digitized Learning Lab to move computer learning under the direct supervision of teachers. In a matter of weeks, everything at every Rocketship school changed dramatically. Any teacher who dislikes revolutionary change should probably avoid Rocketship and, instead, settle into the comfort zone of a traditional district job prescribed by a bible-thick union contract.

Danner realized the unions constantly calculate the odds of organizing any charter school, including Rocketship. "What the union knows is that with every Rocketship school opening there are twenty-five fewer union jobs in their district. So it creates pressure." Almost certainly, says

Danner, unions will try to unionize Rocketship. But he doesn't predict success. "Schools that get organized are not super happy places. Happy people don't do that. Even hard-working teachers, teachers who feel like they're working too hard in their jobs, won't take that step unless they get to the true misery stage." It's Rocketship's job, says Danner, to listen closely to the teachers, to keep them as full participants in revolutionary education reform. (This maxim would get tested during the model change, which was disliked by many teachers.)

For decades, teachers unions have held the upper hand, explains Danner, because they dominate the school board election process in which only the self-interested voters, especially union members, turn up. But Rocketship, he believes, has inserted a disruptive dynamic into the process—parents. Specifically, Latino parents who have their own self-interest cause: their children. He has a point. Anyone who believes the conventional wisdom that Latino parents traditionally defer to school authorities has never witnessed a full turnout of Rocketship parents at a meeting of the Santa Clara County Board of Education—a usually staid gathering observed by a few drab souls suddenly becomes the equivalent of a Friday night pep rally. Only thing missing is the bonfire.

As long as the teachers remain happy, activist parents become the trump card, Danner believes. "Here's my thesis: unions are actually going to be the ones that create the change ultimately because they're membership organizations and they know that if they can't get the result that the population demands they're in huge trouble. School boards, superintendents, they're kind of transient. They come and they go, but those unions and the union representatives, they're often there for a long time, and their negotiating teams come in and they do this for a living." Bottom line, from Danner's viewpoint, is that unions feeling the pressure from parents will make school reform measures stronger than what either school boards or superintendents might recommend. It's a matter of survival.

Undoubtedly, any union leader hearing Danner say this would execute a full eye roll. But that's how startup guys think. Not surprisingly, Stephen McMahon, the (former) president of the San Jose Teachers Association, sees things differently. When told about Danner's comment about the 452-page teacher contract, McMahon walked over to the closet, got a copy, and thumbed through the pages. "I don't know, it's big, at least four hundred pages. There's a lot of pages here about payroll, etc., just basic employee contract issue. Any organization with a human relations department is going to have a lot of procedural language. I think Danner could work with our contract."

As a union leader, McMahon is about as sophisticated as they come. You won't hear any rush-to-the-barricades rhetoric from him about stopping charter schools. And he appeared to rule out "scratch organizing" Rocketship teachers, the union term for going into school uninvited to sell the union. "Unions have an incentive to have a big membership, but I'm not the typical union president. I don't think that's the goal. I'm more interested in public education. The other things will sort themselves out." But if Rocketship teachers sought them out? That's another matter.

For now, relations between Rocketship and the teachers unions can best be described as an uneasy standoff. McMahon believes Rocketship's success is due more to selection bias, the natural advantage of taking only students whose parents want them, than their blended learning instructional formula. And he strongly disapproves of Rocketship getting its charters through the Santa Clara County Board of Education rather than through each district (see "The Pushback Gets Real: The Fight over Tamien"). Individual students might be helped by switching to a Rocketship school, but from a regionwide perspective more harm than good is done when a Rocketship school disrupts life at a nearby neighborhood school, he says.

One certainty: if Rocketship expands as quickly as planned it will eventually encounter union-organizing attempts.

A MOTHER AND DAUGHTER TALK UNIONS

Rarely is there an opportunity to explain Rocketship-union relationships on a personal level, but that opportunity arises with Jenifer Merz, a first-grade teacher at Rocketship Si Se Puede, located in the Alum Rock School District in East San Jose, and her mother, Jocelyn Merz, president of the Alum Rock Educators' Association. Alum Rock and Rocketship share a rocky relationship. The district rejected Rocketship's application to sponsor a charter there, so Rocketship instead went to the county school board to win approval to open a school in the high-poverty area. It is probably safe to observe that the Alum Rock district views Rocketship as a mostly unwelcome intrusion. I first met Jenifer when touring Si Se Puede, and when I learned about her mother's position we joked about the "interesting" Sunday supper discussions they must have. "We do talk about it a lot," said Jenifer at the time. "A lot of those conversations are really interesting. It broadens our perspectives." Other discussions end in "let's not talk about this anymore."

Jocelyn, who graduated from San Jose State University, went into teaching via the traditional pathway, teaching elementary grades in Alum Rock for twenty-three years before getting elected as union president. In 2012 she was in her third year as president. Jenifer, who as a teenager used to help her mother out in her classroom, graduated from UCLA, where she volunteered in a mentoring program for high-poverty kids. Then, she worked for two years as an assistant teacher at a UCLA-run lab elementary school.

"At the last minute I decided to apply for Teach For America," said Jen. "It was the last day of the last deadline. I got wait-listed at first. I was kind of hesitant about TFA. People I had worked with encouraged a more traditional route into teaching. Then I got a call from TFA about interviewing for Rocketship. It seemed really interesting." Jen got hired to teach first grade at Si Se Puede, and in 2012 she was completing her fourth year of teaching. Usually, Rocketship sweeps teachers like Jen into a leadership development program, but she has resisted. She wants to keep teaching first grade. "I love first grade; I love the school."

I asked if there was a chance I could sit down with both of them, and in November 2012, that happened at the end of a day at Si Se Puede.

On Teach For America:

Jocelyn: In our school district I've seen a lot of TFA teachers come in, stay for two years, and then move on. It's just a stepping stone. It's not their career. It's just a way of giving back. They come in with the mind-set that they're the best and the brightest. . . . They come in with the attitude they are going to save the world. Many of our long-haul teachers are thinking, "Wait a minute. I've been here for fifteen years, and you're here with no experience and no credentials and you know better?" Those TFAers take teaching spots that otherwise would go to teachers intending to spend their life as teachers.[1]

Jen: I got some pushback about TFA, and not just from my mother. I was working [at the UCLA school] with more traditional teachers, and their concern was that with TFA I would not get the classroom support I would need. I think that depends on your TFA placement. That was not the case at Rocketship.

Do Rocketship teachers suffer from having no union protection?

Jen: We have a voice. When we have concerns people listen. Yesterday I met with someone from [the] regional team about a change I wanted. I feel like I'm heard within the network without a union.

Are there Rocketship practices unlikely to happen in a unionized district?

Jen: We have the expectation of doing forty home visits per year, which is forty more hours of work. Of course, coming here to Rocketship, and having no other teaching experience, I didn't know [any different], so there was no pushback from me. We were told, "We do home visits, and this is why it is important. We do extended day, and here's why that's important." It's part of the job. I think home visits are important.

Jocelyn: Not having worked in a district that has a union, she is told, "Oh, we teach from 7:55 a.m. to 4:05 p.m.," and she says, "Okay." They are told they have to teach for three weeks longer in June and go back to school earlier. They are told they have to be there Thursday night or be there for the weekend. She didn't know [any different]. Jen doesn't have kids and [a] family to take care of, and knowing who she is she jumps in 100 percent with everything. What happens when the Rocketship teaching force ages and needs to take care of young children? When the Rocketship teachers resemble the more veteran teachers in the Alum Rock schools, how can they work those hours?

Jen: I love the home visits, but is this something I can do ten years from now when I'm married with kids? I don't know. I put in these hours not because I'm told to. I want to. I feel like Rocketship understands that. They have this young, like-minded group of people with similar lives, not families, and it works. But Rocketship also understands teacher retention and is working to make the job more sustainable.

What about Rocketship's higher salaries and salary bonuses?

Jocelyn: Salaries are public records. I'm making about $80,000, and so is Jen. [Jocelyn has twenty-four years of experience, Jen four years.] Plus, Jen gets 100 percent of her medical benefits paid. [Jocelyn's medical expenses are 85 percent covered.]

Jen: Not everyone's salaries went up that much. My salary went up more because my kids did really well on the NWEA [the Northwest Evaluation Association tests, which Rocketship uses for internal evaluation purposes]. I don't entirely agree with our structure for merit pay and I voiced my concerns. I don't like my salary being based on how kids do on the computer, even though I knew they did well. I still felt weird.

What about Rocketship's rapid promotion system (which Jenifer has declined to participate in)?

Jocelyn: I don't think someone is qualified to be a school leader in a couple of years. I see the change my teaching went through in twenty-four years. In order to be an effective school leader you have to be teaching for more than two or three years. I think five minimum.

Does Rocketship "skim" students to get its higher test scores?

Jocelyn: I do think Rocketship is skimming. Not necessarily for better students, I hate to say that, but I think they get families with more parental involvement. And I know Alum Rock gets kids back from Rocketship that couldn't cut it, for whatever reason. [Jocelyn then cites other charter schools in the district that ejected kids for "behavior" reasons.]

Jen: I don't know of a single Rocketship kid who has ever been kicked out for behavior, ever. In fact, I can think of a lot of families with kids with bad academic and behavior issues, who we have begged them to keep their children in Rocketship. Literally.

But does Rocketship skim?

Jen: What I would agree with is that since Rocketship is a school of choice a lot of parents have sought it out. It's not just a district school, so there's a percentage of parents who are more involved, and we know that helps. But we also have a population of kids that don't have parent involvement or have learning disabilities.

What do you two agree on?

Jen: School leadership. I've had really good school leadership at this school. I don't have "charter school" tattooed on me. I have "good school" tattooed on. I have a friend in another school district, not at a Rocketship school, who doesn't get feedback, has no classroom observations, and doesn't feel like she is improving. Here, I feel like I have people helping in class and a place I can go for help. I'm so lucky to have seen what leadership can do. I don't think that's a charter school/[traditional] school issue. We both agree that the leadership makes so much difference.

Update: After this interview, in the 2013–2014 school year, Rocketship took several new actions to make teaching a more sustainable career, says Jenifer Merz: "We have been given increased collaboration time within the school day and additional curriculum [and] resources—these changes contribute to greater teacher sustainability and retention.

NOTE

1. This frequently heard complaint is disputed by TFA, which argues that the (TFA) teaching spot might be taken by a new teacher who quits after a year. Based on internal surveys, two-thirds of TFA teachers remain in the education field, either as educators or in related areas such as policy advocates.

EARLY FALLOUT FROM
MODEL CHANGE

October 2012: San Jose, California

Aylon Samouha, who joined Rocketship in 2010 from Teach For America and had moved into many key roles there, had been warning Danner and Smith that the model change plans were too ambitious. But Danner and Smith wanted to press ahead full speed. "Maybe I've been around too long but I truly cannot follow orders that don't make sense to me. It's not in my constitution." Making things worse was the fact that Samouha lived in Chicago with his family and for two years had commuted to San Jose for the school week. Overseeing a dramatic model change would make that commute even more impossible, so he left Rocketship. "It was definitely mutual. It was like a very good breakup—just deciding to be friends. Not throwing anything on the way out. I felt like the organization was in good hands. It was not irresponsible for me to leave. In fact, it may have been good for them. One cook out of the kitchen."

Update: When I last talked to Samouha the problems from the model change had broken out into the open. He wasn't surprised. "Some of my warnings have now sort of been realized, which is unfortunate; I would've rather been wrong."

THE PUSHBACK GETS REAL
The Fight over Tamien

November 2012: San Jose, California

To San Jose commuters, "Tamien" means just one thing, a train station at Lelong Street and Alma Avenue located in a working-class, Latino neighborhood southwest of downtown San Jose. Its name is taken from the Ohlone Native Americans who once occupied California's central and northern coasts, a territory that today includes what people worldwide know as Silicon Valley. But to the hundreds of commuters who show up here every day, Tamien Station is simply the place with decent parking where you catch Caltrain's "Baby Bullet" and make it to San Francisco in just over an hour.

To educators in San Jose and the sprawling Santa Clara County, however, Tamien has a separate meaning. Rocketship's proposal to open yet another school on a field next to Tamien Station had become ground zero in a local education war zone with national implications. Here at Tamien, San Jose Unified drew a line in the sand and legally challenged Rocketship. For too long, Rocketship had outmaneuvered the local school districts in the county by, from their perspective, going behind their backs and appealing to the county board. That's a belief held not only by San Jose Unified but also by many of the superintendents of surrounding school districts.

So it all came to a head here in a modest-sized plot just below the train station, an uncared-for field of grass and weeds that local residents had always hoped would turn into a park, possibly a soccer field. Here, the right battle emerged at the right time, a throw down neither side was likely to back away from. Eventually, all fast-expanding charter groups will encounter their own version of the Tamien battle. Even for charter school enthusiasts, the questions raised here at Tamien are tricky to answer. It's not always clear who is in the right.

Rocketship proposed to occupy a small corner of the field with a new K–5 school, complete with a playground available to the neighborhood after school hours. Perhaps a soccer field could follow. A lot of people thought that was the best idea ever. San Jose mayor Chuck Reed was all in favor. After the city's environmental review turned up positive, the city's planning commission also gave a big thumbs up. The zoning change allowing a school to be built there was granted by the Santa Clara County Board of Education, a solid supporter of Rocketship. What other schools in the area were demonstrating an ability to close learning gaps between white students and the fast-growing population of Latino students?

But that's just one side of the story. The other side of the story can be found a few blocks from Tamien Station at Washington Elementary School, a San Jose Unified school that already finds itself under siege from two nearby Rocketship schools, the newly opened Alma and Mateo Sheedy. If a third school opened at Tamien Station, Washington could slip into a death spiral.

· · · · · · · · · · · ·

On the day I visited Washington Elementary the fast-moving, larger-than-life principal, Maria Evans, was brightly attired in an overflowing green shawl and about to conduct her weekly madre-a-madre meeting in the spacious, green-carpeted school library. Evans greets me with an effervescent hug as though we were old friends (apparently that's how she greets everyone) and leads me to the front row of seats to face a group of nearly fifty mothers, all of them bundled against the chill, clutching Styrofoam cups of coffee. Few speak fluent English and most have the sturdy appearance of women accustomed to long hours of punishing work. These mothers look a lot like Rocketship mothers but on this day they are about to tell me, mostly via a translator, why they prefer Washington Elementary to Rocketship and why they don't want to see a new Rocketship school open only a few blocks away.

Under the guidance of Evans, Washington Elementary has become a bustling, bilingual school that's brimming with student activities and enjoying active support from parents. At this meeting, parents are shown a graphic asking, "Is your child ready for the future?" The graphic lists the thirty-something clubs offered to students. There's a garden club, pilot's club, Girl Scouts, Boys Scouts—and some unique clubs, such as the Adelante club, a leadership development club open to fourth- and fifth-grade boys that was originally designed as a gang diversion program for at-risk boys. "There are so many clubs that kids have a hard time choosing," said former Washington parent Brett Bymaster, who sits next to me at the front of the assembly.

Bymaster stands out in the school and the neighborhood. At six feet, four inches, Bymaster, thirty-six, is twice the height of some of the moms in the room. He's also alarmingly thin, very white, has an elite education, works as a hearing aid engineer, and can occasionally be seen cruising the neighborhood via Xootr, an adult kick scooter. In this neighborhood, that's definitely standing out. Bymaster is also an intense community activist who sent one of his children to Washington Elementary and is convinced that a new Rocketship school would damage the school and the neighborhood. He has emerged as the key Rocketship opponent. He's highly effective and willing to devote whatever time it takes to stop the new Rocketship school.

There are two other compelling facts about Bymaster: he and Preston Smith attend the same church (awkward) and Bymaster and his physician-wife not only live in a house adjacent to the field where the Rocketship school would be built but also his back property line is about twenty-five feet from the back wall of the proposed school (that's beyond awkward; that's in your face). Unlike Washington, a neighborhood school where most children walk or get walked to school, the new Rocketship school would be open to children all over the city, many or even most of whom would arrive by car. Twice a day, drop off and pick up, his street would get clogged with traffic.

Bymaster agrees that his resistance to Rocketship has the earmarks of personal interest. Who wants that kind of traffic enveloping their home? But the conflict theory doesn't hold, he says. He's not objecting to Rocketship or to charters. Rather, he says what the community really needs is a park. And if a school does get placed next to Tamien Station it should be a high-performing middle school, not another elementary school that would squeeze Washington. "With this proposal we get no park but we do get traffic problems with no benefit to the community. We're using public land to serve Rocketship." Bymaster has a point; the area desperately needs a high-performing middle school, more than it needs another elementary school. Problem is, Rocketship isn't in the middle school business.

One by one, the Washington mothers get invited to say good things about their school. They like that instruction at Washington is bilingual. "I want my child to be able to talk to her teacher in Spanish." At Rocketship, instruction gets delivered only in English. They like the family atmosphere at Washington, as opposed to what they see as the test score–centric Rocketship schools. And they like the pressure-free, homework-light approach at Washington. Said one mother, "I sent my daughter to a Rocketship school and there was so much pressure she used to cry. She was so tired at the end of the day. There's not supposed to be pressure like that in elementary school. I took her out. Some parents here threaten their kids with Rocketship: if you don't start doing better I'm going to send you to Rocketship." And several parents complained about Rocketship recruiting— constant phone calls, door knocking, Rocketship recruiters at churches, supermarkets, anywhere.

After the madre-a-madre meeting I sit down with Evans, Bymaster, and several other Washington Elementary boosters. Here, the discussion turned darker. Although registered as a nonprofit, Rocketship is really a business argued Bymaster and others, interested mostly in land acquisition and software development. There's a lot of money in their software, I was told.[1] I was also told that the purpose of Rocketship is to expand and displace as many seats (in traditional schools) as possible. Conspiracy theories aside, the real tension comes down to whether Washington Elementary, a school they rightly see as a huge plus to the neighborhood, would get enough breathing room to survive. If surrounded by three Rocketship schools, Washington could wither and die. Already, with the nearby Rocketship Alma opening in the 2012–2013 school year, enough Washington families switched to Alma to force Washington to eliminate two kindergarten classes. That was painful. A dearth of kindergartners forecasts an ongoing contraction passing through the grades. It's the worst grade to lose.

So, is Washington Elementary worth saving? The real question, it seems to me, comes down to this: does it make sense to maintain a true neighborhood school despite the fact that it struggles academically? To Brett Bymaster and Maria Evans, that's an easy argument to make. At

Washington Elementary, students and families walk to school. It's *their* school. It's social glue for the neighborhood: five hundred students from kindergarten to fifth grade, nearly all of them Latino and eligible for free and reduced lunches. Three out of four are English language learners. (Again, Washington Elementary looks a lot like neighboring Rocketship schools, a little poorer, but not enough to predict stark differences in student outcomes.)

True, children at Rocketship turn in higher test scores, but since when do higher-scoring elementary school students necessarily become better middle school students, high school students, or students who once they enter college persist to earn a degree? Here at Washington Elementary, advocates employ the term *grit* and *perseverance* a lot, words that have become education buzzwords to mean that higher test scores in high school don't necessarily predict college completion rates. You may have high test scores, but do you have the grit and perseverance to make it through college? The "grit" research can be traced back to KIPP's effort to boost the college completion rates of its graduates. Now, ironically, the jargon has been adopted by charter critics: test scores don't matter that much![2]

Maybe the Washington Elementary advocates are right. At this point, it is unclear what happens to the students from Mateo Sheedy after they enter middle school. Maybe that extra boost of academic confidence fades away. Maybe, but maybe not. In years to come, we will know the answer to that here and in other cities. If high-performing elementary charters spill out thousands of low-income students, over-performing students, what happens? Essentially, one of three things: high-performing middle school charters form to scoop them up, the parents of these children force neighborhood schools with middling academic records to pick up the pace, or neither happens and all that extra work done by elementary charters gets washed away. In San Jose, there's some emerging evidence about that, which will be addressed later in the book.

Essentially, the contrast between Washington Elementary and Rocketship comes down to this question: at what point do higher test scores overwhelm all other factors? With that in mind, let's compare Washington Elementary and Mateo Sheedy, schools with parallel grades and students. (Rocketship Alma, the other competitor to Washington, was too new at this time to produce comparison scores.) In 2012, students at Mateo Sheedy scored a 924 on California's API; Washington Elementary students scored a 798. Only education insiders can figure out API scores. A better comparison is the percent of students scoring proficient or above. At Rocketship Mateo Sheedy, 76 percent of the students test at proficient and above in reading, 93 percent in math. That compares to 54 percent of Washington students scoring proficient in reading, 56 percent in math.[3]

If grit and perseverance, rather than test scores, were the determinants of which is the better school it would be hard to make a call. Both schools seem to be doing a better than adequate job with that. And there's no study tracking the Washington–Mateo Sheedy students into traditional middle schools to determine whether the higher test scores at Mateo Sheedy paid off. So if the grit factors are roughly equal, who's more likely to successfully apply that grit in middle school, high school, and beyond? It's unknowable, but my instinct tells me to go with the students who demonstrate they know basic math skills and can read and write with demonstrated competence.

Something revealing about the two schools emerges from a long e-mail sent out by Bymaster to make an argument on behalf of Washington Elementary. In that e-mail is a chart comparing the schools, which are roughly the same size. Washington, however, has twenty-nine teachers, compared to only sixteen at Mateo Sheedy.[4] Class sizes at Washington are nineteen students for every teacher, compared to Mateo Sheedy, where there are twenty-nine students per teachers. Every single teacher at Washington is credentialed, compared to only half the teachers at Mateo Sheedy. And Washington has a counselor, whereas Mateo Sheedy has none.

In the future, Bymaster might want to add campus size as a comparison. Washington floats in a luxurious island of land: fifty-seven thousand square feet of buildings on 6.4 acres, whereas Mateo Sheedy clings to an acre lot with only twenty-two thousand square feet under roof. Clearly, Bymaster intends this as a comparison that is unflattering to Mateo Sheedy. Wouldn't Washington parents be attracted by the larger, better credentialed teaching staff, smaller class sizes, and spacious campus? Probably. But seen from another perspective a different take away emerges. Mateo Sheedy is a school that significantly outscores Washington despite higher class sizes, fewer credentialed teachers, crammed buildings, and a puny campus. Clearly, the stripped down Mateo Sheedy qualifies as a Fibonacci school.

Round one of the fight between Rocketship and San Jose Unified went to Rocketship, which won approval from San Jose's planning commission and city council. San Jose's blunt-talking mayor, Chuck Reed, has thrown his support behind Rocketship, regardless of opposition from San Jose Unified. "I'm committed to closing achievement gaps. We have some excellent-performing neighborhood schools, and Washington Elementary has done better. But it's easier to replicate a high-performing charter than it is a-high performing district school, which is why I'm supporting Rocketship here." Rocketship also won a key vote from the Santa Clara County Board of Education approving the zoning change needed to build a school.

Round two went to San Jose Unified. Simply filing a lawsuit challenging the authority of the Santa Clara County Board of Education to grant zoning changes was sufficient to prompt Rocketship's lender to pull out of the deal to build a new school. Bymaster not only quarterbacked a separate lawsuit against Rocketship but also started working with Rocketship opponents at other proposed sites. Lacking funding to build, Rocketship had to put the Tamien school construction project on hold.

Round three also went to Bymaster and San Jose Unified. In October 2013, a superior court judge ruled that the county board lacked the authority to exempt Rocketship from zoning rules. "We are pleased that the court has ruled on the commonsense side of the community," said Bymaster. "Adding a third Rocketship to our tiny eight-block community is inappropriate." San Jose Unified superintendent Vincent Matthews said that his objection was not to charter schools but rather to the county board exercising powers it didn't have, according to the judge. "It's important that school sites are thoughtfully planned in our communities by educators, parents, community members, and city leaders."[5]

But the challengers failed to persuade Rocketship to back down. The current strategy is to pursue a zoning green light from the city. "We've gone from 160 kids (with their first school) to 3,800 kids," said Smith, "and we still have wait lists. People want these schools, great schools, and we're not gonna back down. You're going to have to sue us to slow us down, and we're gonna go to court and win. . . . It gets back to *Waiting for*

'*Superman.*' Are we willing to look hundreds of kids and families in the face and say, 'You want to go here, but unfortunately your ball didn't get pulled out of the slot?' As long as there is demand, we will fill it. We have to be clear that the community has spoken. Hundreds of kids want to come here and we're going to do it. We're going to deliver for the kids."

Also not backing down is Bymaster, who says opposition to the Tamien school continues to build among Washington Elementary parents. "Rocketship continues to recruit extremely aggressively, something that we believe is doing great damage to our community. The opposition to Rocketship among Washington families increased significantly through the course of last school year, and this year we plan a more focused recruitment and education effort on some of the core issues with Rocketship."

One certainty that never gets mentioned by either side: competition from the two nearby Rocketship schools is undoubtedly the biggest reason Washington pulled itself out of an academic tailspin.

Update: The final round may have gone to Bymaster and San Jose Unified. In November 2013, the San Jose City Council deadlocked on giving Rocketship approval to build there (after a councilman switched his vote to disapproval). Reconsideration won't happen for another year. That denial gives extended life to Washington Elementary, pleasing everyone who wanted a purely neighborhood bilingual school. But will Washington ever give its students the kind of academic jolt Rocketship provides?

NOTES

1. To prove his point, Bymaster points to Zeal, Danner's new software company, which has its origins in Rocketship.

2. The irony of the criticism is that charter groups such as KIPP, which pioneered research into the college persistence rates of their graduates, are far ahead of their critics in working out ways to overcome that issue. Is Washington doing something to infuse their students with grit that Rocketship isn't doing? Not that I could determine.

3. In 2013 Mateo Sheedy students dropped dramatically on the state test and Washington students rose slightly. In 2013 52 percent of

Washington's students scored proficient or better in reading, 60 percent in math. At Mateo Sheedy, 57 percent of the students scored proficient or better in reading, 82 percent in math.

4. In addition, each Rocketship school employs six "individualized learning specialists" who handle many instructional duties.

5. Sharon Noguchi, "Rocketship Schools' Growth in Santa Clara County Could Be Slowed by Legal Ruling," *San Jose Mercury News* (October 17, 2013).

PART IV

THE PUSH TO EXPAND OUTSIDE SAN JOSE

Welcome to South Milwaukee

November 2012: Milwaukee, Wisconsin

The first awkward moment came when John Danner arrived at the front door of the warehouse Rocketship bought to convert into its first school launched outside California. It should have been an auspicious moment. With Danner was Timothy Sheehy, president of the Metropolitan Milwaukee Association of Commerce, who was a key player in recruiting Rocketship to this city; Kristoffer Haines, Rocketship's head of national expansion; and Antonio Gonzales who represents Canyon-Agassi Charter School Facilities Fund, which was taking on the conversion project. But the door was locked, and nobody could come up with a key.

That was definitely awkward, but it also gave everyone an opportunity to survey the neighborhood scene. Across the street was a modest house with a backyard surrounded by a solid wood fence that had to be at least six feet tall. And yet, every few seconds you could see the head of an angry, barking German shepherd pop above the fence for just a moment. Was the dog on a trampoline? If this menacing dog was upset by our small group, wait until a few hundred children get dropped off to and picked up from school every day. What would happen then?

The street outside was a major shortcut that cars zoom through with little apparent fear of a speed trap. Would they ever learn to slow down in a newly posted school zone? And the warehouse designated to be a school was even odder; it was a props company, bristling with unusual displays. Want to stage a luau? This company had it all for rent. A Star Wars theme for your kid's birthday? Definitely have that. What was this business doing in a South Milwaukee neighborhood? Could it ever be turned into a school?

And then, things got even stranger when a been-around-the-block middle-aged woman attired in a tricked-out motorcycle jacket nosed her worn-out sedan to the curb next to the distinguished group shuffling around on the sidewalk trying in vain to get into the front door. Oblivious to the traffic behind her, she reached over the considerable clutter in the passenger seat, rolled down the window, studied the group, and asked, "Are you buying this place?" Somehow, she had correctly singled out Danner as the key player to address.

Years of tangling with hostile superintendents, school boards, and teachers unions had not been wasted on Danner. Instinctively, he hedged. "We're thinking of it," he answered. Well, the lady said, you had better clean up all the deer carcasses stacked in the back next to the train tracks. Deer carcasses? She had an explanation. "I find those deer carcasses when I'm out at night trapping wild cats." Trapping wild cats? This time she offered no explanation. It was all left to the imagination.

After she delivered her ultimatum and drove off, we checked it out. Sure enough, hunters (we assumed) used the secluded, weedy area as a place to dump the carcasses. Welcome to South Milwaukee, John Danner. Palo Alto this isn't.

An omen about rough times ahead in Milwaukee? At the moment, the deer carcass lecture from the cat-hunting lady in the motorcycle jacket was nothing more than a great story for entertaining others. But, in fact, trying times were ahead in Milwaukee. Maybe the wild cat lady knew something.

A POWER PLAY BACKFIRES

November 2012: Santa Clara County, California

Usually, campaigns to win a seat on the Santa Clara County Board of Education are sleepy affairs. At most, a challenger or incumbent might spend $30,000 on a campaign. Why bother? The board is not the key education player in the San Jose area. That role falls to the thirty-one districts within the county. But in 2006 all that changed when the county board approved the first Rocketship charter school—the same school that had been rejected by San Jose Unified. That approval led to more approvals, adding up to the equivalent of granting Rocketship its own school district within the county. To charter school advocates, the county board was a slender lifeline, a lifeline that by 2011 was looking a bit tenuous. That year, when the board took the startling step of granting twenty new schools to Rocketship, the approval vote was uncomfortably close. Could the support for charters dry up? The 2012 school board election could determine that.

Fearing future setbacks, a pro-charter Political Action Committee (PAC) formed (an initiative of the California Charter School Association) and began raising money to support pro-charter candidates and attack the key anti-Rocketship member, Anna Song, an activist in the state Democratic party and the first Korean-born female to be elected to a California school board.[1] The PAC's considerable success revealed much about the tech muscle in the valley that backed Rocketship and other charters. Reed Hastings chipped in $50,000; Gap heir John Fisher another $50,000; Laurene Powell Jobs $40,000 (through her nonprofit, Emerson Collective), and Rocketship board member Timothy Ranzetta another $10,000. In all, the PAC raised nearly $200,000, much of it spent on auto-dial calls and fliers criticizing Song and supporting her pro-charter challenger.[2]

Song was shocked. "It's an outrageous amount of money to take out one school board member." Song was not alone in being shocked by the power play. "What they are doing could be very significant," said Terry Christensen, professor emeritus at San Jose State who tracks local politics. That heavy slug of political spending dwarfs what is usually spent on the county school board races. "It wouldn't take much to have an influence."[3]

But the outsized spending campaign backfired. Song survived. Nationally, the news of Song's survival made her an instant cause célèbre in the bitter education wars. School reform critic Diane Ravitch singled out Song in a speech before the National School Boards Association, asking her to stand up and take a bow to celebrate winning a showdown with the evil "entrepreneurs" who, in Ravitch's eyes, threaten traditional public education.[4]

In truth, the election could be better described as a draw. Pro-charter board member Grace Mah, also backed by the PAC, prevailed as well, beating her charter-critic opponent. Maybe it was just an election when voters decided to back female candidates, suggested John Danner, pointing out that both opponents were male. One lesson for Danner: building strong relationships with parents carries more weight than cultivating political leaders. "That lets everyone know that this is a community that really cares. That will have more impact for Rocketship than whether we can get the right number of people to support a given candidate." But that may be Danner putting a positive spin on a clear public relations setback. If the pro-Rocketship PAC had succeeded in defeating Song, the national story still would have been about bully billionaires "privatizing" our public education system. But at least they would have shored up their support on the only school board that would allow them to grow in the San Jose area. Song's survival triggered a lose-lose for Rocketship. Song became a Joan of Arc, and Rocketship became a national target in the toxic education wars, which odds favor coming back to haunt them.

NOTES

1. The source of Song's opposition to Rocketship has always been murky. Press reports suggested she thinks Rocketship is "untrustworthy" for various reasons. Song's critics say she decided to side with

the unions. On several occasions, Song agreed to be interviewed by me, but then always backed out.

2. Sharon Noguchi, "PAC Money Floods Local School Board Races," *San Jose Mercury News* (October 31, 2012).

3. Ibid.

4. Song was not present to take a bow.

SCHOOL STARTS IN SEVEN MONTHS—BUT ONLY THREE SIGN-UPS!

January 2013: South Side Milwaukee, Wisconsin

When it comes to recruiting Latino parents in the dead of winter in Milwaukee, there are lessons to be learned. First, look for indoor places to find the parents. Going door to door in this weather can be brutal. Laundromats, it turns out, can be promising. Many low-income Latino couples here lack washers and dryers at home, so they come to laundromats. Here on Milwaukee's South Side, the Blue Kangaroo Laundromat chain is the place to go. Clean, well lit, chock-full of Latino moms and grandmothers and staffed by friendly attendants willing to let you post notices about wanting to recruit parents. The insider tip about recruiting in laundromats: approach the moms while they are folding clothes—the one time in the process when they are captive audiences.

Despite employing smart laundromat strategies, Vanessa Solis and Rodney Lynk have a tough time recruiting this day. Solis and Lynk make an odd-couple recruiting team. Solis, twenty-eight at this time, was raised by a single mother in Chicago's South Side. Only Spanish was spoken at home, so she speaks Spanish fluently and English without a trace of Spanish accent. She is impeccably outfitted in fashionable knee-high leather boots and blessed with a light-up-the-room smile. Next year she will teach in the first Rocketship school here. She looks the part of a teacher. Lynk, twenty-six, African American, wears a Green Bay Packers hoody, not-so-fresh-looking jeans, and clumpy Bean boots. When he emerges from his dirt-streaked, cluttered Pontiac, Lynk looks like a union organizer working the docks. You would never guess Lynk is a math and chess wiz with an elite education, someone tapped to open up Rocketship's second school in North Side Milwaukee where Lynk grew up and still lives in the duplex where he was raised. This was his blue-collar, man-of-the-people look. I'm not sure it's working as intended.

On this day, Solis and Lynk have a serious problem that, if it isn't keeping them up at night, it probably should. To date, they have only three sign-ups by parents interested in the yet-to-be-named school. When asked what their recruiting goal was at this point on the calendar, Solis and Lynk artfully change the subject. They'd rather not think about that. No wonder. In seven months the first Milwaukee school is supposed to open with 485 students in grades K–3. Within two years, the school is supposed to grow to 650 K–5 students. By way of comparison, the proposed Tamien school in San Jose, which at this point in time lacks final approval, exists only as a field of spotty turf and is likely to be the target of lawsuits trying to stop it, but it has several hundred sign-ups.[1]

Nobody expected Milwaukee to be easy. In San Jose, it would be hard to find a Latino parent who hadn't heard of Rocketship. In Milwaukee, the opposite was true. That difficulty is apparent today. When it comes to school reform, Milwaukee has seen it all and, frankly, nothing has worked out that well. Parents are nonplussed. Rocketship? Big deal. Plus, the Milwaukee school choice program offers publicly funded spots at parochial schools, many of them located on the South Side. The academic results there aren't always the best, but who wants to cross the priest by pulling out your kids to send them to a Rocketship school?

At the first Blue Kangaroo, nobody has heard of Rocketship; nobody wants to sign up for anything. "There were a couple of people who were receptive," said Solis hopefully as we left the laundromat. "But that's the thing that's hardest," said Lynk. "We can pass out information but that's not enough to get them in. We're trying to 'deputize' the laundry workers (the Blue Kangaroo employees who sit behind a half doorway and keep an eye on things). Charming the laundry workers is a task that falls to Lynk. He tries to converse in his limited Spanish, and they praise his effort and try to help out. It seems to be working. "She has gotten to know me," Lynk says pointing to one Blue Kangaroo worker. "We keep Rocketship fliers in the back of the laundromat and they don't get thrown away, like in some other places."

For an organization reputed to be the hottest charter school group in the country, recently profiled on PBS and lauded on the front page of the

Washington Post, an organization conceived by a Silicon Valley software entrepreneur, this canvassing effort is surprisingly unsophisticated. Solis and Lynk have no short videos on iPods to flash to potential parents showing Rocketship's success in San Jose. They even lack simple color fliers explaining Rocketship. The most they have to offer is a black-and-white form about a "Family Fun Event & Coloring Contest" coming up, where the top prize is an iPod shuffle (prize at the time worth $49). The day of laundromat visits ends with no new sign-ups. Not a good sign.

NOTE

1. At this point in time, 581 new parents had signed up for a Rocketship school in the San Jose area. Among those, 130 listed Tamien as their first-choice school.

DANNER STEPS DOWN; SMITH STEPS UP

January 2013: Redwood City, California

The *San Jose Mercury News* carries the story of Danner's departure and Smith taking over as chief executive of Rocketship. To many outsiders, the news was a surprise. In truth, the changeover has been planned for a very long time.[1] To mark the occasion, Smith and Danner wrote praiseful letters to one another that were released only inside the organization. Danner departed to launch Zeal, an online learning startup drawing on lessons learned from searching for software for Rocketship students.[2] Their twin messages were perfectly synched. But in the coming months Smith and Danner's relationship will fall out of synch.

NOTES

1. The exact timing of Danner's departure, however, remains an issue. Based on comments he made to the Rocketship staff, it appears he may have left on the early side, in part because of the controversy over the model change.
2. The alpha version of Zeal became ready in September 2013.

Mateo Sheedy principal Maricela Guerrero leading morning launch

Mateo Sheedy teacher Marcello Sgambelluri

Parent leader Karen Martinez outside Rocketship Mateo Sheedy

Rocketship cofounder John Danner

Reed Hastings, Netflix founder, an important Rocketship supporter

"Kickout crew" member Amy Filsinger teaching in Discovery Prep's combined classroom, part of the controversial model change

Sharon Kim, a Teach For America corps member put on a fast-track path for school leadership, at her new school, Rocketship Alma Academy

Aspire's Allison Leslie at Hanley Elementary in Memphis

Washington Elementary principal Maria Evans leading a madre-a-madre meeting

Brett Bymaster with Washington Elementary supporters who cooked lunch for me. From left, Graciela Leon, Maria Marcelo, Zully Ortega Hernandez, and Mirna Sandoval.

Tim Sheehy, Kristoffer Haines, John Danner, and construction coordinator Antonio Gonzalez from Canyon Agassi at the deer carcass site

Milwaukee Rocketship supporter Roberto Montemayor at his Monterrey Market

Milwaukee recruiter Vanessa Solis with Conchita

Vanessa Solis recruiting a parent at the laundromat

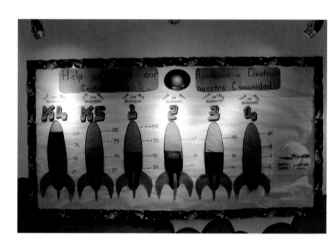

The Southside Prep recruiting goals (and shortfalls), laid out by grade

Anti-Rocketship poster plastered to a lamppost outside Southside Prep, the tip targeting Milwaukee Public Schools

Milwaukee principal Brittany Kinser speaking to parents about recruiting more students

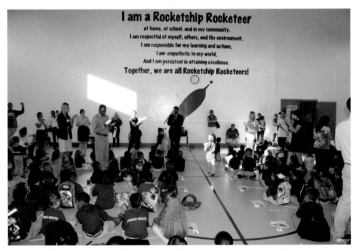

Principals and teachers leading the launch at Southside Prep

Preston Smith meeting with Milwaukee Latino leaders

Rocketship critic (and Milwaukee Public Schools board member) Tatiana Joseph meeting me for coffee

A family of educators, the mother, a union president; the daughter, a charter school teacher: Jocelyn Merz and daughter Jenifer Merz

All photos by Richard Whitmire except for Reed Hastings (supplied by Netflix) and John Danner (supplied by family).

Milwaukee Gets a Shakeup

January 2013: Milwaukee, Wisconsin

Not long after my visit to Milwaukee Preston Smith arrives and observes what I had seen earlier. Recruiting is off to a slow start, an alarmingly slow start. After flying back to San Jose, Smith took immediate action, which led to a resignation. Kristoffer Haines, who oversees Rocketship's national expansion, was temporarily put in charge of recruitment—and pretty much everything else about Milwaukee that would determine whether the new schools would be successful.

And then, as soon as Smith took that action he regretted the way he did it. He should have taken more time with the current manager to explain why things weren't working. But he didn't. He acted summarily and the blowback was significant. Rocketship was getting a reputation for tolerating a cutthroat front office and this didn't help. Probably, Danner could have gotten away with it. But Danner always had the advantage of managing from ten thousand feet. He was the genius software entrepreneur who came up with the Rocketship model. Smith, however, was different. He was a mere mortal, a teacher-principal seen by Rocketship folks as one of them. Possibly fallible. As in this case. The fact that this all played out just days before Danner stepped down as Rocketship chief and handed the reins to Smith was worrisome. Smith got that.

But there were no regrets about deciding to pour more resources into Milwaukee. All eyes were on Milwaukee. If Rocketship couldn't pull off its first successful launch outside California what hope was there to reach twenty-five thousand students in five years? While in Milwaukee, Smith approved a powerful new tool for the recruiters there: prekindergarten for four-year-olds. Prior to the Smith visit, the new school was limited to five-year-olds. This shift was huge. Rocketship's competitor schools all offered K–4 classes. To parents weighing school choices, K–4 means child care, and that means everything to families in which many parents work double jobs just to stay afloat.[1]

Within days of Smith's visit Solis visited a South Side Head Start program and walked away with nine applicants. Plus, some of the laundromat contacts come through. By mid-January, Rocketship had seventeen applications. With each day, Solis sharpened her recruiting skills. One breakthrough came from discovering the Spanish edition of the Great Schools guide, which lays out the facts about Milwaukee schools and offers an easy-to-grasp rating. Solis began taking that book to laundromat visits. When a mother brings up the school her child attends, they look it up together to check on test scores. Is the school above or below state average on math and reading? Is the rate of improvement above or below the state average? Two elementary schools near the new Rocketship school that get mentioned a lot during laundromat visits: Allen-Field and Forest Home. Solis can open the book and show the parent the ratings: Allen-Field, a rating of three out of ten, falls into the below-average category. For Forest Home, the rating is even grimmer: a two. Suddenly, the conversation changes. Suddenly, moms are more interested in hearing about a school that might produce better academic results.

Watching these parents weigh school choices reminds Solis of her own childhood. In Chicago, she was able to attend a Catholic school during her elementary and middle school years, but the family had no money for a private high school. Her neighborhood high school was low performing, but she got lucky in the lottery and won a spot at a magnet school. There, she entered into an International Baccalaureate program, which in turn led to a full scholarship at the University of Wisconsin, Madison. She hit the education jackpot, a jackpot that eludes most poor, Latino children growing up in South Side. Admission to oversubscribed charter schools is done by lottery, the same kind of lottery she faced in Chicago, the same kind of lottery documented in *Waiting for "Superman."* "I know very well what it's like seeing if your number is called, seeing if the trajectory of your life is about to change."

But although recruiting picked up a bit, it was still not clear that Rocketship Milwaukee would ever reach the point when a lottery was needed. At this point, finding 485 students to enroll seemed an impossible dream.

NOTE

1. On opening day, this move would prove to be prescient.

STRETCHING TO LURE
TOP CHARTERS
The San Antonio Story

February 2013: San Antonio, Texas

On this day, Victoria Rico drives me around San Antonio to visit charter schools. Blond, outfitted in a black power suit complete with high heels, and steering a massive black SUV, Rico looks the part of an aggressive power player. But close up she's anything but intimidating. In truth she's a bit shy, preferring to let the charter school operators do the talking. Maybe that's because, frankly speaking, her grand plan to create eighty thousand seats for San Antonio kids in high-performing charters by the year 2026 seems, to put it politely, a stretch. Think about the logic: in a mere thirteen years, Rico envisions a fourth of students in San Antonio, a city few realize ranks as the nation's seventh largest, attending not just any charter but a "high-performing" charter capable of quick expansion, a Fibonacci school.

Nationally, the supply of charter management organizations capable of spinning off Fibonacci schools is limited. Everyone wants them to come to their city. Why should they favor San Antonio, a city that barely registers on the national charter scene? When it comes to charter schools, San Antonio can't compare to New Orleans, a city that courtesy of Hurricane Katrina probably leads the pack, educating seven out of every ten students via charters. Charter schools were a key innovation in New York City, where former chancellor Joel Klein had the enthusiastic backing of his boss, former mayor Michael Bloomberg, in drawing in the best charter groups in the country—Achievement First, Uncommon Schools, and KIPP. The catnip: $1-a-year rents in existing school buildings. In Washington, DC, a unique school-reform law passed by Congress cleared the path for the rapid expansion of charter schools. Today, the charter district educates thirty-five thousand students and is growing faster (and posting better academic results) than the traditional school system there.[1]

Making San Antonio's bid even more improbable is Rico herself. She's never taught school, never launched a charter school. In the education world, she's a newbie. Despite all of that, I can easily envision her bold plan coming true. She appears to have the right vision at the right time with the right financial backing. Rico was born and raised in San Antonio in a family of prominent lawyers. Her grandfather was Leroy Denman Jr., who earned his law degree from the University of Texas and served as attorney for the famed King Ranch, one of the world's largest ranches. Her grandfather also chaired the board for the Ewing Halsell Foundation, a philanthropic heavy hitter in San Antonio and a foundation playing a big role in Rico's vision of building a charter school colossus. Her father, James Branton, is a prominent trial attorney in San Antonio. Rico, a Harvard graduate who earned her law degree from the University of Texas, continues that legal tradition, only in a very different direction.

In 2009 Rico was working with her husband's online corporate training business and handling immigration cases pro bono when she got an offer to become a trustee of the somewhat musty George W. Brackenridge Foundation. Despite being pregnant with a son due in three weeks she accepted. Even by Texas standards, George Brackenridge (1832–1920) was a unique character. A prominent banker and business leader, also known as a patron saint to the University of Texas, Brackenridge became a philanthropist known for looking out for the less privileged of Texas. Keep in mind, this was Texas at the turn of the century; that had to be against the grain. That philanthropic bent survives to this day, and it's a bent that attracted Rico, who was transformed by her immigration work. How does this nation offer its newest generation of immigrants a fair shake at the American Dream? It all comes down to education, she concluded. And based on what Rico saw around her in traditional San Antonio schools, the answer didn't appear to lie there. One of the largest school districts in San Antonio, San Antonio Independent School District, draws a ranking of only three on the one-to-ten scale drawn up by greatschools.org. Clearly, the kind of students George W. Brackenridge cared about weren't getting cared for in San Antonio.

With about $25 million in assets, the Brackenridge Foundation was able to give away roughly $1 million a year in grants. Most of that money had been going to after-school programs, summer camps, arts programs, field trips, and mentorships. All good programs, of course, but the impact was nowhere to be seen. The question Rico kept asking herself was how the foundation, with its modest grants, could become a change agent in improving education. The answer revealed itself during her first visit to a local KIPP charter school. "I thought that school was amazing. Then I saw *Waiting for 'Superman'* and realized there were more like KIPP out there, schools that can replicate quickly." Fibonacci schools. Rico and other San Antonio philanthropists were players in luring an IDEA charter school to San Antonio, a charter group that earned its spurs in the Rio Grande Valley.

Rico's vision was to fund rapid local expansion of IDEA and KIPP, the existing Fibonacci charters in San Antonio, and draw in several charter operators operating elsewhere in the country. But which ones could be induced to come to San Antonio? Rico had heard about Rocketship, so when she heard John Danner speak at a conference in San Francisco she waited anxiously for a chance to pull him aside. But Danner was swarmed after speaking, and she almost missed that opportunity. Not until she chased him into the stairwell did she get a chance to pitch Danner on bringing Rocketship to San Antonio. She must have said something right. Danner told her to get in touch with Kristoffer Haines, the head of national expansion for Rocketship.

These days Rico and Haines are in regular contact. Rico is selling what Rocketship is buying: plenty of low-income kids attending schools that do them few favors in return; philanthropies able to pony up startup costs; and a well-connected, legally savvy Sherpa, a fixer, if you will, to navigate state charter school laws, zoning quagmires, and local political pushback. That would be Rico. In East Palo Alto, San Francisco, and Oakland, John Danner and Preston Smith learned their lesson well. Don't go where you aren't wanted. There are plenty of poor, minority kids in cities where you are wanted. Cities such as San Antonio.

Here's the plan Rico settled on, called Choose to Succeed: convince other foundations to buy into a plan to help KIPP and IDEA expand while drawing in four great charter organizations: Rocketship; BASIS (an Arizona-based charter group known for giving students a curriculum far more challenging than most traditional educators believe is possible); Carpe Diem (also Arizona based, which specializes on a mix of coaches and online learning; subject mastery, not course completion, is what's important here); and Great Hearts Academies (yet another Arizona charter that appeals to middle class families; best described as a "free" private school).

What's interesting about the plan here is that it also offers options to middle-class families. Even in the wealthy suburban districts on the north side of San Antonio there are students falling short of meeting state standards, says Matthew Randazzo, president of Choose to Succeed. And there are large numbers of low-income minority students in those suburbs. Plus, getting suburban "soccer moms" to back charters will open doors for all students. "If we have middle class white moms advocating for the same thing that low-income Latino moms are advocating it makes the movement grow faster."

The new charters would join the rapidly expanding charters already in San Antonio. Mark Larson, the founder and chief of the KIPP network in San Antonio, plans to expand from four to fifteen schools by 2023. That's going from 1,200 students to 9,000. IDEA's expansion plans for San Antonio are even more aggressive: twenty schools serving fourteen thousand students by 2022.

What the grand vision takes is money and that's where Rico plays a major role. Through a campaign of persistent persuasion, Rico convinced several major money players in San Antonio, including foundations far larger than Brackenridge, to join hands in the single cause of ramping up available seats in high-performing charters. Brackenridge pledged $7 million over the next seven years toward the cause, which accounts for all their gifts. The Ewing Halsell Foundation pledged $21 million to the cause. To date, $32.5 million has been raised. If that number reaches $90 million, seats for more than eighty thousand students would open up.

Rico's plan appears to be unfolding on schedule. Already, BASIS and Great Hearts won chartering approval from the state. A new BASIS school opened in San Antonio in 2013, with a Great Hearts school and a second BASIS school opening in 2014. Choose to Succeed expects applications from Rocketship and Carpe Diem to win chartering approval.

How badly are those seats needed? Randazzo came up with a unique way of measuring "quality" in San Antonio. Based on the percentage of students passing state exams, a mere 22 percent of seats in this city qualify as high quality; 65 percent fall into his low-quality category. That's 65 percent of 315,000 students in San Antonio. Translated: 204,750 students that deserve better. So is there room for 80,000 seats in high-performing charters? It would appear so.

Update: Rocketship failed to win approval from the state to open in 2014 and is looking at 2015 as the earliest launch date there. The approval process in Texas is murky; the reviewers don't have to reveal their objections. But it appears one major player was Rocketship's insistence on keeping English as the language of instruction.

NOTE

1. That share would soon rise to 44 percent.

SMITH'S WORST MONDAY EVER

February 2013: Redwood City, California

The unhappiness that led to the big showdown meeting at Rocketship's headquarters had been percolating for months. The tension first spilled out publicly several months earlier when the executive staff gathered with Preston Smith for drinks and dinner at the Los Gatos Brewing Co. on Santa Cruz Avenue in San Jose. The plan was to enjoy some craft beers, have dinner, and watch the Giants play the Tigers. It was a big game; the Giants were in the playoffs that year. But nobody watched much baseball that night. Instead, Smith heard a lot of griping about how Rocketship was run.

John Danner, they said, was pushing too hard on the model change—trying to make all grades at all schools change over in a single year. Moving that fast was ill-advised, they said. The school staff was not trained for a move of that magnitude and the facilities were not ready. Morale, they warned, was at a breaking point. Worst of all, they say, Smith appeared to be defending Danner while not truly believing it was a wise move. "You could even hear Preston mouthing things that were John's words," said Stern. "John's a strong personality. . . . We all knew it was awkward and felt sorry for Preston." What they really wanted to know from Smith was when was he going to stand up to Danner? There was no resolution to the issue that night, allowing the tension to simmer for another few months.

At the school level, the push to convert all the schools appeared to be taking principals away from their primary tasks as instructional leaders. "Through December principals were not focused on things that make schools great," said Melissa McGonegle, a key Rocketship veteran who ended up leaving due to strains among top managers. "It's hard to run a school when you're all about how many laptops you need and when the walls are going up," she said, referring to the attempt to combine grades in larger classrooms. "The previous year we had the best [teacher] retention ever. I would be shocked if this didn't have an effect on retention."

For Danner, however, this was a textbook example of startup decision making. Once you decide on your business future and know the steps needed to get there you move immediately and filter out dissonant voices. In one conversation I had with Danner he approvingly cited the controversial decision his friend Reed Hastings made with Netflix. Once Hastings concluded that streaming, not mail-order DVDs, was the future, he immediately rearranged the company to pursue that strategy— a decision that sent the company's stock price into a plunge made famous in business school studies. "A lot of customers wanted to lynch him," said Danner. "But when you look at the results of that today, Hastings was right. The streaming business is scalable; the DVD business is not, so he is getting more leverage on his resources with efforts toward streaming." Netflix's recent stock gains also signal that Hastings was right. To Danner it seemed clear that combining grades in larger spaces and placing the teachers in charge of online learning was the future: let's go there sooner than later.

All this put Smith in the middle. Did he listen to Danner or listen to his team? Problem was, the executive team would decide something and then Smith would meet with Danner who would try to reverse the decision. "We would say, 'Wait, didn't we just spend four hours discussing this, and now it's changing?'" said Kristoffer Haines. "John put Preston in purgatory." Especially caught in the middle were Kate Mehr, chief schools officer, and Lynn Liao, chief programs officer. The two had to oversee the model change but Smith kept overruling them. Said Mehr: "Preston kept revising with Lynn and me, saying, 'I think we should do this' or, 'What do you mean not all the grades this year?'" Said Liao, "It was awkward. It was like, 'Who's really in charge here?'"

Finally, after several attempts to change Smith's mind, Andy Stern brought it to a head. "I walked into the office and sent Preston an e-mail saying, 'I'm quitting.'" Stern, a veteran of several Silicon Valley startups, liked working at an education startup. But in truth, he didn't need the job and the stress he saw at the Rocketship headquarters was pushing him over the edge. All that set the stage for the now-famous Monday 8:30 a.m. staff meeting at Rocketship on February 25. Attendees: Smith, Stern,

Liao, executive coach Jill Wear, and, by phone, Haines and Mehr. "We told Preston that we were tired of John ruling through him, controlling him," said Stern. "We didn't know who we were talking to. Even if Preston agreed with us, he would then go talk to John and come back with a different view."

Stern was not alone in leading the assault on Smith. Mehr, who had seen Smith overturn some of her decisions, was just as blunt. "God bless the man, we beat the crap out of him. We told him that if he kept this up he was going to lose the majority of the leadership team. We told him if he leads that way we can't be effective. To me, it felt like a big leadership moment for him." Changing all the classrooms to open spaces by the end of year was too risky, says Mehr, who told Smith she was channeling the opinions of the principals she oversaw. "We just didn't know enough to do all the grades. I felt like we didn't have a game plan. We hadn't begun to define what all this looks like, let alone the support, the type of teachers you need."

Everyone at the meeting agreed not to leave the meeting until everything got worked out, which meant the morning meeting stretched into the afternoon. Smith, for the most part, just listened, a wise move. "That Monday was the worst professional day of my life," Smith told me weeks later. "Three quarters of my executive team was ready to go out the door. . . . If they had walked out—I have to be realistic—principals would have walked out." Had that happened, word would get out that Rocketship leaders up and down the chain were jumping ship. Naturally, outsiders would conclude that everyone was leaving because they trusted Danner, not Smith. Erroneous, perhaps, but that's what people would assume. That kind of plunge in prestige for a new leader could have proven disastrous not just for Smith, but for Rocketship.

How Smith reacted to the barrage of criticism from his executive staff changed the direction of Rocketship. He could have accepted Stern's resignation. He could have fired him. He could have watched others walk out the door and replaced them as well. Instead, Smith absorbed the unanimous criticism and incorporated the lessons learned. "The lesson I learned is that you had better be an authentic leader or you don't lead," said Smith. "There were months where every conversation I had to take the party line. It's tough, and my team saw that."

Only a few days later, on February 28, Rocketship's board met and plunged into an unexplained, lengthy, closed-door session. I was sitting outside waiting to hear the board's public session to learn what it had decided to do about the legal challenge at Tamien (see "The Pushback Gets Real: The Fight over Tamien"). Only later would I learn that Tamien had little to do with the private discussion. Rather, Smith was laying down reality as he saw it. Translated: you board members need to make the transition in loyalty from John to me, because I'm about to change direction here. Sitting with me outside waiting to get into the public session was Danner. If he knew the true nature of the discussion inside he wasn't letting on. Nothing but smiles and amiable discussions with staff members who would stop by our sofa just outside the meeting room.

In short, the board threw its support behind Smith. In the days that followed what emerged was a new launch for Rocketship. During the 2012–2013 school year, different Rocketship schools had been implementing the model change for different grades, an experiment that roiled the schools but was supposed to prepare the system for a complete switchover the following year. No longer. Instead, the model change would evolve gradually. Only grades 4 and 5 would become common "flexible" classrooms the following year. Students in the lower grades would continue to rotate into digital Learning Labs. And the expansion rate officially slowed, a move that Danner agreed was necessary. Rocketship would launch only two new schools, one in San Jose, the second in Milwaukee. Most important, Rocketship would take an "investment year" with each school receiving an infusion of money—money that in previous years had gone toward expanding Rocketship elsewhere. That next year, Rocketship schools would only break even, shifting the money toward investments such as an extra assistant principal and an on-site business manager, enabling principals to focus more on instruction. Of most significance to the teachers: no more scrambling to come up with your own instructional materials. This would be the year Rocketship teachers would adopt common literacy and math instructional programs.

During my year of following Rocketship the only critical words I ever heard Danner and Smith say about one another arose from that confrontation, and even those words were carefully chosen. Once the dust settled, two outcomes became clear. In only a few years Smith had gone from managing a small school with a dozen or so young teachers to managing an $18 million enterprise run by an executive team that was older and, in most ways, more experienced than he was. After the "worst Monday ever," Smith became his own boss with the backing of the Rocketship executive team and board. He was no longer the "kid" running Rocketship. That was a good thing. Also clear was that Rocketship, now with seven schools and poised to go national, was looking less like a startup and more like any other high-performing charter group.

Exactly What Kind of a Difference Can a Fibonacci School Make?

March 2013: Princeton, New Jersey

Students attending KIPP charter schools score "substantially" better than their counterparts, the independent and respected Mathematica Policy Research concludes in a study sponsored by KIPP. Bottom line: over a three-year period KIPP middle school students gained an extra eleven months of learning in math, eight more in reading, fourteen more in science, and eleven more in social studies. In probably the most in-depth study ever done on a high-performing charter school group, researchers found no evidence to support critics who maintain that KIPP achieves those gains by pushing out troublesome students. The attrition rate among the KIPP students was the same as the rate among the students in the comparison group.

MILWAUKEE LOOKING UP (A BIT)

April 2013: Milwaukee, Wisconsin

We arrive at 3 p.m., about twenty minutes before release time at Holy Wisdom Academy, a stolid yellow brick parochial school on Milwaukee's South Side. There's Rocketship startup principal Brittany Kinser; Elsy Villafuentes, hired to be Rocketship's office manager; and me, following along as an observer. I feel a bit like a vulture. We're here because of turmoil at the school that erupted after the longtime principal at the school, Richard Mason, was fired. A lot of unhappy parents here. In March, 150 Holy Wisdom parents signed a petition demanding that Mason be returned, some of them marching in front of the school carrying signs on the snow-cleared sidewalks. It was enough of a news event to make the *Milwaukee Journal Sentinel.* Add it all up, and you have the perfect opportunity to pick up some unhappy parents who might be interested in switching to the new Rocketship school opening here in August.

There's an art to this in-your-face recruitment. Arriving at just the right time, while parents are waiting to pick up their children, is key. And focusing only on parents picking up by car is just as important. Rocketship will not offer bus service, so parents who lack transportation will be difficult to recruit. The first vehicle, a well-worn SUV, turns up an interested couple. Villafuentes is the key recruiter here; most parents speak only Spanish. Kinser hovers nearby in a supporting role, showing them photos of the new school from her iPhone. They sign up, which means they will get a home visit, which usually leads to filling out an application, and applications often lead to enrollment. One by one the team makes its way along the line of parked cars. In only twenty minutes, they get seven names. Not bad.

"Initially they are nervous about giving us their names, but Elsy makes them feel comfortable and then they say they want to learn more," said Kinser. "We will phone them to ask about meeting in person, at their house, or office, a McDonald's, coffee shop, anywhere." A few Holy Wisdom parents get offers to visit Rocketship schools in San Jose, trips funded by Rocketship. Many of those parents also sign on. And they help recruit others. It was an easy sell: test scores at Holy Wisdom are unimpressive. In California, Rocketship schools draw national attention for their academic results.

One parent unhappy about losing Mason at Holy Wisdom is Nelly Hernandez, a mother of three with two attending school there. Hernandez works as a community organizer for Great Schools, which rates schools and advises parents on choosing the best school for their children. "The parents wanted to know what was going on so we requested a meeting with the priest. He wouldn't give any explanation to the parents. He just said it was his decision, and if we didn't like it we could leave." In April, Rocketship invited Hernandez and several other parents to San Jose to tour Rocketship schools there. "I was very surprised," said Hernandez about her visits there. On the Great Schools ranking, Rocketship is rated a 9, which means the kids are very advanced in what they are learning. We toured four schools and we could see the students were doing math work that was much higher than what we see at Holy Wisdom. As a result, she decided to switch schools. And her decision to switch prompted her two sisters to do the same. And several other Holy Wisdom parents followed her lead.

At a lunch earlier that day when Smith talked with local Latino leaders, I ended up sitting next to none other than the fired principal Richard Mason, who had been tapped by Rocketship to help recruit students. And next to Mason was Nelly Hernandez. This is how the recruiting game is played. Suddenly, Milwaukee was starting to look more like San Jose.

A clear sell to many Hispanic parents in San Jose and Milwaukee is that Rocketship is neither a bilingual nor dual-language school. Nearly all the current Rocketship students are Latino, with mostly Spanish spoken at home, but at Rocketship schools all lessons are conducted in English. The only Spanish you will hear is when parents visit the school and headsets get passed out for instant translations. These are not parents worried about "preserving" Spanish culture. These are first-generation parents worried their children will never compete for good jobs unless they are fluent enough in English to win first-class educations. The last parent Kinser spoke to that day outside Holy Wisdom was a father dismayed at his son's lack of progress in learning English. "My son is not moving back to Mexico," the father told Kinser. "He needs English to be successful here."

Securing sixty-three enrollments, with another ninety applications, was a different picture from my January visit when the total enrollment sat at three. But both numbers are a long way from the goal set for the August opening: 485 students from pre-K through third grade, growing to 650 pre-K through fifth grade within two years. Will they open up too lightly enrolled? That's possible, acknowledges Preston Smith, who was in Milwaukee that day. Rocketship's problems in Milwaukee stem back to getting a slow start with community engagement. "You can't recruit kids if you're not in touch with the community. In fact, you probably shouldn't open a school, either." In short: visiting laundromats should never be the linchpin of your recruiting strategy.

Despite being incredibly important—Rocketship's first school launch outside California—a lot fell through the cracks in setting up Milwaukee properly. Much of the problem can be traced directly back to the trauma at the California schools about the model change. On this day, Smith's sense of the recruiting pace was they would end up pulling in between 350 and 380 students for the first-year launch—a figure that at the time he wanted me to keep to myself. Officially pulling back from a goal of 485 would only sap energy from the recruitment campaign. That lower number would be painful, he says. Not only would that diminish revenue to a break-even status, but the students recruited in later years to fully flesh out the grades would be first-year Rocketeers and therefore need more remedial assistance.

In truth, Rocketship was lucky to be only a little behind at this point, probably a testament to Haines stepping in to take over. But in future launches, Nashville, DC, and beyond, Rocketship won't be able to rely on Haines to make things work. He can't be everywhere. Nobody knows that more than Smith. Regardless, Smith feels a lot better today than he did in January when he visited Milwaukee and discovered only three enrollments and no community outreach. "At the time I was thinking, "Oh . . . this is going to be bad."

The first Milwaukee Rocketship School may not draw the 485 students they wanted for the first year, says Hernandez. "A lot of people don't know anything about Rocketship, so they are afraid to transfer their kids. Some schools here open, then don't do well, and close within two years. But if the Rocketship school here does as well as the ones I saw in San Jose, by the second year there will be a waiting list." I suspect she's right, but still, this was a painful lesson for Rocketship.

Two Charters Make the Top-Five List

April 2013: Washington, DC

*T*wo charter schools, both BASIS schools located in Arizona, rank among the nation's top five high schools on the U.S. News & World Report annual list. BASIS Tucson and BASIS Scottsdale are among the BASIS schools created by Michael and Olga Block. The BASIS curriculum is pegged to the highest standards found in European and Asian countries.

If Rocketship Is the Digital Future Why Do Its Schools Look so Ordinary?

April 2013, Scottsdale, Arizona

Here at the five-star Phoenician Hotel, sprouting from 250 acres at the foot of Camelback Mountain, few of the hundreds of people attending the annual ASU/GSV[1] Education Innovation Summit paid much attention to the twenty-seven-hole golf course, the elaborate pool "complex," or the Centre for Well Being with its spa pampering. This was about networking, not about Arizona sun and fun. In theory, the gathering was about education. After all, "education" was part of the conference's title. But there were few educators here. Rather, these are the "suits" of education technology, the digital inventors looking for venture capital and venture capitalists looking for the next Coursera (offers online university courses) or Knewton (designs adaptive learning digital courses). These are the people Diane Ravitch has in mind when she warns of dark forces trying to "privatize" education. In truth, there were few privatizers in this crowd. They were just aspiring capitalists trying to make a buck off the hundreds of billions spent each year on K–12 and college education. They don't care whether the spending is public or private; they just want a slice of the market, just as textbook writers, lunch providers, classroom furniture makers, and, yes, the teachers unions, have exhibited for decades. Diane Ravitch included.

The difference with this group is its focus on digital innovations. These "disruptive" technologies, they argue, will change the face of education. And they're right. Soon, all students will participate in the kind of blended learning Rocketship and others pioneered. Given the proliferation of smartphones and tablets, any alternative future for education is unimaginable. The most crowded events here are the technology demonstration breakout sessions where you get to know the up-and-coming stars in the field: Smart Sparrow (a platform for creating adaptive courseware), Catapult Learning (programs for professional development and tutoring aimed at closing achievement gaps), Chegg (connects students to textbooks, homework materials), Educurious (enables project learning connected to real experts), Wowzers (meshes education and gaming), MindSnacks (teaches foreign language via gaming), and Schoolzilla (a school data management platform).

In theory, John Danner should have been a star at this meeting. In all likelihood, he was the most successful startup guy in the room, at least measured by what he earned after DoubleClick bought his startup. And he had to be one of the few digital guys here who had actually spent time in a classroom. To be fair, many of these startup outfits have a core educator on their founding team. But still, looking around the rooms it was hard to imagine any of these entrepreneurs coping with the inner-city kids Danner taught in Nashville. What made Danner a true rarity here is he was someone who had actually put it all together, meshing his lessons learned from teaching with fresh technology to launch actual schools. Real disruptors on the ground in San Jose, not just hypothetical disruptors transmitted as mobile apps.

But in truth Danner seemed a bit uncomfortable here. He knew that few at this gathering had any idea of what life was like in a challenging classroom. And he knew that few here had a snowball's chance of making it big. Most were just beginning to learn the hard lessons of peddling technology to district superintendents: unless you are one of the few education biggies, such as Pearson, you weren't going to get an audience with school superintendents. The best shot most of these entrepreneurs had was catching the attention of a big company that would snap them up.

There is something revolutionary playing out in Rocketship schools and it is drawn from the startup culture in Silicon Valley. But it has little to do with hardware or software. Rather, it has to do with inventing a way to do personalized learning (Danner's big lesson from his teaching experience in Nashville) in a way that's lean enough to take it national. Take those crowded classrooms, for example. Rocketship figured out a way to build schools for half the cost of traditional schools and then thrive on the measly $7,500 per student offered up by California. Rocketship teachers specialize in math or literacy and each day most of them teach four classes with at each thirty kids. Same lesson, over and over, with a lot of names to learn. Teachers in neighboring schools enjoy far smaller class sizes, and they also teach in so-called self-contained classes, where they get to teach the full range of subjects, from math to social studies. That's far more pleasant for the teacher, but also a classic example of schools being organized for the adults in the system, not the children. The Rocketship style takes a toll on the teachers, but in practice teachers who specialize in math get really, really good at teaching those lessons. And those class rotations, also stressful on the teacher, allow one rotation per day into the less-expensive computerized Learning Lab, which means fewer teachers are needed. Given that each teacher costs roughly $100,000, that's a lot of savings. That lean model not only produces more academic success but also gives Rocketship what few high-performing charters have: scalability.

Schools have a lot to learn from Rocketship, but it's not just about the software and hardware they use. Rather, it's how a school can model itself on the strategies used by the most successful Silicon Valley companies, companies that know the game is all about getting top talent, targeting customers with the exact product they need, and then keeping the best talent while constantly adapting the original model. The secret here is not just the adaptive software; it's the adaptive school culture. In some cases, using an adaptive culture means moving away from online learning a bit, away from the isolated Learning Labs and placing the computers under the control of the classroom teachers, who know how to maintain classroom culture and know exactly what each student can gain (or not) via DreamBox or other instructional programs.

If you are a parent with small children, blended learning is coming your way shortly, in force. But the biggest digital breakthroughs won't come from the suits gathered here at the Phoenician. Rather, they will come from principals such as Rocketship's Adam Nadeau, who managed to open up Rocketship Mosaic at full enrollment on the first day of school, nearly all the students from high-poverty families and speaking English as a second language, and yet turn in striking test scores that very first year. Technology was a player at Mosaic, but the bigger player was Nadeau knowing exactly when technology should be used, how to structure a school to maximize its potential, and when not to use technology.

Adam Nadeau wasn't at the Phoenician that day; he was in Nashville making plans to open up the first of eight Rocketship schools in that city. That's too bad. The suits could have used his classroom perspective.

NOTE

1. Arizona State University/Global Silicon Valley. The event bills itself as the "Davos of the Desert" for education technology.

Fibonacci Developments in Massachusetts

May 2013: Boston, Massachusetts

*S*tudents in Boston charter schools significantly outperform students in regular schools, concludes a study that compared students who "won" the school lottery to get a charter school spot to those who did not win a seat and enrolled in regular public schools. The study, carried out by the School Effectiveness & Inequality Initiative at the Massachusetts Institute of Technology, found that the charter students outperform their counterparts on the state test, the SAT, and Advanced Placement exams. The only downside: charter students had a slightly lower graduation rate. Some of the score differences were significant. Charter school students scored one hundred points higher on the SAT. The charter students were twice as likely to take an Advanced Placement exam. The study is significant in part because Massachusetts boasts the best school-reform effort in the country, with regular public schools in that state outperforming schools in other states.

More Progress
in Milwaukee

May 2013: Milwaukee, Wisconsin

By late May Rocketship had 119 enrollment packages, sure bets for actual students showing up for classes in August. During the week of May 13, Rocketship pulled in thirty applications, a record to date. The enrollments include about fifteen students from Holy Wisdom, which continues to be a steady source of applicants from parents unhappy about the leadership change there. Another big break came from general "neighborhood buzz" from people seeing the Rocketship fliers. One parent leads to another.

An intense push to blanket Head Start centers and talk to parents is paying off, along with the much-used tactic of visiting with parents waiting to pick up their children at low-performing Milwaukee schools. Another boost arrives courtesy of the very popular Bruce-Guadalupe Community School. That charter school, which belongs to the Schools That Can network that helped draw Rocketship into Milwaukee, recommended that the waiting-list parents at their school consider Rocketship.

So do 119 enrollments at this date indicate momentum that Rocketship will fill its 485-student goal on the first day of school? No. Making that goal means pulling in thirty-six applications a week. And any week they don't get thirty-six they need to attract extra in the following week. On this date, the Milwaukee launch is still looking a bit shaky.

A Day in the Life
Rocketship's Flagship School, Mateo Sheedy

May 2013: San Jose, California

7:55 a.m. "Morning launch" is a must-do ritual at every Rocketship school, a time when students pack into tight lines, dance like crazy to loud music, shout out support for Rocketeers winning prizes, and compete to see which side achieves the highest decibel rating while reciting the Rocketship character-shaping code. On this day, the 591 Rocketeers (grades K–5, 85 percent low income, 68 percent speak English as a second language) pack into tight lines on the tiny paved playground, along with all teachers and a fair number of parents.

This Monday is especially stressful. The following Tuesday the Rocketeers take the all-important California achievement test, a test that will determine whether Mateo Sheedy's score of last year, a 924 was a one-year wonder or a wonder with legs. Lots of final scrubbing of academic skills will take place over the next few days.

"Launch is about building community," said principal Maricela Guerrero. "It's a time to set the foundation for the rest of the day." There are awards for personifying Rocketship values (showing respect, for example), awards for exemplary behavior in the digital Learning Lab, awards for pretty much any values school leaders want to see reinforced.

Watching on this day are parents Rosanna Lara, whose daughter, Giselle, is a kindergartner, and Rocio Luna who has twin sons in kindergarten, Marc and Adyson. Both mothers chose Mateo Sheedy for its high test scores. In math, Mateo Sheedy students score as well as students in many elementary schools located in the posh neighborhoods of Silicon Valley, schools that serve white and Asian professional families. There's a price to be paid: each drives over a half hour through notorious San Jose rush hour traffic to reach Mateo Sheedy.

Luna acknowledges the high academic demands put on Rocketeers can be stressful. "In the beginning I was ready to pull my daughter because it was overwhelming. She didn't go to preschool. We would pick her up at 6 p.m. and it would be like, hurry up, eat, get to the homework. It was too much. But she adapted. I'm glad I didn't pull her out." Rocio likes being surrounded by parents who have learned to advocate not just for their children but for better schools beyond Rocketship's K–5 grades. "In some ways Rocketship is like a private school. There's a flexibility to try new things. And I like the idea of nonunion teachers. If there's a bad teacher here, they'll address it. That's so critical to the success of the school."

The school is named after Father Mateo Sheedy, pastor of nearby Sacred Heart Church. In 1999 Father Sheedy was tapped by Santa Clara University to find neighborhood students who, with the help of the university's Juan Diego Scholarship program, could graduate from the university. He couldn't find a single candidate; all were too far behind in their neighborhood San Jose Unified schools to possibly survive the academic rigors of Santa Clara University. Dismayed by his finding, Father Sheedy set out to establish schools that would succeed with the Latino students from Washington Guadalupe. Rocketship Mateo Sheedy became one of those solution schools.

9:15 First-grade math teacher Sherri Dairiki, thirty-one, checks weekend homework for "quality work" while her twenty-eight students busy themselves with a "do-now" sheet of subtraction exercises that reviews already-learned skills, but adds a new twist. "I'm pushing them to think about reasonable estimates. Is 39 closer to 40 or 30?"

Dairiki is a mix of Japanese and Chinese. Her grandparents spent World War II in a US internment camp. Her father is a dentist, her mother a pharmacist. After graduating from the University of California at Davis with a degree in economics, Dairiki went to work for Gallo Wineries as a forecast analyst. "Then I realized I wanted to contribute more to the world." Prior to joining Gallo she had worked as a tutor in West Oakland. She recalls getting assigned an eighth-grade boy who had no idea how to multiply. When she inquired how he could have made it to eighth grade, she was told he was promoted from grade to grade due to his "effort." That astonished Dairiki. "How could anyone get to eighth grade without knowing anything?"

Dairiki left Gallo to complete the coursework needed to become a dentist, taking on two part-time jobs, one of them working at a Starbucks on University Avenue in downtown Palo Alto, a favorite stopping place for John Danner. The two chatted at times, and one day Danner invited her to submit her résumé to Rocketship. She got hired for administrative jobs but yearned to teach. Danner and Smith paved the way for her entry into Teach For America, which trained her and got her started on earning the needed teaching credential. This year, 2013, was her first year teaching.

By having large class sizes, teaching four classes the same subject, and having one class always rotating into the Learning Lab for an hour and forty minutes, Rocketship gets by with one less teacher per grade. That money goes into paying teachers more and preparing for national expansion. The downside of the Rocketship formula, Dairiki readily admits is the repetitiveness, creating a "teacher sustainability" challenge. The plus side she acknowledges, is that as the day progresses she gets a little better at teaching the same lesson. When Dairiki meets teachers from traditional schools they are astonished that she has 110 first-graders. "They say that's crazy. . . . This is more intense than regular schools."

9:31 A timer goes off in Dairiki's class, a signal for her to scan the classroom to make sure all students are on task. The timer was a suggestion made by her coach. Dairiki is older than most first-year teachers, which she says makes her more accepting of the strenuous demands. "I realize that new teachers right out of college don't understand the structure of organizations. When they get handed things they don't want to do, it's an adjustment." During multiple observations, Dairiki ran her first classes with the aplomb of a veteran teacher. Teaching appears to be a good fit. "It's an awesome opportunity that John [Danner] gave me. He gave me [the] opportunity to find my passion. I even have an after-school session with the low [performing] students. I do it on my own. I choose all the first-graders who are low and bring them in from 4 p.m. to 5 p.m."

10:00 Principal Maricela Guerrero arrives with not-so-good news. A substitute kindergarten teacher failed to show up to replace a teacher out on training, which meant that Dairiki and other first-grade teachers have to each take in a small batch of younger students for the rest of the day. Already, she was tap dancing through the near-impossible challenge of personalizing the math instruction for each of her 110 students. How, exactly, do you do that while also coming up with instruction for kindergartners? Dairiki appears to embrace the challenge, assigning a first-grade "mentor" to each of the kindergartners. But somewhere behind the smiles she had to be thinking, "Wow, Mondays are always a special challenge. This Monday just got more Monday-like."

10:30 A schoolwide fire alarm goes off. False alarm! Yes, it truly is a Monday.

10:45 Principal Guerrero pauses briefly to lay out the tribulations of the day so far. A missing kindergarten substitute, a mystery fire alarm. "It just went off randomly. We have no idea why. We went around and checked everything before calling the alarm company and the fire department." And, of course, the pressure of the soon-to-arrive California achievement tests. Will Mateo Sheedy retain its lofty test score status? "If you are asking me right now, I will predict that we're gonna be in the 900s, pretty much the same." Last year's score of 924 ranked Mateo Sheedy as the fifth-highest scoring school in the state serving high-poverty children. (Her prediction will prove to be optimistic.)

Guerrero doesn't really fit the mold of a Rocketship teacher or principal. She didn't go to an elite university. Didn't enter from Teach For America. She grew up in South Central Los Angeles, graduated from the University of California at Santa Cruz, and started teaching third grade in Alum Rock, a high-poverty district just north of San Jose. When she found herself short of the required teacher credentials she shifted to subbing while getting additional credentials. One day she got a call to substitute at an Alum Rock alternative school founded by Rocketship cofounder Preston Smith. She ended up staying there for three years. And when Smith left to become principal of the first Rocketship school, he asked her to come along. She agreed, and although teaching conditions in the downtown church that served as home that first year (see "Opening Mateo Sheedy: Tough Times") were difficult, she and Smith teaching together landed that startup school as a top-ranked high-poverty school.

12:30 p.m. I walk by Guerrero's office to see her closeted with an out-of-control boy, screaming and shouting. The cause is unclear. More signs that it is Monday.

1:40 Academic dean Hana Bass heads off to observe a first-year teacher, someone who last year worked as an ILS (independent learning specialist), the teacher aides who work in the Learning Lab. As with any school, teacher quality here is uneven. This young woman falls short of mastery. Kids get the giggles a lot and there's some chatter. "This talking needs to stop," said the teacher, who several times walked to the behavior-rating chart and moved two clothespins (each pin has a student name) lower on the chart—two boys now hover barely above the danger zone. Rather than pausing to regain complete control of the class, she grimly presses on with the lesson.

Bass takes lots of notes and after about fifteen minutes we leave. Bass was there for a specific purpose. During her last observation in that class, Bass saw that when a student came up with a wrong answer the teacher immediately skipped to another student who might have the right answer. Not pausing to help struggling students shows low expectations. Bass thought the teacher was improving on her questioning, but also noted what I saw—the students not paying attention to the teacher and the grim delivery. "The instruction wasn't celebratory; she wasn't bringing in the joy factor. We can work on that."

Bass, twenty-six, graduated from the University of California at Irvine, joined Teach For America, and got assigned to a school in New York's South Bronx where she worked with pre-kindergarten children. Bass said she did her best to prepare the young children for elementary school but she lacked confidence that the school "bureaucracy" would make that happen. "I had heard about charter schools and a TFA alum got me in touch with some Bay Area charters. I researched them and decided I was on the same page as Rocketship." After only one year as a Rocketship teacher Bass got tapped for the fast-track leadership trajectory—principal within two years. "I don't want to rush, but I have a lot of professional development. I have a coach who coaches all the academic deans, one to one." Next year she will be an assistant principal, then principal. It's the Rocketship way.

2:00 A little boy stands sheepishly across from the reception desk. Long dark stains stretch almost to his shoes. "He peed in his pants," one little girl helpfully offered. No question about it; this is Monday.

2:43 Fifth-grade literacy teacher Marcello Sgambelluri lays down a showcase performance of what it means to teach with both joy and expertise. The students, without a single exception, respond. It may be test time, but you won't see test prep going on in this class. "It's not really a time for grinding on skills. Now, it's about engaging them, looking back on the work we've done together. Last week we had a discussion about hard work and today we're going to push more on that idea, which I've talked about before, [Malcolm] Gladwell's ten-thousand-hour mark for hard work. If you look at geniuses, and what they do, bar none, they have spent at least ten thousand hours on it. My students can do anything through dedication and hard work, period. We're all born with a clean slate. What we do from there is up to us. You need to put the power in the students' hands."

In theory, Sgambelluri's class is discussing slavery but every minute or so the lesson briefly veers into short-duration brain teasers that keep every student in rapture. "What goes up but never goes down? I'll give you thirty seconds." A cascade of not-quite-right answers pours forth—clouds? Earth? Plants? At the thirty-second mark, he gives enough hints for the answer to emerge: your age. The class is juiced.

Sgambelluri grew up in Washington state, the son of two teachers. At the University of Washington he majored in economics and minored in social sciences and political science. His original plan, to teach high school social studies, veered in a different direction after working one summer with special education students. "That shifted what I thought about education and disadvantaged populations. You see a kid who's sitting in the hallway, disconnected, and when you sit down and talk to him or her you see a fire in his or her eyes emerge. The people that humanity pushes out are usually the most humane. They have the greatest passion and empathy, maybe because they've seen the worst sides of it." That summer experience led Sgambelluri to Teach For America, which led to teaching in a Washington, DC, charter school, which then led to Rocketship. Although this is his first year at Rocketship, his considerable teaching skills honed from experience are evident.

The emphasis Mateo Sheedy places on doing well on the upcoming state tests doesn't bother Sgambelluri. The criticism that Rocketship-like schools are nothing but test-prep factories that fail to educate the "whole child" makes no sense to him. The wealthy kids from Palo Alto and Menlo Park turn in high scores, he says, but nobody criticizes them for failing to educate the whole child. "The skills on the state tests are fact-of-life skills that are needed on college admission tests and later in life. The basic skills needed on tests, as basic as they are, are a foundation to more advanced skills. It's not about the test, it's about the skills they get through being proficient on the test. Standardized tests are, and I tell my students this, just another box you have to be able to work within: SAT, MCAT, LSAT. They will be there your whole life. In order to connect testing to students' lives we think about critical thinking within test taking: this question is trying to trick me in this way. . . . This answer is wrong because of this. Then we link back to real-world examples of critical thinking: when Mark Zuckerberg started Facebook he was thinking about the problem of people wanting to communicate but it's hard for everyone to be in the same coffee shop. He solved the issue through critical thinking and problem solving."

All day Both small-group tutoring and Response to Intervention[1] instruction go on during the entire school day. Those, along with teachers breaking their classes into constantly shifting groups that may need either remedial or accelerated instruction and the adaptive learning software in the Learning Lab—DreamBox and ST Math for math skills, i-Ready for literacy skills—constitute the Rocketship arsenal of personalized learning

3:00 Kindergartners are dismissed. They remain in the play area for "structured fitness" until 3:45 p.m.

3:12 Sgambelluri's students are in the Learning Lab using i-Ready to work on literacy skills. The experience is unimpressive. There's lot of milling around, asking for bathroom passes, and aimless perusing of the computer software. The instructional learning specialist running the class seems to lack the respect of the students and issues vague threats while spending most of her time trying to solve technical glitches, such as the girl who kept scoring 90 percent on the exercise but the software still wouldn't let her advance.

3:30 Guerrero catches me up on the day's excitement. The kindergarten boy needing restraint has "sensory" issues that often end up in screams and shouts. "We try to calm him down. We have a behavior plan for him. We restrain him for a bit and offer him the 'right choice' of sitting in a chair. He did. Because he has sensory issues we massage his hands. Today, it took forty-five minutes to calm him down. That's pretty normal."

As for the little boy peeing in his pants, that crisis never makes it to the principal's level. The office manager taps into her supply of back-up clothes. Crisis over.

Despite the unplanned events, Guerrero still managed to teach two small-group math sessions that day, one on multiplication and another on the same topic, which targeted "BB and FBB" students (below basic and far-below basic).

I tell Guerrero what I observed in the Learning Lab and she agrees that some of the Learning Lab experiences are less than great, especially for the older students. "The ILSs are not certified teachers. We try to work with them on classroom management issues. We have a challenge on this campus. The kids can identify who the teachers are, those with true authority, and those without." Teachers, for example, have visited all the homes and met the parents. "The kids know the ILSs are not their teachers and they don't know their parents. That makes a huge difference."

When I tell Sgambelluri what I observed in the Learning Lab, he said part of the problem arises from the model change Rocketship experimented with this school year. The back-and-forth about how to mix blended learning with teacher-driven instruction produced some unevenness in how the digital learning takes place. Next year, all Rocketship schools will settle on identical models, with the emphasis on teachers orchestrating the blended learning. Then he said something equally interesting: "That all being said, the onus is on me just as much as the ILS. This is something a majority of teachers in America deal with, pushing our students to make the right decision regardless of the space they're in or adult that's working with them. If my students are in an empty field with no one around and they see a piece of trash or a wallet, I hope to give them the life skills to throw away the trash and find the owner of the wallet, regardless of who sees them. Many students are there—some are not, and I continue to push all of them to be their best selves. They still are children and we need to give them high expectations and strong structure." Lessons on grit.

4:00 First- and second-graders are dismissed.

4:10 Students in grades 3–5 are dismissed. The full-school PA system kicks in: "A Honda CRV is in the roundabout. Please move it!" Some things about schools translate everywhere. Do not mess up the balletic end-of-school pick-up traffic flow.

4:15 Xzavier Diaz, eleven, and Leslie Martinez, ten, students in Sgambelluri's class, stay behind to talk to me. Asked about the highlights of their day, Diaz answered, "I remember dancing in the morning for launch. And then we went to the park to play for PE. We played dodgeball and ran. And I got my science test back and got eighteen of nineteen right." For Martinez, "learning about riddles" was the high point of the day—other than getting nineteen of nineteen right on the science test.

Both students said they love Sgambelluri's class but don't think much of Learning Lab. "It gets boring sometimes," said Diaz. "In computer lab you're more on your own. I like class better." Martinez agreed. "In the lab I get distracted by the surroundings. I end up chatting rather than doing my own work." The students acknowledged that going to Rocketship meant longer school hours and more homework—something their neighborhood friends always point out when asking why they don't transfer to regular public schools. "They think it's not cool," said Diaz. Would they prefer switching out of Rocketship? "No," said Martinez. "I know this school will make me better than them. I'll be more mature, smarter. I'll succeed more." Diaz agreed. "This is hard, with longer hours. But I want to succeed. I want to have a good job."

4:00–6:00 The YMCA runs an after-school program on campus.

Note

1. An academic intervention model designed for struggling learners.

FRESH TURBULENCE
IN MILWAUKEE

June 2013: Milwaukee, Wisconsin

In early June, a time when Rocketship recruiters were already running well behind their goal in student sign-ups, a clue arrived that might explain some of their difficulties: pamphlets that cautioned, "Parents, Be Careful"; Rocketship schools are "privately run" schools from California with monstrous expansion plans designed to duck "democratically elected school boards." Rocketship schools, the pamphlet advised, save money by shunning art and music and sticking their kids in front of computers for one hundred minutes a day for digital instruction that's "not working." Once the eight Rocketship schools are up and running, each school will send $600,000 a year back to Rocketship's California's headquarters: "That means $4.8 million dollars will leave Milwaukee's economy every year," read the unsigned paper.

Those pamphlets were just a crude beginning. Soon after they appeared, Rocketship employees showed up for work and discovered highly sophisticated posters plastered to lampposts around the school and a bridge overpass near their headquarters. This time, the artwork was striking in its detail—a Rocketship, complete with its working parts, headed straight into the ground. Actually, not the ground. The poster showed the rocket detonating on Milwaukee Public Schools (MPS). Ouch. Each stage of the rocket carried messages in Spanish: Rocketship has no local control; it sends money from Milwaukee back to California; it employs teachers with no certifications; the president lives in California and the school uses drill-and-kill worksheets. The lamppost posters at the school were deemed to be graffiti, so the city quickly removed them. The posters on the highway overpass were on county property. That took a bit more effort to get those removed.

Soon, it became clear that the pamphlets and posters were just the tip of a barely-below-the-surface whisper campaign designed to keep parents from switching to Rocketship. What was interesting was the absence of anyone taking responsibility. Was it MPS teachers? It certainly looked that way to Rocketship's Rodney Lynk, slated to be the assistant principal at the new school, who chatted up some protestors handing out pamphlets at Rocketship's office. Turned out they were MPS bilingual teachers. My initial reporting turned up a more likely culprit: Tatiana Joseph, a former high school Spanish teacher now working as an instructor at the University of Wisconsin–Milwaukee—and a newly elected member (with union support) of the Milwaukee School Board.[1] Joseph and Tony Baez, president of Centro Hispano, are champions of a bilingual education system established long ago in Milwaukee at the request of the Latino community. That effort paid off in numerous K–8 bilingual schools scattered around the South Side, schools now experiencing a slackening enrollment as voucher schools such as the parochial powerhouse St. Anthony School picked off their students. English immersion, not bilingual, was the strategy there. Rocketship was just the latest intruder arguing English immersion was the way to go. For Rocketship, this was beginning to look a lot like the fight in San Jose as it tried to open another charter in the orbit of Washington Elementary, a bilingual school fiercely championed by many advocates.

It was becoming clear that the political and business leaders who recruited Rocketship to come to Milwaukee left a few people off that corporate jet: anyone from MPS, the teachers union, or Centro Hispano. The business leaders had looked at Rocketship as a game changer. What they envisioned was Rocketship opening one school in a Latino neighborhood on the South Side and then expanding to the African American North Side, building a network of eight schools throughout Milwaukee. If Milwaukee proved to be anything like San Jose, soon there would be charter middle schools to take in the higher-performing Latino and African American students graduating from Rocketship schools, and that would lead to new and better high schools as well. But the players missing from the plane that day were not looking for a game changer. What they wanted was to hold onto the game that was already slipping away from them: students in traditional Milwaukee schools, especially the bilingual schools on the South Side.

Although Tatiana Joseph might have been the key organizer of the pushback movement aimed at Rocketship, she was really just part of a coalition deciding that Rocketship had to be stopped. The union and Centro Hispano, the key player in lobbying for bilingual schools, were all part of the word-of-mouth campaign aimed at Rocketship. The union benefitted whenever a nonunionized charter school suffered a setback, thereby steadying enrollments at the unionized MPS bilingual schools. And Centro Hispano benefitted by arresting enrollment declines at bilingual schools, which they believed was the right path for Latino families to choose. What really upset people such as Baez were reports of "aggressive recruiting" by Rocketship organizers, in which recruiters didn't just hand out brochures outside schools and Head Start centers but went inside. Parents are offended, he says, by recruiters passing out literature that claims their schools are lousy and Rocketship schools are great. That's what triggered the pushback movement against Rocketship, Baez says, with the pamphlets and posters.

In a lot of ways the Rocketship critics had a point. When it came to recruiting students, newcomer Rocketship was violating all the informal "rules." Traditional Milwaukee rules: you weren't supposed to stake out parents on sidewalks outside low-performing schools; you weren't supposed to point out test score differences; you weren't supposed to mess with the popular voucher system keeping Milwaukee parochial schools off life support. Rather, you were supposed to show up at organized school fairs scheduled for the summer before the next school year and put your brochures out on a folding table, allowing parents to walk by and choose which school they wanted. Showing up at laundromats in the middle of winter and badmouthing other schools was verboten! Welcome to in-your-face Rocketship recruiting. May the best school win. Breaking the rules is what the city leaders had in mind when they flew to San Jose to do everything possible to lure Rocketship to Milwaukee.

The Milwaukee teachers union reveled in the dustup. One morning, after failing to get a response from the union president, I cold-called Dave Weingrod, a part-time union employee who, as he put it, "does their political stuff." He willingly engaged in an unusually blunt on-the-record conversation about school politics. "Rocketship pissed off a lot of people in the last month," he said, referring to Rocketship's recruiting practices. Photos of the posters flew around a Facebook exchange shared by anti-Rocketship partisans, he says. The union totally supports the Rocketship pushback, says Weingrod, who acknowledges that teachers and retired teachers are among those handing out brochures and pasting posters. "As much as possible we want to work with community groups that want to reject something like Rocketship." But the union is not quarterbacking the resistance, he says. "When the union comes in to dominate everything, it becomes our agenda and it doesn't work out as effectively." Better to sit back and enjoy the show.

For the record, the union has objections to Rocketship that go beyond recruiting students from their schools. Young children should not be spending that much time in front of a computer, says Weingrod. "You sit for a couple of hours in front of a computer and who knows what's going to happen. It seems like a factory model where they use machines to replace teachers. There's not a single software engineer in California who sends their kids to a school like that." Turning teaching over to software is a way of "deskilling" teachers, says Weingrod, using a term that was new to me.

Weingrod also raised the issue of Rocketship sending money back to its central office to be used for national expansion. "The number I've heard is that after the first three years they will send $600,000 per school back to California. Officially, Rocketship is probably a nonprofit, but they are acting more like a for-profit company. The people at the administrative top are getting really large wages and they are probably using money from all over the country." The union would feel differently about Rocketship had its charter come from the school district rather than the city, a difference that costs the school district between $1,000 and $1,500 per child—money that could be used to cover "legacy costs," he says referring to teacher pensions.

The union is suspicious of the grand plan laid out by the city business and political leaders to create twenty thousand "high-quality" school seats by the year 2020, a plan that calls for improving the best schools already in Milwaukee and bringing in high-performing charter schools. "They openly talk about setting up a school district for twenty thousand of the best kids, so I think they are very conscious of who are they are going to take in and who they are going to exclude and sort of leave the rest for public schools."[2]

The pamphlets and posters set off an immediate reaction at Rocketship. Within days, a letter went out to every contact Rocketship had in Milwaukee, a response that spoke to the whisper campaign and posters. A three-page "Milwaukee Fact Sheet":

Q. Why was Rocketship asked to come to Milwaukee?
A. Milwaukee parents lack options for good schools. Only 62 percent of Latino students and 60 percent of African American students earn their high school degrees on time.
Q. Do Rocketship schools offer art and music?
A. Rocketship students have a daily enrichment block that includes art and music and dance.
Q. Does Rocketship accept special needs students?
A. Absolutely.
Q. Do Rocketship schools make a profit?
A. Rocketship is a not-for-profit organization, so we don't make a profit.
Q. What are Rocketship plans for Milwaukee?
A. We will open eight schools, but only if the existing Rocketship schools in Milwaukee are high performing.[3]

Kristoffer Haines, who is overseeing the Milwaukee launch for Rocketship, says he doubts the anti-Rocketship campaign is hurting enrollment. "The unidentified groups, muscling in and not showing their faces, are doing themselves no favor. Most parents just want the facts. Anyone who saw the flier can see right through it, the way it's written, the tone, that they are talking in falsities. We sat down with our parent leaders and talked with them about it. Our parents are equally pissed. The fact they are not showing their face and engaging is telling. It gets parents fired up in our direction."

There are some positives arising out of the pushback movement. During my visit shortly after the fliers appeared, the attacks seemed to galvanize the staff and parents; the pushback was a sign they were working on something important. Lynk said he has no apologies to offer about the aggressive recruitment. "They might feel it's a form of intimidation," said Lynk, "but I feel like it's a form of inspiration. We're out there making some type of noise and holding everyone accountable." Lynk, who once worked for Milwaukee Public Schools, says the message to his former school district is,

"Hey, you need to ensure that kids are learning. If you don't, then people are going to find a better school."

McGonegle, who now works in Milwaukee coaching school leaders, predicts success for Rocketship in Milwaukee (despite her strained departure). "The more time I've spent in schools here the more shocked I am about how far behind they are in [data-driven] instruction." Rocketship, she predicted, would have no problem rising quickly to the top as a top-performing school. "Rocketship is very good at thinking on the fly and finding what works and doesn't work." The Milwaukee Rocketship school will enjoy another advantage, says McGonegle: the ability to focus on nothing but academics, a half-continent away from office politics spilling out of Rocketship's central office in California—the politics that triggered her departure. "They'll get to focus just on running a great school."

Rocketship's slow recruiting has to be put into perspective, says several outside charter experts. Most charter schools would never aim as high as 485 students on opening day and 650 two years later. Only Rocketship would aim that high. And Rocketship's recruiting record compares favorably to other new schools opening in Milwaukee. "At this time of enrollment, Rocketship has been more successful than any of the other new schools opening here," said Jodi Goldberg from Great Schools Milwaukee, which ranks and reviews schools. "There have been so many new schools in the last ten years." Opening in August with one hundred fewer students than hoped for should not be viewed as a defeat, says Goldberg. "If they do they will have been wildly successful. If they have a top-notch first year, the rest of the recruiting will be easier."

Notes

1. Joseph, at this time, declined to respond to e-mails and phone messages. (Later, after the controversy ebbed, she agreed to an interview and told me she had no idea who made the posters.)

2. Union president Bob Peterson never returned my phone messages or e-mails.

3. Not addressed directly in the fact sheet was the assertion that Rocket-ship transfers $600,000 per school back to headquarters for expansion efforts. Typically, the figure is closer to $400,000, said Haines. "It goes for everything national does to support its regions: leadership development, budgeting, accounts payable, accounts receivable, school model design, legal, compliance, etc."

Surprise Shift
on TFA

June 2013: Redwood City, California

In 2008 Danner and Smith had settled on a unique approach to hiring teachers: Let Teach For America handle the initial selection and training. The rationale for making TFA Rocketship's de facto personnel department hinged on two bets: that Rocketship could quickly turn these first-year teachers into effective teachers and, through quick promotions and higher pay, could hang onto teachers who otherwise would leave for law school, business school, or other pursuits. The strategy worked . . . until it didn't, and in 2013 Rocketship cut back on first-year TFA recruits.

It wasn't that those two bets didn't work out. Rocketship was able to make most of the new teachers into effective teachers, and it was able to keep more through higher pay and promotions. What they hadn't counted on, however, was the effort it took to make those teachers effective. "Principals were pouring a lot of effort into coaching new TFA members and not paying attention to the other teachers," said Lynn Liao, who oversees talent recruitment for Rocketship. The new strategy, says Liao, is to hire only two new TFA recruits per school (rather than the previous four). Not only will that reduce the coaching load but fewer hires increases the odds of taking in better teachers who will need less coaching, she said. For the upcoming 2013–2014 school, for example, Rocketship will take in seventeen new TFA recruits, compared to the usual thirty-two. Another thirty-five experienced teachers will be hired.

Hiring more outside teachers meant Rocketship had to build an internal recruiting team. "That team will also handle leader recruitment, which is a huge priority for us, to fuel our growth." The Rocketship model of rapid promotion of teachers is working, says Liao, pointing to a sizable list of teachers promoted to assistant principal for next year. The Rocketship model of fast growth always assumed that roughly a fifth of new school leaders would have to be hired from the outside. When asked about the shift, Smith emphasized that the TFA decision was made by members of his executive team, Liao and Kate Mehr, the chief schools officer. "There's a new sheriff in town," said Smith, referring to the change in leadership he swore to after the blowup meeting (see "Smith's Worst Monday Ever"). The new credo after that meeting: don't second-guess or overrule your leaders when they make decisions. And this is what Liao and Mehr wanted. But Smith supported their decision. The new instructional model, with combined classrooms in fourth and fifth grades, creates specialty teaching positions requiring more training and experience—and therefore less suitable for a rookie teacher, says Smith.

Sharon Kim (see "How Many Sharon Kims Are out There"), who at the age of twenty-five became a startup principal for Rocketship, opening Alma Academy, sees both sides of the TFA issue. A TFAer herself, she received considerable coaching her first year as a Rocketship teacher. Now, as a principal, she estimates that she, along with her academic dean and assistant principal, devote as much as 70 percent of their coaching time to the school's four, first-year corps members, especially during the first three months of the 2012–2013 school year. That coaching pays off, she says. Based on end-of-the-year data, the students in those classrooms made greater gains than the students in the classes taught by the more veteran teachers. Cutting back on TFA hires will redirect the coaching to the rest of the staff, she said. But for the next school year, Kim will cut back only slightly—taking three rather than four first-year TFA teachers. In short, she liked what she saw during her interviews with the TFA candidates and chose one more than the other schools were taking.

"I enjoy having TFA members," said Kim. "It's rough in the beginning, but they are very eager to soak up whatever coaching we provide them. Because of that spongelike quality, they grow at very high speeds, which has been exciting for me to see."

MILWAUKEE PARENTS
NAME THEIR SCHOOL
Southside Prep

June 2013: Milwaukee, Wisconsin

Founding principal Brittany Kinser and her recruiting team may have been running short on their recruitment goal at this time, but the roughly two hundred families already signed up showed up in force on this Friday afternoon for the naming ceremony. There were barely enough folding chairs to set up in the new gym. The parents got introduced to the newly hired teachers and the leadership team. They also got an early taste of Rocketship culture. Not only did they vote on a school name, a Rocketship tradition—the name "Rocketship Southside Prep" was introduced with a drum roll simulated by hands slapping on knees—but they experienced a simulated Rocketship "launch," the first-in-the-morning ceremony that includes lots of dancing, singing, and chanting the school goals. All the teachers and school leaders formed a line in front of the parents and, together with some incoming students, waved their arms in the air as they danced to high-decibel music.

Kinser invited all the parents back to the school Saturday morning and asked that they bring neighbors, friends, or relatives who have children who might be interested in coming to Rocketship. There's urgency here, Kinser told the parents: we need to recruit another three hundred students. That comment triggered lots of quizzical and worried looks among the parents. Three hundred? Southside Prep might be a bit behind on its recruiting goal, but the reason it has roughly two hundred students enrolled at this point, and the reason turnout was so good this day, probably has less to do with Kinser, her assistant principals, her teachers, and the Rocketship national team than it has to do with the most critical hire made to date: the office manager. I first met Elsy Villafuentes as she was helping Kinser recruit parents from Holy Wisdom Academy (see "Milwaukee Looking Up [a Bit]").

Finding Villafuentes wasn't easy; it took a lot of shoe leather work by a key member of the Rocketship recruiting team, Vanessa Solis, a native Spanish speaker and Teach For America recruit slated to be a Rocketship teacher in Milwaukee. Months earlier in the middle of a very cold Milwaukee winter day, Solis and Kinser went door knocking together, leaving brochures when they found no one home. Villafuentes saw the brochure but was only slightly interested. "I was worried that this would be just another charter that closed down." Then, Solis returned to the neighborhood alone during a snow storm. This time Villafuentes was home. "I let her in to sit down. It was snowing really hard. She showed me a video of a Rocketship school and I agreed to fill out an application for my seven-year-old daughter. But I told her I couldn't promise her anything, and she said that was fine."

Solis's door-to-door persistence impressed Villafuentes, who then conducted her own research into Rocketship. She liked what she saw. What sealed the deal was an offer from Rocketship to fly her to California to see schools there. "When I saw the morning launch I had tears in my eyes." Not only did she embrace what she saw in San Jose and agree to enroll her daughter, Jocelyn, but she also accepted an offer to work for Rocketship. Villafuentes had the perfect skill set: local, a native Spanish speaker, savvy about education statistics, and invaluable people skills from her previous job doing home visits for a Milwaukee foundation. Anyone meeting Villafuentes immediately knows the importance of getting her onboard. Look into her eyes and you can see the calm, confident, long-view perspective of someone who has experienced the always-challenging road to making it in America as a nonnative, especially in snowy, racially divided Milwaukee.

Villafuentes didn't buy into the view held by many Latino leaders that bilingual education was the best way to go. She studied the bilingual schools in Milwaukee, which are making respectable but incremental gains, and concluded that was not the path for her daughter. For Jocelyn, and other young children of Latino families in Milwaukee like her, Villafuentes wants a path into the future: college and a good career. To her, Rocketship's aggressive, English-only academic program looked like the right path for Jocelyn to accomplish that.

Rocketship may offer Villafuentes and Jocelyn something promising, but for Rocketship, the Latino mother offers something even more promising: an insider's path into who really matters on Milwaukee's South Side. It was through her that Rocketship pulled in its best recruiter, Conchita, someone who doesn't even work for Rocketship. Her real name is Maria Conception Gonzales Sandoval. But everyone knows her as Conchita. Born in Mexico, she immigrated to the United States long ago and for the last seventeen years has lived in Milwaukee, where her husband found a factory job. When she first arrived on the South Side, she was surrounded by Polish families. At her church, St. Vincent de Paul, she was one of ten Latino families. Today, there are only ten Polish families remaining at the church and all the other parishioners are Latino. Sandoval tried to learn English, but it never took. But on the South Side, she has no problem surviving without English skills. In fact, she's thriving; taking several leadership roles at the church (she has the keys to everything in the church). Of special importance is her role overseeing Quinceañera, the Latina ceremony celebrating a girl's fifteenth birthday, a transition from childhood to womanhood.

All that means that when Sandoval offers advice, her words are taken seriously. And the advice she was passing along in spring 2013 was this: enroll at Rocketship. Her first contact with Rocketship was through Villafuentes. "I had known her since she was a child, and she started telling me about Rocketship," said Sandoval (through Vanessa Solis acting as translator). Sandoval has three children, including an eight-year-old daughter. "My daughter was struggling in school and I went to the teacher, but the teacher never had time for me. She would close the door on me. I went to the principal and the principal would not follow up." Her daughter was born late in life, making her education outcome especially precious. "I want to be very involved with her schooling."

So when Villafuentes urged her to look at Rocketship she was eager to learn more. Everything she learned about Rocketship was encouraging, and when her sister who lives in California reported back that the schools had a good reputation there, Sandoval decided to make a change. And she concluded that other families should consider a change as well. When Sandoval recommends, people listen. To date, about forty of the two hundred families signing up for Rocketship have been direct referrals from

Sandoval. She's a recruiting powerhouse. Solis jokes that Sandoval will take away her job as a Rocketship recruiter.

Sandoval became one of the parent leaders for Southside Prep, a key group of local supporters who can step into political confrontations with authority. That also describes Roberto Montemayor, owner of Monterrey Market, a South Side Latino grocery. On the afternoon before the school-naming ceremony I met Montemayor at the market. This is not Safeway, Giant, or Piggly Wiggly. Here you find foods here you won't find at the big box stores: fajitas, tamales, and chicharron. And here, everybody knows your name. Montemayor is a burly, fast-talking guy with a politician's gift of gab. Everyone has a little something to say to him as they pass through.

Montemayor first noticed Rocketship when the old party props warehouse was under construction. "I noticed the sign and thought, 'Rocketship,' that's an odd name. He was curious enough to check on it and ended up talking by phone with Solis. Eventually, that led to an invite to visit the Rocketship schools in San Jose. Roberto and his wife, Leonora, recall getting a look at a first-grader's homework packet. "It was amazing. Here was this first-grader doing stuff that kids don't get here until third or fourth grade. That's going to benefit them for the rest of their lives; they are going to be a year or two ahead of the game."

After that trip, they not only decided to send their youngest child to Rocketship but also agreed to become parent leaders. Montemayor's grocery turned into a mini-recruiting station for Rocketship with available brochures and sign-up sheets. One winter day he turned his store into a Rocketship BBQ event, with hot dogs, giveaways, and a Spanish radio station broadcasting from the store, encouraging everyone to come to the store to check out the new school. That drew forty or fifty people and triggered several applications. Even more important, when Rocketship sent out the letter taking on the anti-Rocketship campaign of unsigned fliers and posters, Montemayor was one of the three people signing the letter.

Local credibility: priceless.

RUMOR JUST IN
Rocketship Falls through the Ice

June 2013: San Jose, California

In late June some Rocketship teachers heard rumors that their school scores took significant dips on the latest, yet-to-be-publicly released California Academic Performance Index. And not just a couple of Rocketship schools—all of them. Was it true? Yes, answered Preston Smith when I reached him by phone. The precise rumor teachers had heard, that each school dipped roughly about fifteen points was "relatively accurate," he says.

Fifteen points on a thousand-point scale doesn't sound like much. The staff at most traditional public schools wouldn't be happy about it, but life would go on unchanged. For Rocketship, however, across-the-board setbacks might prove disastrous. Media darlings have a way of getting taken down, brutally. Just ask Michelle Rhee, the former DC schools chancellor.

Smith insisted the score dips were not related to the model change, pointing to encouraging test results in the grades where Rocketship placed all students in one grade into a single classroom. "The new model is not responsible for this. It did not tear us down. You could argue that it definitely shifted focus, and that's a valid argument."

To Smith, the score dips were evidence that Rocketship spent too many years eating its seed corn, focusing on rapid expansion and sophisticated learning software rather than giving teachers a curriculum to work with. "For the past few years we just haven't invested in our academic systems. If you ask teachers in one school how they teach phonics and then ask the same question of teachers in another school, you are going to get two different answers." That all changes this coming year, with Rocketship settling on a single literacy instruction program for all the schools. Long before these scores arrived, the 2013–2014 school year was designated a rebuilding year at Rocketship, strengthening curriculum and instruction and opening only two new schools, Southside Prep in Milwaukee and Spark Academy in San Jose.

"This smacked us hard this year," said Smith, "and we deserve it. We need the humility and we need the reminder that, whoa, this is really hard work. If you don't have your systems in place, you are going to get smacked." Smith seemed confident that Rocketship was prepared to bounce back from a year that, as he put it, "The ice broke." But if the bounce doesn't happen, he is prepared to take personal responsibility. "In August I will tell the board that if we don't deliver next school year I am going to step down. I'll walk away, because I don't give a crap about the position. I'm in this for Rocketship and kids to be successful and, you know, if we're not doing it then, I am going to be out."

When was the last time you heard a traditional school superintendent vow to fall on his sword if student learning didn't improve in the next school year?

A Fibonacci Charter
Group Is Honored

July 2013: Washington, DC

For top-performing charter school networks, the annual Broad Prize for Public Charter Schools has become something of an Academy Award. Who's the best of the best, as measured by successfully educating low-income minority students? This year, the several thousand charter school advocates who swarmed into the Washington Convention Center for a conference organized by the National Alliance for Public Charter Schools learned the honor would go to Uncommon Schools, a network located in the Northeast. The award brings not just bragging rights but a $250,000 prize to be used for boosting college readiness.

From my perspective, Broad could not have picked a better winner. I first came across Uncommon Schools while researching a book about boys struggling in school. While following boys at the Excellence Boys Charter School in Bedford-Stuyvesant I found a school that impressed me during every visit. Then, while researching a book for the College Board about schools that work for poor, minority students, I visited another school run by Uncommon Schools, the True North Troy Preparatory School just a few miles outside Albany, New York. There, one of the stars of Uncommon Schools, Doug Lemov, author of the hot-selling Teach Like a Champion, *designed a school that makes full use of the book's findings.[1] Lemov and other leaders at Uncommon Schools have put together a stunning track record. Their schools serve African American and Latino students, 80 percent of whom are low income. All of Uncommon's seniors took the SAT in 2012, earning an average score of 1570, which is 20 points higher than the college readiness standards set by the College Board.*

Do the top charters have a special technique that other charters or traditional schools can't possibly replicate? Not really. YES Prep, which won the Broad Prize last year, achieved its success with this short list of practices:

- *A challenging curriculum guided by the material on Advanced Placement exams*
- *A longer school day*
- *Hiring teachers based on a profile of previous hires who turned into great teachers for YES Prep*
- *Regular teacher professional development*
- *Hiring administrators based on past successful YES Prep hires*
- *Character building and community service*
- *Preparing students to thrive in a college culture*
- *Supporting graduates after they enter college*
- *Using continuous improvement strategies[2]*

Doing all those things well is incredibly hard. But those are knowable practices, already used by the other charter networks in the top 15 percent. These top charters get there mostly because they execute better, not unlike a modestly talented football team that year after year makes it into the championship round.

NOTES

1. San Francisco: Jossey-Bass, 2010.
2. YES Prep study issued by the Broad Prize for Public Charter Schools.

BUILD, MEASURE, LEARN . . .
RINSE, REPEAT

July 2013: Palo Alto, California

Like many startup guys, John Danner finds a lot to like about "build, measure, learn," the mantra pushed by startup guy Eric Ries, author of *The Lean Startup*.[1] The cover blurb accurately advises, "Mandatory reading for entrepreneurs." What's important, Ries argues persuasively, is not coming out of the blocks with a finished product that's perfect for the customer—"castles in the sky," as he describes them. That approach wastes far too much development time and money. Ries, a cofounder of the social network IMVU, describes the untold hours he spent building a "castle," an early version of the network that he thought was sophisticated enough to merit respect among other startup guys, only to be told by consumers that what they wanted was a very different kind of castle. "I wondered, in light of the fact that my work turned out to be a waste of time and energy, would the company have been just as well off if I had spent the past six months on a beach sipping umbrella drinks?"[2]

Rather than building a castle, the idea is to follow the three-step process of building, measuring, and learning. Better put, listen to your customer, then rebuild, debug, and roll out a new product. Then, rinse and repeat. That's something Danner gets on a personal level. When launching NetGravity the joke among the sales staff as they headed out for the day was they were selling "vaporware." To them, that meant software that existed mostly in the, well, formative stage. Had Danner waited until NetGravity engineers produced the perfect software castle the competition in this fast-expanding field would have eaten him alive. Only when NetGravity landed a customer did the real work commence: adapting the software to the customer, debugging, learning new lessons, rinsing, repeating. It worked.

Understandably, Danner wanted Rocketship to follow that philosophy, and in many ways it did. In 2007 when Danner and Smith opened the first Rocketship, truly adaptive software—the kind of program that really tracked the learning habits of each student and could thus act as a teacher—was a bit of a fantasy. At that point, most learning programs weren't even online, let along adaptive. Essentially, Rocketship was feeding vaporware to its students. As described in the chapters about developing DreamBox, Danner became a demanding customer for DreamBox and other providers, insisting that they build, measure, learn. The message: give us *exactly* what we need. In math, the lean startup approach paid off quickly and had a huge impact with Latino students at Mateo Sheedy turning in impressive math scores. Makes sense. Math programs are not only the most logical to write, but they can be entirely visual—English language skills not entirely necessary. As all educators know, reading is another story. That's deeply rooted in out-of-school experiences dating back to birth. Even as late as 2013, online reading software remained a work in progress.

Another lean startup success emerged from its lean building design-and-construction strategy, which was crucial to keep expenses low and scalability high. Had Rocketship instead pursued the strategy of leasing existing unused buildings from schools districts (the recommendation of some of its board members), that scalability would have been lost. New construction was a risky move—Rocketship had to get it right from the get-go—but one that paid off.

From a broader perspective, however, there are many ways the startup culture proved to be an oil-and-water fit with school culture. What Danner discovered is what other startup guys will find, at least those brave enough to take on education reform, so it's important to draw up a list:

Metrics. In weighing whether to fund tech startups, venture capitalists rely on relatively simple performance metrics such as growth and revenue predictability. From those metrics, they make go or no-go decisions on funding the startup. For nonprofit charter school startups, foundations take the place of venture capitalists. But foundations take a different approach to performance metrics. What made sense to Danner was something startup simple: growth and student achievement. But foundations want far more. "Among all the grants we received, people were trying to hold us to hundreds of metrics, based on whatever they thought was important, instead of the business drivers. That causes a loss of focus."

Take teacher turnover rates. Funders expect teacher turnover to remain low. To them, that's an important marker for school stability and the likelihood a charter group can expand quickly. But that metric can get in the way of ensuring school quality, says Danner. "If you were a struggling charter management organization trying to make funders happy you wouldn't fire low-performing teachers because that's going to count against your attrition rate."

Focus. In the startup tech world, once the right product-market mix gets settled on, the challenge is to resist wandering from that right focus. In the school world, it is nearly impossible to keep a tight focus. "At any point in time you can only do two or three things really well as an organization. Those objectives have to be really clear, repeated often, and resources need to be aligned to them. At Rocketship, because of the complexity of the business, I found this to be tremendously difficult. We had real estate issues, talent issues, political issues, regional issues, and academic model issues. It was very difficult not to deal with all of those every day. I think ultimately this complexity is what makes it difficult to scale any nontech business, but especially ones where regulatory and political issues are a big-time sink. If I had to do it over again, I would be stronger on focusing on one thing at a time in each of these areas and getting it right to build up our capacity over time. But that's very hard compared to software businesses that are insanely simple, where you build the product, get users, make them happy, and get them to pay."

With schools, for example, there's a need to simultaneously develop principals, teachers, and the academic model. From a management perspective, it would make sense to prioritize those three, but then pick one, let's say choosing principals as the top priority, and work on that until you have it right before moving to the other two. In the school world, you don't have that luxury. All three have to be developed at once. Inevitably, that means something gets shortchanged. "We did too many things at once and so some of them, academic systems being the big one, never got done to completion with clear metrics."

Paying talent. In both startup and school worlds, getting the right talent means everything. In the startup world, talented coders and product development engineers can be attracted and retained through a combination of salary and stock equity. The stock equity distributions enable the startup business to ease the demand on the company's invaluable cash flow while also retaining top talent. But in the nonprofit world, equity distributions aren't possible. As a result, Danner said, "You are capping people's upside." The only option for recruiting and motivating teachers and principals is to pay them more each year.

But there's an obvious catch-22 here: the more you grow, and the better you become at retaining great talent, the more cash you burn through. "In nonprofits, the talent problem continues to work against you." Is there a way around that hurdle? "The only thing I could figure out was to create a culture and public image that was strong enough to attract for-profit people," said Danner, referring to the desire to attract what he saw as the deeper talent pool from the for-profit world. "I'm not sure we really pulled this off. I think Teach For America has done a better job with that."

Capital. In the tech startup world, if you are executing well on your metrics, capital is abundant. In the nonprofit startup world, however, just the opposite plays out, especially for an organization such as Rocketship that wants to grow fast. "Since foundations lose money any time they invest in you, it doesn't really matter how well you are executing—the incentive for them to invest in you doesn't get any greater. And yet you need more capital to grow."

Risk aversion. Here, foundations and venture capitalists are at polar opposites. Venture capitalists are often comfortable with one-in-a-hundred bets, especially when the "one" reveals itself as the new Facebook, a home run that makes all the failed bets look a lot better. Foundations, by contrast, are under pressure to make every bet look good. For them, one home run doesn't make up for a string of washouts. "This risk aversion creates friction for people doing innovative things because they are riskier." In the beginning, Rocketship's design looked riskier because it was. As a result, Rocketship didn't receive any foundation support for three years. Even the nation's most "out-there" charter school investor, NewSchools, took a pass on Rocketship in those early years. "If our model had not been so efficient, and if we hadn't had a few good angels [donors such as Reed Hastings], we would not have gotten off the ground."

Board management. In tech startups, boards are simple and stream-lined. Maybe five people with technical expertise and a couple of funders. Nonprofit boards, by contrast, often number about fifteen members picked for their fund-raising potential. Having that many board members with so little expertise in the core business exacerbates the focus challenge. "At Rocketship we resisted this. We chose for expertise."

NOTES

1. New York: Crown Business, 2011.
2. *Inc.* (October 2011).

ONE MONTH BEFORE SOUTHSIDE PREP OPENS

July 2013: Milwaukee, Wisconsin

On July 19, exactly one month before school was to open, enrollment stood at 240. The original goal, 485 students on opening day, seemed impossibly distant. Even the informal hoped-for goal of 350 seemed pretty challenging. It appeared Rocketship leaders accepted that they would launch the first out-of-California school underenrolled. "We're prepared to start at less than full capacity in the first year, and what will govern our growth is execution and performance," said Tim Sheehy, the local chamber president who was instrumental in convincing Rocketship to come to Milwaukee and also serves on the Rocketship national board, when interviewed by the *Milwaukee Journal Sentinel*.[1] "The families that are in it will become tremendous advocates for the school, and enrollment will take care of itself."

And the campaign to convince parents to avoid Rocketship continued as well. Milwaukee school board member Tatiana Joseph passed out anti-Rocketship leaflets at a July 4 carnival sponsored by Rocketship to reach out to parents who might be interested in the new school. Briefly, Joseph and Southside Prep Brittany Kinser exchanged some pointed words while standing on opposite sides of the street, with Kinser accusing Joseph of spreading falsehoods. "I wasn't yelling," said Joseph. "I was just saying that Rocketship isn't as peachy as its sounds and people should know the other side of the story."

NOTE

1. Erin Richards, "California-Based Charter Network Raises Eyebrows with Results, Aggressive Tactics," *Journal Sentinel,* July 13, 2013, http://www.jsonline.com/news/education/rocketship-pushes-to-enter-milwaukee-school-orbit-b9950297z1-215395661.html.

How Many Sharon Kims
Are out There?

July 2013: San Jose, California

I first met Sharon Kim in 2011 when she was a Teach For America newbie just placed at Rocketship Mateo Sheedy. Nothing from her four years at Cornell University or TFA training truly prepared her for that first day of school to teach four classes of kindergarten math, thirty students per class. "I was so confident walking into that classroom. I knew exactly what I wanted to teach." But that plan got tossed. What she found in her first class were thirty students who lacked what educators call "school-readiness skills," starting with the basics of how to sit at a desk, how to raise your hand, how to use the school bathroom. Nearly all her students spoke English as a second language and only a few had been to preschool. "Those first few days were extremely difficult. . . . I had to learn all their names, but within the first hour they ripped up the name tags and threw them away."

Kim seemed an unlikely candidate to arrive at a Rocketship school in San Jose. The daughter of Korean immigrants, Kim grew up in Dallas, where her father was a pastor and her mother was a postal clerk. Saving enough money to send their daughter to Cornell wasn't easy, so when Kim began thinking about a career her parents hoped she would choose a field with promising financial rewards. Law school or medical school, which were at the top of her list, was fine with them. But at Cornell Kim was struck by what she was learning about the nation's achievement gap. She attended some lectures by Jonathan Kozol, read his *Savage Inequities*[1] book, worked in a summer program at some of the New York City schools Kozol wrote about, and decided to apply for Teach For America. Her parents had serious concerns about her career choice, but Kim stuck to it. She wanted to teach in San Francisco but mistakenly checked "South Bay" on her TFA application, which landed her at Rocketship Mateo Sheedy, Rocketship's flagship school in San Jose.

To Rocketship, Kim was everything they hoped for in a TFA candidate. As conceived by John Danner and Preston Smith, the plan was to recruit great candidates from TFA and then, through exacting guidance delivered by a teaching coach in the back of the room, often speaking wirelessly to ear bud–wearing teachers, turn them into effective first-year teachers.

With Kim, that all came true. She visited students' homes, which fueled her desire to act with urgency. "It's a reminder that many of my students lived in a room with seven other children and grandma. That's where he would do his homework." And she responded well to coaching by the assistant principals, which meant that her students started scoring well on tests. Most of all, she seemed to know how to pace herself. It's not just students who need to acquire grit and perseverance; it's teachers as well. Kim often reminded herself of an adage she had learned: "You should forgive yourself at night and recommit yourself in the morning."

During her second year of teaching Rocketship tapped Kim for its emerging leaders program, and by her third year she was promoted to assistant principal at Rocketship Discovery Prep. By her fourth year Kim was handed the prestigious assignment of becoming a launch principal for a new school, Alma Academy. Four years out of Cornell and Kim had her own school.

Even by Rocketship standards, this was an extraordinary rise. If Danner and Smith were right about extra pay and rapid promotions, and if there were enough Sharon Kims out there, Rocketship could generate its own principals internally for its rapid expansion. Were they right? Only partly. With benefit of hindsight, Kim turned out to be more extraordinary than ordinary. Principals, especially startup principals, are tough to find. In 2013 Rocketship appeared to be running short on principals. When Adam Nadeau left to start Rocketship schools in Nashville there were few internal candidates to take his place at Rocketship Mosaic and Rocketship advertised for outside candidates.[2] Danner was partly right about Rocketship's ability to bring most first-year TFAers up to full teaching speed.

The last part of the Danner-Smith personnel theory may be the most interesting: can you persuade good teachers to stay longer by paying them a premium and basing part of the pay on job performance? The answer, again, is mixed. I came across teachers who stuck longer with Rocketship because of the pay, and others who left at roughly the five-year mark to teach elsewhere even though that meant taking a pay cut.

In 2013 Rocketship's teacher retention dipped from 77 to 73 percent. But considering the turmoil that year, the dip was not as big as top leaders feared. Schools such as Si Se Puede, which went through the most trauma over the model change (three iterations, according to Lynn Liao) saw the highest number of departures. There, retention fell to 63 percent. But that's not necessarily proof of dissatisfaction over the model change, says Liao. That school is Rocketship's second oldest, and several teachers there were ready to move on. "When you're the second school you are used to doing things you own way," said Liao, pointing out that some of the teachers there fondly recall the days when they would head out to lunch with Preston Smith to discuss school matters. As Rocketship grows, that just isn't going to happen, she says.

Rocketship may be entering a pattern seen at other high-performing charters. At both KIPP and Success Academy Charter Schools, the latter run by former New York City councilwoman Eva Moskowitz, teachers stay in the classroom for about four years. At YES Prep, teachers stay in the classroom an average of 2.5 years. At Achievement First, the figure is 2.3 years.[3] At these charters, school leaders hope for five years on the job and then aren't surprised to see the teachers move on. Teachers who begin their careers at Rocketship stay an average of 2.9 years.

By comparison, teachers at traditional public schools stay an average of fourteen years. School administrators take pride in keeping career teachers on the job, as do the teachers unions, which have negotiated contracts that peg salary to longevity on the job. Isn't it obvious that more experience equates to more effective teaching? Actually, other than documenting that first-year teachers struggle, the data are slippery. In teaching, experience and excellence are not necessarily connected.[4] As Sharon Kim discovered at Alma Academy, her rookie teachers may have needed special guidance but they proved to be her strongest teachers.

Kim's school did well in 2013. The test scores were good and there are waiting lists for every grade. The retention rate among teachers at Alma was 75 percent, says Kim, a rate she was comfortable with—while pushing for even higher retention. Several of her teachers aspire to be school leaders, she says, including one first-year Teach For America corps member. Despite her rapid rise, Kim does not consider herself an outlier. In short, she thinks the Rocketship personnel system is both workable and sustainable.

What is barely sustainable, Kim says, is the personal strain. "I remember getting the offer letter from Preston to become a principal, and the first thing that went through my mind was, 'Oh, my gosh, the next two years are going to be very intense. I remember telling my family that it was going to be a steep learning curve and they had to help keep me in check, to make sure that I didn't do this at the expense of my health, friendships, and relationships with my family and church community." Has she succeeded in maintaining an outside life? "It's not where I want it to be. It's still something I need to better handle. But it's better than what I thought it might have been."

Teaching at Rocketship

While researching the book I met many Rocketship teachers during multiple school visits. Some conversations I had were official, as in part of an arranged school visit. Others were conducted privately, over the phone. These four short profiles represent a rough range of the attitudes I came across.

Juan Mateos

Mateos grew up in Oxnard, an hour's drive north of Los Angeles, in a neighborhood that was nearly entirely Latino. He graduated from Stanford University. While on an internship in Washington, DC, working in a congressional office he was struck by the paucity of Latinos either serving in office or working as staffers. "Decisions were being made that didn't reflect what was real." Mateos concluded that until the education system improved few Latinos would find their way into the upper levels of government. Mateos applied to Teach For America and got placed at Washington Elementary, a school that's close to two Rocketship Schools (see "The Pushback Gets Real: The Fight over Tamien"), where he taught bilingual classes. He recalls feeling very proud of the progress he was making with one second-grade girl who toward the end of the year was reading on a fourth-grade level. Then one day her older sister, a fourth-grader, came into their class and did some homework with her little sister. The older sister read at only a second-grade level. Clearly, quality instruction and learning wasn't taking place throughout the building. "It made me think about having an impact beyond just my class."

And so when Preston Smith contacted Mateos (Rocketship keeps tabs on the successful TFAers in the neighborhood) about switching to Rocketship, Mateos was more than willing to listen. "I met with Preston and we talked about his idea of growth and scale." To Mateos, joining an organization dedicated to scaling up quickly seemed an ideal way to have an impact beyond one classroom. He signed on with Rocketship and became a teacher at Rocketship Mateo Sheedy.

Given the tension and rivalry between the two schools, it was interesting to hear Mateos compare the two schools. Parent involvement is very different, he said. At Washington, parents are eager to volunteer and come to the school events, he says. At Mateo Sheedy, parents are more attuned to academic issues. "Parents are viewed more as stakeholders. I've had parents audit my classroom to make sure students are getting the best education. They hold us a little more accountable."

The teacher turnover is starkly different, he says, with significant turnover at Rocketship and very little turnover at Washington. "At Washington the same teachers come back year after year." There are several reasons for the turnover difference, he says. Some Rocketship teachers leave for law or business school. The added responsibility at Rocketship is another factor, he says, with Rocketship teachers expected to achieve a year-and-a-half of learning for each child, every year. That demand, which is felt by every teacher, creates a sense of urgency that isn't seen in most schools. But that year-and-a-half of learning carries a price tag for teachers. "That means a lot of work, a lot of hours."

The rotating classes, with teachers seeing 60 or 120 students a day, are more stressful than teaching self-contained classes at Washington or any other traditional elementary. [Those rotating classes, where teachers who specialize in either math or literacy deliver the same lessons four times a day, may be stressful on teachers but they probably account for much of Rocketship's success, probably more than the blended learning, which usually gets the credit from the media. By the second rotation, teachers get better at delivering the material.]

(continued)

Some teachers just aren't cut out for that level of stress, says Mateos, which is the reason many Rocketship teachers move on. That's not the case with Mateos, however, who finished his second year at Rocketship during the 2012–2013 school year. He is joining the emerging leaders program at Rocketship with the hope of becoming an assistant principal the following year. "I'd like to stay."

Andrea Chrisman

Chrisman grew up in Oklahoma and graduated from the University of Oklahoma. After joining Teach For America she was assigned to Rocketship, the first year Mateo Sheedy moved into its new building. She then shifted to another Rocketship school, Los Suenos, and then briefly left Rocketship and returned home to Oklahoma. Three weeks after returning to Oklahoma she got a call from Rocketship: "We need a third-grade teacher for Si Se Puede." She agreed. "I missed California, the friends, and the life I had here." So Chrisman returned to the Bay Area and taught for two more years. "I've taught at more schools than anyone else and taught more grades than anyone else. It's been a crazy ride."

The turmoil over the model change, however, ended her five-year Rocketship career. This time, she says, she has quit Rocketship for good. The open classroom, with all the students from one grade in one space, didn't work for her. Nor did it work for all the students, she says. "I'd say for the kids who were super high on math and reading, it served them very well because they were in one classroom with other students who were challenging themselves. But for the lowest kids, it was not serving them well." Working with low-performing students was Chrisman's specialty. The Rocketship combined-classroom strategy was supposed to help the slower readers by carving out time for small groups to experience "guided reading" with the teacher. But that happens just as well in a self-contained classroom of thirty, says Chrisman.

Chrisman said that she was interviewing at other schools, including a KIPP charter school, even though that meant a significant pay cut. Rocketship, she predicted, will have a tough time meeting its ambitious expansion plans. Quickly promoting teachers to school leaders, she says, means principals have limited teaching experience, which limits their abilities to be instructional leaders. What does a principal with two years of teaching experience have to offer in the role of coach?

Becky Johnson

Johnson was raised in Southern California and graduated from the University of Southern California. She next spent a year working at a school in the Watts neighborhood of Los Angeles for teen moms and pregnant moms. Following that, she entered the New York City Teaching Fellows program (similar to TFA, a program where she also earned a master's degree in special education) and taught in the South Bronx, working in a self-contained classroom for emotionally and behaviorally disturbed children. Returning to California in 2011, she joined Rocketship, where at first she was a special education teacher covering two schools.

"I was excited to come to a program that was full inclusion," said Johnson, "that had students mainstreamed throughout the day and really pushed teachers to embrace all types of learners in the classroom." When Johnson first arrived at Rocketship the schools lacked the resources to accomplish that goal, but that changed quickly. Still, Rocketship draws only about half the special education population as the surrounding traditional schools. The perception that Rocketship isn't for special education kids is changing quickly, she says, partly due to community awareness efforts. "We are getting tons of new [special education] kids next year," said Johnson.

For the 2013–2014 school year, Johnson will become an assistant principal at Discovery Prep, a school that took a big morale hit the year before, partly due to the rushed model change. "I think we are figuring out the kinks to that. Individualized education is just that," said Johnson, referring to the constant refrain anyone would hear from Danner and Smith. "It has to be individualized." The open classroom works for many students, she says, allowing more targeted instruction. "I've had other students for whom it was very distracting." For those students, the heightened noise levels and lessened personal contact with a single teacher were problems, she says.

Johnson says she thinks she knows why the teacher turnover for the 2012–2013 school year wasn't as awful as expected [due to the model change]. "One thing Rocketship has done well is build community. Teachers are embedded in this community. We know their families. We've been to visit their houses. We go to birthday parties. This is our community. I think teachers aren't willing to leave that community because of turbulence from the top," said Johnson, referring to the disagreements in the central office over how fast to move ahead on the model change.

(continued)

The sustainability issue—can Rocketship maintain its core of great teachers while expanding quickly—is something Johnson has thought about. The teachers who stay at Rocketship are those with a high tolerance for enduring innovation and change, she said. Plus a willingness to work long hours. "When I was in New York your day ended at 3:27 p.m. and that was just it. Everyone was out of the building. That's not how it works at Rocketship." A huge Rocketship change that should improve sustainability, she says, is the new literacy program that will be adopted by all Rocketship schools in the 2013–2014 school year. Asking teachers to visit each student's home, become a part of the community, work long hours—and also come up with their own day-to-day literacy curriculum—was too much to ask.

Kimberly Menendez

Menendez grew up in Los Angeles, or, more important, in the low-income neighborhood of Watts. She managed to make it into a magnet high school so when it came to colleges she had her pick. Although she was accepted at both UC Berkeley and UCLA, neither school offered enough scholarship money to see her through. Pomona, a highly selective, small private college, offered her a full ride and she accepted. For four years, the only thing she paid for were books. While at Pomona she worked at summer teaching programs, half academics, half summer camp, and decided to try teaching. She applied to Teach For America and ended up as a founding teacher at Rocketship Los Suenos, teaching kindergarten literacy. After finishing her two-year TFA commitment she stayed with Rocketship, shifting to second-grade math. Her plans call for returning there for one more year, and then looking for a teaching or school administrator's job in her home city of LA.

Overall, she gives good ratings to her Rocketship experience. "But there have also been a lot of rough times. It demands a lot of us. I work long hours and we have a lot of kids in our classes. At one point I had thirty-one kids in my class. Menendez teaches in rotating classes, so she sees 120 students each day. "My favorite part of the job is that Rocketship is very community oriented. There's a lot of parent support, so if I ever need anything I call parents and say I need them to grade papers, and they grade the papers. Or, they will come on field trips. Sometimes I will ask a parent to come and hang out in the class so there's an extra body, and they come."

The model change at Los Suenos involved only the third grade, so Menendez avoided that drama. "The third-grade teachers definitely went through a lot this past year. I could see they did not have a good year, and that's because nothing was really established. There was just 'Oh, let's try this. . . . Oh, that didn't work; let's try this.' It felt like a big experiment."

Menendez has questions about the sustainability part of Rocketship's teacher philosophy. "It's not a place for teachers who want to teach for the rest of their lives. I don't feel like you could do more than five years." She knows a teacher who left Rocketship for that reason—she wanted a lifelong teaching career and Rocketship was burning her out. Menendez says she gets to school at about 7 a.m. and then puts in a ten-hour day. On Sundays, she spends time getting materials ready for the upcoming week. "So it's maybe like sixty-five hours a week."

Notes

1. New York: Crown Publishers, 1991.

2. Those advertisements were withdrawn after the principal at Discovery Prep switched to Mosaic and a Discovery Prep teacher was appointed principal there.

3. Mokoto Rich, "At Charter Schools, Short Careers by Choice," *New York Times* (August 26, 2013).

4. In 2013 the National Bureau of Research released a report by two Cornell researchers who documented a rise in student achievement when Illinois teachers fifty and older were offered attractive early retirement packages. The result: the average age of the teachers dropped sharply and student achievement rose.

Eva Makes Life Hard
for Her Many Critics

August 2013: New York City

Generally the news out of New York where students took Common Core–related tests for the first time was universally dismal as test scores plummeted. Exceptions were the Success Academy Charter Schools run by former New York City Council member Eva Moskowitz. The students at her schools, which serve low-income minority children, aced the tests. Success Academy students scored in the top 1 percent of all New York schools in math and in the top 7 percent in English, with 82 percent achieving math proficiency and 58 percent passing English standards. Among the seven test-eligible schools (five in Harlem, two in the Bronx), African American and Hispanic students outperformed white students in the state by fifty-one points in math and twenty-seven points in English.

The results so impressed the Eli and Edythe Broad Foundation that the foundation immediately announced a $5 million gift. The gift prompted a vow from Success Academy leaders that by the end of the decade they would operate one hundred schools in New York.[1]

NOTE

1. The positive scores are unlikely to settle any debates about her schools in New York, however, where critics say the schools succeed by pushing out low-performing students and not replacing them, a charge denied by Moskowitz.

Opening Week at
Southside Prep

August 2013: Milwaukee, Wisconsin

It is Friday, the last day of launch week here, and things are settling down nicely. The number of "criers" whose mothers needed calling fell off dramatically by midweek. That was a relief. The pickups and drop-offs, always a bit chaotic at any school, are calmer. The neighbors aren't happy about the extra traffic and street parking, but they are getting over it. The anti-Rocketship protesters appear to have run out of enthusiasm, brochures, or both. Nobody's seen them for several weeks. The best news of all was visible during the wildly enthusiastic morning launch. On the first day of school, only the teachers danced to Katy Perry's "Firework" as the kids watched in stunned silence. This is school? But today all the kids were dancing and singing along, even some of the parents who lined the back walls. Yes, this is school . . . Rocketship style.

About the only discouraging news was enrollment. On the first day of school, enrollment stood at 270. By the end of the week that rose to 300, but that's still nearly 200 students shy of the first-year goal of 485 students. Even though Rocketship knew its enrollment numbers were running short, the school opened at full staffing. Even assuming a best-case scenario, that principal Brittany Kinser and her recruiters get the enrollment number up to 350 by early September, that still means the school will be short 135 students, which translates into a deficit of roughly $1 million that Rocketship must foot.

"In a typical school," said Rocketship CFO Andy Stern, "if we knew we were opening at three hundred we wouldn't fully staff it." But Milwaukee was different, the first Rocketship launch outside California. Everyone was watching. The Rocketship brand was at stake. With that kind of visibility Rocketship couldn't fully staff the school and then lay off unneeded teachers. What teacher would sign up at the other launch cities?

So Rocketship decided to take the loss. An investment in the future, an investment in the brand.

Honestly, having all those extra adults around the first week—not just the spare teachers but a surge from the national staff in Redwood City—came in handy, especially considering the higher-than-expected number of special education students, roughly 20 percent. In Rocketship schools in San Jose, the special education percentage is a fourth of that. Having assistant teachers to take over a class while the teacher takes an "acting-out" child for a walk around the hallways proved to be invaluable.

Startup principal Brittany Kinser, a Midwesterner herself, is steely as hell with a runner's endurance. During her first parent coffee Kinser clearly left the parents impressed, handling the toughest question of the morning with aplomb. "I hesitate to send my daughter here because then she would have to go to MPS for middle school," said one mother, referring to a very real dilemma: Rocketship only goes to fifth grade. What then? Very few MPS middle schools are viewed as desirable, at least by these parents. If that mother enrolled her daughter in a parochial school she would have a pipeline leading through the high school years.

"We know that is a great concern for our families," answered Kinser. "It was a concern among our parents in San Jose as well." Two things happened there, says Kinser. First, a group of Rocketship parents helped bring a high-performing charter school to San Jose. Second, high-performing charter schools form partnerships with the better middle school. Already, there are signs of that playing out in Milwaukee, says Kinser, who told the parents about how the principals of two nearby middle schools had reached out to her to recruit future Rocketship graduates to their schools. "They want our Rocketeers," said Kinser, "because they see the family involvement."

Kinser's strength is probably why Rocketship was comfortable with her taking on three assistant principals who before this year had no experience as school leaders. The APs, as they call them, were chosen based on their leadership potential rather than proven management experience. Considering the high visibility of Rocketship's launch here, that was a gutsy decision (typical of Rocketship) but one that is likely to pay dividends in the future, at least based on what I saw during my visits. My guess is that all three are likely to become principals soon.

California Test
Scores Released

August, 2013: Redwood City

The score declines rumored in July get confirmed: Rocketship schools took a hit. But what seemed like a calamity back in July appears less so today. A lot of California schools dipped. Overall test scores for California schools dropped for the first time in a decade, and elementary schools such as Rocketship suffered the biggest declines. True, Rocketship still ranked in the top 5 percent of state districts serving low-income families, but score declines aren't supposed to happen at Rocketship. That's for other school districts. The highest fliers in the Rocketship system, such as Mateo Sheedy, suffered the biggest declines, falling 73 points from 924 to 851. Mosaic fell 36 points to 836.

Not surprisingly, the search for blame starts with the traumatic model change when schools knocked down walls, scrambled schedules, and moved computers to combine some grades into a single class (different schools experimented with different grades) with multiple teachers. The news here is mixed. Scrubbing the numbers by each grade at each school showed that the grades going through the model change were generally not the cause; it was the other grades.

That doesn't surprise teachers such as Joe Connor, a 2010 graduate of Duke University who joined Rocketship a year after teaching for a KIPP school in Washington, DC. He thought he was moving to a charter school group that offered teachers a better life-work balance and arrived at Mateo Sheedy just in time for the model change. "It's hard to overemphasize how disruptive that was," said Connor, who left Rocketship after just one year to enter law school. "Everything from the way it was presented to the way it was enacted was bad." The teachers directly involved in the model change complained about what they saw as a lack of research behind the crash reform. For Connor, who taught third-grade literacy, a grade that wasn't part of the experiment, the model change meant that coaching for teachers like him dried up. Too many emergencies elsewhere in the building. Whatever merits the model change might have had, the resources weren't there to carry it off.

Nor does it surprise Smith. "We were not focused on all grades, and we were not focused on kids far behind." That's what the numbers show: the number of Rocketship students scoring at proficient and advanced held steady; it was the struggling learners that fell further behind. Smith does his best to put a positive spin on it. As a school network, Rocketship is still doing well. And the fact that Rocketship endured its roughest year ever, attempting major changes during a year when budgets had been cut by 15 percent and still emerged with limited damage is a "miracle," says Smith. And the fact that the model-change grades did okay on the tests is proof that Rocketship is headed in the right direction, he contends.

Based on the multiple corrections Rocketship put in place to bolster teaching—the tightly targeted model change affecting only the upper grades, more administrators, and a standardized math and literacy curriculum—Smith has drawn a line in the sand. We took a beating in 2013; bet against us in 2014 at your own risk.

PART V

THE FUTURE FOR ROCKETSHIP AND OTHER HIGH PERFORMERS

Answering the
Fibonacci Question
Will Rocketship Make It Big?

September 2013: Arlington, Virginia

Rocketship founder John Danner cited the Fibonacci sequence, as described in the introduction, while imagining how his charter schools might burst into big numbers as they spread, with each new city opening at least eight Rocketship charters. Is that likely to happen with Rocketship? Is it likely to happen with the other top groups, such as KIPP, Uncommon Schools, YES Prep, and Aspire?

Answering the second question is easy (I think it will; see "Conclusion"). The first question, whether Rocketship charters will be major players in that story, requires more discussion. Rocketship's original goal of educating a million students by 2030 got shaved back in 2013. It's the one big lesson I learned while following Rocketship for a year and a half: this stuff is not easy. Given the setbacks I witnessed—test scores dropping at each school in 2013, bitterness over rapid turnover in the leadership team, unexpected drama playing out as Danner stepped down, the hurry-up model change stressing its teachers, a shortage of leaders to take over schools—it might seem logical to dismiss Rocketship's growth potential. After all, they opened a mere two new schools in the 2013–2014 school year. And although Rocketship continues to open up in new regions—within a couple of years there will be Rocketship schools in Nashville; Washington, DC; and Indianapolis along with more schools in San Jose and a second school in Milwaukee—the pacing falls short of explosive.

But I saw more than growing pains during my time watching Rocketship. I saw a small group of charter schools do something rarely seen in the education world: shoot big (who wins twenty new countywide charter schools in a single vote?) and embrace disruption. The latter is probably more impressive than the former. Only schools started by a startup guy would willingly take on that stress. Rocketship could serve as a chapter in *The Innovator's Dilemma*. Rocketship could have sat on its considerable gains. In 2012 it ranked in the top 5 percent of California school districts serving low-income students. That year, 77 percent of Rocketeers scored proficient or advanced in math, compared to 86 percent scored by the most affluent school districts in California. Resting on gains worked for Sears, Xerox, and Bucyrus Erie . . . until it didn't.

In the 2012–2013 school year Rocketship leaders decided to shake up their success, aiming for a "model change" that would reduce costs and boost student learning. Trying to push that dramatic change in a single year didn't go smoothly and in the end, after much strife in the front office, Preston Smith and his top leaders backed off a bit. That turmoil was messy and fractious. Some top leaders resigned; others threatened to resign. With the benefit of hindsight, one can conclude that John Danner pushed too hard to keep Rocketship as a pure startup enterprise. A group of charter schools attempting to reverse achievement gaps among low-income Latinos doesn't always respond like a business startup. Not enough school supports were in place to handle that rapid change. Lacking was the training for teachers expected to take over these large combined classrooms, resources to continue mentoring teachers not involved in the model change, and an established curriculum in math and reading that's a must-do when trying to grow a successful model quickly.

Defining Rocketship's Chemistry

Trying to assign blame for Rocketship's difficult year wrestling with the model change misses the point. In the traditional education world, who even tries such radical change? In that world, failing schools often go untouched for decades. And if something appears to be working, even if "working" means you get tiny, nearly useless gains every year, you leave the model untouched. That's not how it works at Rocketship, which operates by backward mapping: first define your long-term goal, then decide how you will measure it, and then determine the steps that will get you there. At Rocketship, the startup philosophy is so radical that at times even those on the inside can forget they are doing something that few adventurous educators even dream of trying. Rich Billings, the former business manager for Rocketship who now holds a similar position at the Charter School Growth Fund, tells the story of going out for a drink with Rocketship board member Alex Hernandez, now his colleague at the Growth Fund. Billings shared his to-do list with Hernandez, the ten things he was supposed to accomplish that year. Hernandez was struck by the list: six of the ten on that list had never been done by a charter organization (a complicated bond deal, winning twenty countywide charters, and more), he pointed out to Billings. "I only accomplished three of them, so I felt like a failure," said Billings, "but it was still three that had never been done before."

To Danner, a veteran of the sharp-elbowed Silicon Valley startup world, the model change turmoil barely qualified as turmoil. That kind of stuff happens routinely. And the transition issues that broke out while passing the leadership torch to Smith were nothing special. "One way to look at CEO transitions is that they are about as messy as acquisitions," said Danner. "Preston acquired Rocketship, and no amount of planning or preparation makes up for the change people feel and how people will act until roles and goals get clear again." To Danner, "Smith's Worst Monday Ever" will be forgotten in a year or two, barely worth a footnote in Rocketship's history.

Looking at the departure of several high-profile Rocketship executives in 2013 it is fair to observe that Rocketship proved to be better at student culture than adult culture. But the departures, which are not uncommon among nonprofits, have to be kept in perspective. The brutal truth is the people who got you "there" are not necessarily the people who get you to the next step. Rocketship, says Billings, was more willing to face that than most organizations. His own departure was a mix of wanting to leave and getting pushed out, he says. "I had a conversation with John [Danner] at the beginning, telling him I was happy to be chief financial officer, but at some point Rocketship is going to need someone who has done this before. When that time comes let's have a hard conversation about it and get to the right outcome." When that time came, and it did, Billings helped search for his own replacement [Andy Stern].

Rocketship may fall short of serving a million kids by 2030, but by other measures the startup has already achieved something unique. Through his Rocketship charter schools, Danner demonstrated that schools can be nearly as nimble as any Silicon Valley dot-com. Rocketship, for example, has figured out a way to build new schools, from the first shovel in the ground to the first student walking through the door, in half the time and half the cost of most traditional public schools. Even more startling, Rocketship shoehorns entire schools into plots of land that regular elementary schools would devote just to the cafeteria and gym. And, the first class of students entering that hastily constructed, inexpensive school will walk out of that school at the end of the school year with impressive proficiency rates likely to embarrass the traditional school just down the block, a school serving the same mix of low-income minority kids targeted by Rocketship.

Most educators think about Rocketship as a pioneer in so-called blended learning, in which online learning gets woven into traditional instruction. That's true, but blended learning is not actually what defines Rocketship. These days, hundreds of schools experiment with some flavor of blended learning (with greatly varying degrees of competence). Rather, what distinguishes Rocketship is its willingness to reinvent itself. When things don't seem completely on course, the Rocketship leaders plunge immediately into reinventing their schools, sometimes in a matter of a few months, even if it means combining classes, revamping software, and tearing down walls. Just like the dot-com startups peppered around Silicon Valley. Everything about Rocketship challenges the way traditional schools have done business for generations. Who says a teacher with only a couple of years of experience can't become a startup principal in a new Rocketship school? Who says that struggling principals need to be given a year or two to find their feet? Maybe what's best for the kids is to yank that principal immediately. Who says that a Rocketship school shouldn't be built a couple of blocks from a traditional elementary school? Maybe parents should be given the choice of which school to send their kids. Who says a small school system can't pioneer its own adaptive learning software or at least force the big providers to give them what they need?

Those are Rocketship practices. They sound controversial, but what makes Rocketship truly controversial is a not a set of practices but rather a philosophy. Rocketship raises a question that most traditional educators consider downright dangerous: what if the conventional wisdom about repairing struggling schools is wrong? Currently, superintendents try to "fix" low-performing schools by pouring in local, state, and federal anti-poverty money to buy more resources: reading coaches, tutoring, classroom aides, and so on. In addition to the surge in extra resources, they might try a new principal, perhaps a "turnaround" expert who then brings in a fresh set of teachers. But what if that widespread conventional wisdom is wrong? What if you pump in all those extra resources, all those extra people, and all you get, at best, are tiny annual increases in math and reading skills? Sure, everyone applauds the progress, but if 80 percent of your students still fail to reach proficiency levels was that extra effort and money truly worth it? Maybe what's needed is an in-your-face school like Rocketship putting down roots only a few blocks from that struggling school. Give parents a choice and see what happens. Most school superintendents hate that option, which explains why among educators John Danner and cofounder Preston Smith aren't the most popular guys in San Jose, the home base for Rocketship. Smith once confided that he avoids certain coffee shops just because he knows his most outspoken detractors hang out there. Why put up with the abuse when all you want is some fresh coffee?

It's the Bell Schedule, Stupid

Rocketship's talent at reinventing itself is why I'm guessing that Rocketship will pull through a tough year, endure the criticism of being an over-sold golden child, and once again start killing it in San Jose. The same, I predict, will happen in Milwaukee and the startups in Nashville, DC, and Indianapolis. And I'm also assuming that Rocketship will successfully get through what I see as perhaps its biggest transition, entering African American neighborhoods. That will happen first in Nashville, followed by DC, and Milwaukee. That success broadening from Latino to African American students will grow out of Rocketship's baked-in ability to adapt quickly, part of its startup culture. Nobody learns like Rocketship, which is why its school leaders will adapt early and often as they enter neighborhoods new to them. The very reason Rocketship ran into trouble in 2013, a determination to avoid the innovator's dilemma, is the reason why they will create great schools in African American neighborhoods as well.

And finally, despite the trauma that played out as Danner left and Smith took the reins, I would argue that Smith is the right leader for the next phase. Smith gets something that scores of advocates of blended learning, online learning—all flavors of digital learning—don't always get: it's all about the bell schedule. Just as James Carville whipped his campaign troops with the mantra, "The economy, stupid," educational entrepreneurs need to keep chanting, "The bell schedule, stupid." Anyone designing schools knows the bell schedule, wrapped around great teaching talent, determines everything. It's how you spend precious student time: what they are taught for how long and by whom. Only educators know how to build a bell schedule, which means that educators, not startup guys, will determine if the shiny digital goods delivered by the startup guys, ranging from adaptive learning to learning by gaming, will get expertly wrapped into a bell schedule that works for students.

Silicon Valley can't save public education. But someone infused with a startup mentality and who is rooted in the education world can pick and choose the best of Silicon Valley and wrap it into an effective bell schedule. That pretty much describes Preston Smith. And nobody knows how to build bell schedules like Smith. Rocketship is likely to be the first charter to evolve the most effective use of blended learning. In 2013 when Rocketship principals embarked on a drastic revamping of how students engage with online learning, that wasn't a criticism of blended learning; it was bell schedule planning.

Will Rocketship make its new goal of educating twenty-five thousand students by 2017? Despite the setbacks of 2013, I wouldn't bet against them. Does it matter if Rocketship comes up short? Not when Aspire, Uncommon Schools, IDEA, KIPP, and others are expanding at ever-faster rates. Rocketship doesn't have to go it alone. And as we will see in the next three chapters, the best charter groups in the nation are moving in the direction of less confrontation, thus enabling charter-district collaboration. "We've grown up," said Dacia Toll, the co-CEO of Achievement First. The swagger that top charters had several years ago when they could create one or two schools with soaring test scores has mostly disappeared. The explanation from Toll: "We (Achievement First) faced serious challenges of our own, and it was humbling. Trying to maintain that success record while growing was much harder than anticipated. We hit our tough spot at about twelve schools"—about the same growth period when Rocketship experienced its setback year. "We've learned from it and our performance has improved. But we certainly now appreciate how hard this work is, especially at scale."

The 2012–2013 school year will probably be remembered as the year Rocketship lost its swagger and gained its long-term legs.

FIBONACCI CHARTERS
SUMMONED TO MEMPHIS

September 2013: Memphis, Tennessee

The decade-long squabble between charter schools and traditional schools is well rehearsed. When newspaper reporters write about top charters outperforming side-by-side traditional schools, charter critics cite the usual complaints: charter schools do better only because they select their students and serve fewer special education students. All those criticisms have merit. At Rocketship, parents do have to sign up and agree to thirty volunteer hours per year at the school and their schools do serve fewer special education students. To me, however, those differences never explain away the wide scoring gap differences. At Rocketship, for example, I found just as many parents who chose their school for child-care reasons (longer school day) rather than academic excellence. And I watched the careful individualized instruction that steers many young Rocketeers away from needing special education, thus making their school's special education rate appear lower. Still, the criticism has enough merit to produce a political stalemate. But try to imagine a scenario in which high-performing charter schools take over entire failing schools, every single student, with no parent applications required. Plus, the charters sweep up all the special education students who were there the year before.

Actually, that's not hard to imagine: welcome to Memphis.

Those who think New Orleans was the nation's great experiment in charter schools taking over a school district are only partially right. Hurricane Katrina created conditions unlikely to play out in any other city. In New Orleans, everything got turned inside out. Here in Memphis, by contrast, nothing gets turned upside down, at least on the surface. This is a far better test of the potential of high-performing charters. The newly formed Achievement School District, supported by grants from the federal Race to the Top program, focuses exclusively on the state's lowest-performing schools, those in the bottom 5 percent. That adds up to eighty-five schools; sixty-eight of which are here in Memphis. The goal: within five years, push those failing schools up into the top 25 percent, using schools run by local charters, national charters, or newly created schools that soon will morph into their own charter brand.

Sounds fantastical, right? It may well be. Who makes those kinds of gains with long-failing schools? But if anyone can make it happen it would be Chris Barbic, founder of the successful YES Prep charter schools in Houston. Barbic, who was a roommate with KIPP founders Dave Levin and Mike Feinberg while training to become Teach For America teachers, is one of the best-known charter operators in the country. Think of Barbic as the president of a club that consists of others who founded top charters. When Barbic puts the arm on his fellow buddies to bring their high-performing charters to Memphis, they come. Who could turn down Chris Barbic? That dynamic explains the gathering of the charter eagles. Already, KIPP operates schools here and plans to expand. Aspire Public Schools just opened a school with nine more to come. Green Dot is on the way. Barbic's own YES Prep arrives in 2015 and Rocketship is cleared to open eight schools here. Nobody else could convince those top charters to gather in one spot. And nobody else could convince some of those charters to suspend many of their practices, such as "opt in" where parents have to agree to send their kids. Of course there's a small quid pro quo to encourage those suspensions: if you act like an ordinary school and take over a failing school with no strings attached—serving every student in the attendance zone—you get an entire building, rent free. That's enough to make any charter operator salivate (and if not, really question itself). Almost overnight, Memphis becomes the Silicon Valley of school reform. Who could have called that?

As we sit across from one another at the Bar-B-Q Shop dining on ribs, pulled pork, and BBQ spaghetti (yes, there is a such a thing, and definitely worth a try), Barbic, tall and bald with a face framed by wire-rimmed glasses, acknowledges the outsized ambitiousness of his endeavor. "The hypothesis is this: if we hire great educators and give them the freedom, power, and resources to do whatever it takes for kids—the hallmarks of proven charter schools—our kids, no matter where they're from, will achieve at incredibly high levels." Judging whether the ambitious undertaking is successful is a year or two out in the future. But it's not too early to judge whether the pieces are coming together. They are. Not only are the nation's top charters jumping into Memphis but some very promising locally created charters are part of the grand experiment. High-performing local charters such as Gestalt Community Schools founded by Derwin Sisnett appear likely to help the Achievement School District evade the missteps in New Orleans, where the out-of-town charters hired mostly white teachers from out-of-town selective colleges. Most of those new teachers were talented and driven, quick to work the longer hours and able to fold quickly into the exacting charter instruction models. But in the end there was no getting around the fact there were a lot of young, white out-of-towners teaching in classrooms filled with all-black students. To those accustomed to seeing mostly black teachers in their schools, that made the charter schools look like destroyers of the black middle class in New Orleans. In Memphis, Barbic aims at keeping between 20 and 30 percent of the teachers who were there before.

Barbic is more than aware of the many pitfalls he faces. Although Barbic is too polite and politically savvy to lay out his challenge in real terms, I am constrained by neither. Memphis is a city of limited resources. This is not San Francisco, which is knee-deep in great colleges and glamorous places to live while commuting to San Jose or Oakland to teach in challenging schools. No problem attracting top talent there. And it's not just glamour that Memphis lacks. It's also short on colleges producing great teachers. Also short on any middle class neighborhoods that can share the educational burden. Also short on jobs that offer much hope to the adults who barely survive in the sprawling low-income black neighborhoods here. It is no accident that in 2011 the Memphis Public Schools raised the white flag by giving up their charter to be independent, an act driven by reasons of poor funding prospects and awful student performance, and forced themselves into the supposed shelter of Shelby County Schools, which includes the suburban districts. We give up, the district told Shelby County; take us in. Legally, Shelby County had no choice, but in 2013 the six suburban towns that made up the Shelby district voted to create their own districts, neatly separating themselves from the thousands of ill-educated black children sent their way. When the music finally stops, Memphis kids will be left with a school district that resembles the failing district it always was. Welcome to race politics Memphis style. The sole exception: Barbic's Achievement School District.

If Barbic succeeds, he will have succeeded in possibly the most difficult setting in the country. And he will have succeeded because his "club" of high-performing charters demonstrated what critics said they would never achieve: academic success the old-fashioned way, one neighborhood school after another, no strings attached. How will we know if Chris Barbic's hypothesis is on its way to being proven? I think we'll have a pretty good idea by the end of the 2013–2014 school year. My personal barometer will focus on the outcome at just one school within his network of troubled schools.

HANLEY ELEMENTARY SCHOOL

On November 5, 2012, Orange Mound residents got some really depressing news: Hanley Elementary faced a state takeover as one of the state's lowest-performing schools. The fact that Hanley appeared on the list of failing schools to be swept in the Achievement School District was embarrassing to many in the proud Orange Mound neighborhood of Memphis. Orange Mound is named after the Osage Orange hedges that lined the Deaderick Plantation that once sprawled through the area. In the late nineteenth century a developer carved out part of the planation to deliberately create a segregated black neighborhood: 982 shotgun houses that at the time sold for less than one hundred dollars each. Orange Mound became the nation's largest neighborhood of homes owned by African Americans. It was home to laborers as well as teachers, attorneys, and doctors. When African American entertainers came to Memphis, and were denied rooms in downtown hotels, Orange Mound is where they stayed. Families moving from the rural South to urban South often ended up in Orange Mound as their first stop. The alumni associations at the local high school maintain who's who lists of famous Orange Mound graduates. The 1980s and 1990s, however, were not kind to Orange Mound, as the crack epidemic drove out the families that had made the neighborhood an African American success story. But as crime moved to other neighborhoods, Orange Mound had a chance to repair itself.

The news about Hanley certainly came as a surprise to Teresena Wright, who sent her adopted niece, Emiley Ann Sutton, to Hanley. Wright and other parents had no idea students there were bottom performers—the principal had never told the parents. "Not only was hearing that a shock, it was hurtful. We were not aware that only one in ten students was proficient in reading. The parents were not aware of what was going on." After the announcement the Hanley principal did her best to convince the parents that students were actually doing better, but it was hard to spin the cold facts of state testing data. Worried about her niece, Wright stepped forward to become an activist, inviting the possible takeover candidates to appear before a meeting of parents at Hanley.

One of those takeover candidates invited to the meeting was Aspire Public Schools, the highly regarded group of California-based charter schools that had picked Memphis as its first school launch outside California. Aspire was a perfect fit. In California, Aspire earned its spurs with bold-and-risky moves avoided by other top charters, such as taking over existing schools with no opt-in requirements (more on that in the "Conclusion"). The Hanley principal, who considered Aspire as a special threat, forbade Aspire from presenting to the parents—a decision she made at 10 a.m. on the day of the meeting. That fiat came as a surprise to Allison Leslie, an Aspire veteran who a year before had moved from Oakland to Memphis to manage the first and follow-on schools in Memphis. Leslie had singled out Hanley as a good fit for Aspire and had flown in a mother and father who sent their children to Aspire schools in Los Angeles so they could talk to the Hanley parents. It took some pointed phone conversations, including a call to Barbic, to get Aspire in the door. Even then, the principal objected when the Aspire parents spoke up.

That was just the beginning of the resistance to an Aspire takeover. Soon, a billboard appeared in the neighborhood: No charters in Orange Mound. But Aspire was relentless, hiring Nick Manning, who grew up in an adjacent neighborhood but attended the Greater Hope Baptist Church in Orange Mound, as a community organizer. Manning, a former teacher and principal in Memphis, said that the process to win over the community started small and grew slowly. One small meeting after another. There were two key breakthroughs. The first came when Aspire decided to fly its biggest neighborhood critics, eight in total, to Oakland, to visit four Aspire schools there. After that trip to Oakland, where they saw low-income African American students achieving academic success unheard of in Orange Mound, the momentum swung to Aspire. "Those who went saw that we are who we say we are," said Leslie. The clinching swing in momentum came from a communitywide campaign to erect a fenced playground on Hanley's grounds. "Folks donated tools," said Manning. "We had University of Memphis athletes here. Lowe's had thirty people here and Lowe's donated a fence worth nearly $5,000. We scheduled for 250 volunteers to help out, and we ended up having to order fifty more lunches." Suddenly, Hanley was a community school, only run by Aspire.

On opening day, Aspire welcomed six hundred students—fifty more than had attended Hanley the previous year. Considering the resistance that could have arisen, the launch has gone smoothly. Aspire hired forty-two teachers, ten of whom taught there the previous year, which falls into the range Barbic hoped for. (Hanley is divided into two schools, with two principals. In one school, 66 percent of the teachers are minorities; in the other, 43 percent.) The school has that distinctive Aspire feel to it. Among the high-performing charters, Aspire has a reputation for being the least traditionally strict of the bunch. Yes, students wear uniforms, but nobody gets upset if students don't tuck in their shirts. In most "no excuses" charters, that would be a cause for a hall stop. Yes, Aspire students are taught to carry out quiet and orderly hallway transitions, but they don't take it to extremes. Students don't have to puff out their cheeks (a technique used by many charters to prevent talking) or walk with their hands either behind their backs or cupped in front. There are no student-teacher formal introductions at the door, another "no excuses" tradition in which each incoming student steps off a line to make eye conduct with the teacher while shaking hands and getting a welcome. School hours are a little longer, forty-five minutes longer than the old Hanley, but students get dismissed at 3:30 p.m., not the 5:30 you see at many charters. Aspire doesn't mandate that teachers do home visits; that's done on a need-only basis. Hanley feels comfortable, relaxed, homey, which is the way Leslie likes it. "There is structure here, but students also have a voice and students feel cared for and loved and have this really good relationship with their teachers." Summing up the Aspire philosophy, Leslie added, "Kids work hard for you if they like you."

But "like" only goes so far. So if Aspire falls short on the tough-love, no-excuses scale, how exactly does it get its gains? Data is their expertise. Aspire knows exactly which students need which skill rehearsed at which time. So their secret becomes a two-stop dance: first the data, then the differentiated teaching. Sounds simple, but it isn't. Getting really good at this is what makes Aspire a Fibonacci school. Everything you need to know about Aspire is revealed in its July 2013 launch of Schoolzilla, a highly unusual spinoff in which Aspire made its data system available as a startup business. Aspire got so good at tracking individual students—Want to know which students miss schools on which days of the week and how to intervene? Want to know which student needs what kind of phonics intervention and when?—that it made its system available to all schools.

Impressive, but none of that means that Aspire will succeed here. We'll know soon enough. Although the Achievement School District has asked for 8 percent gains in the first year, Aspire has doubled the goal: 16 percent gains in math and reading. By the end of the school year, Aspire expects to see 38 percent of its students proficient in math and 28 percent in reading. So there's the barometer for the entire Memphis experiment, at least from my perspective. If Aspire makes that ambitious goal, the other incoming charters will achieve roughly the same and Barbic's grand experiment is likely to succeed. If Aspire falls far short of that—especially if Hanley falls short of the 8 percent goal—then the Achievement School District faces political challenges. In this arena, short-term success means everything. Without it, the opposing forces will eat your lunch.

It's clear that history will be made here in Memphis. "Chris was definitely a factor in our decision to come here," said Leslie. "But I think what is happening in Memphis right now is bigger than all of us. We are taking a citywide approach to this work, which is very different from what you see nationally."

HOUSTON'S SPRING BRANCH SCHOOLS
The Future?

September 2013: Houston, Texas

You can find pieces of what the future looks like in New Orleans; Washington, DC; Memphis; or Denver. Or, you can come to Spring Branch Independent School District and see all the pieces of the likely future already lined up and starting to work together. On the surface, this is an odd place for breaking new ground on melding Fibonacci charter schools with a traditional school district. Who has even heard of Spring Branch? It's an odd duck of a place, a "district," not even a city, tucked into the Houston sprawl, known primarily for attracting Hispanics and Koreans. But its school district is independent and its size, about thirty-five thousand students, including many high-income whites and low-income Hispanics, makes Spring Branch an ideal proving ground; it's about the same size as hundreds of other school districts and facing similar demographic challenges.

What makes Spring Branch unique is its superintendent, Duncan Klussmann, who several years ago did something traditional school superintendents rarely do; he visited a nearby high-performing charter school, YES Prep. He met with YES Prep founder Chris Barbic, toured a school, and liked what he saw. "I was really impressed with the culture, the environment, the interaction with the kids. As I tell people, I often gauge things by whether my own three kids are missing out on something by not being part of a really good program." About a year later, Klussmann accepted an offer to visit a KIPP school. Again, he liked what he saw. Those two visits launched a series of discussions about how Klussmann could fold both charter school groups into his system. That may sound like a logical response, but it's an action you rarely see other superintendents taking.

Klussmann wasn't just looking for great charter schools; the district already started two successful charters. He was looking for something unique, a way to marry KIPP and YES Prep with his own schools while preserving the best of what neighborhood schools are all about, giving Spring Branch students a neighborhood-connected education offering everything from sports to challenging academics. The most interesting part of the district's plan, called the SKY Partnership (named for the first letters of Spring Branch, KIPP, and Yes Prep), is its goal, a single metric by which all Spring Branch educators would be guided. The idea of a single metric arose from Continental Airline's long-ago successful campaign to upgrade its image as a second-class airline. Continental settled on a single metric: on-time departures. It worked. Klussmann chose his single, Continental-like metric carefully: double the number of Spring Branch students who successfully complete some form of higher education—a technical certificate, a two-year degree, or four-year degree. Klussmann wants to achieve that goal, pushing it from 36 percent to 72 percent, in five years. Notice what's not part of the goal: pushing up test scores or getting more Spring Branch students admitted into college. What's the point of higher tests scores if they don't lead to college success? And make that true college success—not just admittance, but graduation.

What Klussmann and YES Prep and KIPP settled on is a unique merger between the charters and two Spring Branch middle schools, Landrum and Northbrook, with the charters operating independently out of both schools. Eventually, as the charters add more grades YES Prep will open a high school to be housed within Northbrook High. On the surface, this sounds like the forced sharing in New York City where former schools chancellor Joel Klein lured top charters into the city with $1-a-year leases. Klein's strategy worked beautifully in achieving its goal—high-performing charter schools poured into the city's poorest neighborhoods. But it also led to have–have not resentments, with some teachers and parents at the traditional schools left feeling like second-class citizens, especially when school report cards came out trumpeting the higher test scores turned in by the charter students.

That's not how it feels at Spring Branch, however, where Klussmann and the building principals worked hard to design cooperative leadership teams willing to learn from one another. When I visited Landrum Middle

School both principals, KIPP Courage principal Eric Schmidt and Landrum principal Luis Pratts, seemed joined at the hip. They spoke to me together, conducted a tour together, educated similar students in similar ways and appeared to be producing similar results. No surprise; Pratts graduated from the five-week KIPP school leadership program. "I was able to get KIPPnotized. I learned their lingo, their culture, and how they did their data mining." It was a new experience for Pratts; many of the speakers at the KIPP program were business leaders, not educators. "And we spent a whole week on culture development, which is a lot of KIPP's strength." No wonder the two schools look the same during the tour. It's almost impossible to tell the KIPP half from the Landrum half.

More interesting is Northbrook, which got a later start on the melding. At this school the two sides seem father apart, thus offering more insights into the learning process. Northbrook principal Valerie Johnson was eager to start on the experiment; she wasn't getting YES Prep–type results from her students. What's the secret she could borrow from YES Prep to push her proficiency rates far above the 50 percent level she was experiencing? "I love this community, and the teachers here work hard," said Johnson, "but we weren't being successful. If there's something [in the charter collaboration] that can make a difference, who am I to say we shouldn't try it?"

Johnson isn't pretending the experiment has been bump free; the school lost eighteen staffers the summer before the merger. "People were worried, asking 'What does this mean for me?'" The teachers who left were a mix of ages, she says. What many had in common were years of making long commutes to work at the school. "Those commutes had always been a pain to them, and they decided now was the time to make a break." Johnson immediately changed her hiring practices, bringing in five Teach For America teachers. Before, she had never hired a TFAer, but when touring KIPP and YES Prep schools to prepare for the partnership, she saw how many TFA teachers they used. So far, she's happy with the new hires. "My impression is they are driven people. Teaching is like a social cause for them."

Johnson also changed her thinking about the most experienced teachers always being the best teachers. Experience matters, she told me, especially when it comes to classroom management. But having an open mind about trying new techniques and not accepting poverty as an excuse matters a lot, she says, and those don't necessarily correlate to time spent in the classroom. "It's always easier to blame kids than to hold up a mirror."

On her side of the school the biggest change has been a new emphasis on school and class culture. In high-performing charters, the first week of school is usually devoted to culture, including the small stuff such as how to transition from class to class efficiently. Now, Northbrook does the same. Johnson knows that she has to imitate the urgency she saw in YES Prep schools, but that has proven to be tricky. After a year sharing the building with YES Prep the district reading scores were released, revealing that YES Prep Northbrook students scored thirty points higher in reading than regular Northbrook students. Johnson doesn't blame it on demographics. Their student bodies are identical, she says.

What made the difference, says Johnson, was a reading program that YES Prep was using, a program that Northbrook students started using the next year. But YES Prep Northbrook principal Cendie Stanford, a former assistant principal in the Spring Branch system, said (when interviewed separately) that she doubted the curriculum was the major player in the reading score gap. The real difference: urgency. Earlier in that school year it became clear that the YES Prep students at Northbrook were not making as much progress in reading as students on other YES Prep campuses. That set off internal alarms, which triggered intensive coaching for the language arts teachers, as much as three hours a week. That coaching, aimed at how to teach the specific skills that her YES Prep students were lacking, explains the scoring difference, says Stanford, not the curriculum. I'm betting that eventually Johnson rearranges her testing schedule and budget so that Northbrook sixth-graders get the same early scans followed by tightly targeted teacher coaching. But if Johnson and Stanford weren't in the same building, that lesson would never get absorbed.

The Spring Branch compact with the two charters goes beyond the two middle schools and soon-to-be formed YES Prep high school. Klussmann hired veteran KIPP leader Elliott Witney as director of strategic initiatives and innovation, a long title that involves figuring out how to infuse KIPP and Yes Prep charter DNA into a traditional school district. How else could Klussmann possibly expect to double the college graduation rate in only five years? That would take more than two invigorated middle schools and a new high school option. Witney came on board in

2012 and to date he hasn't encountered any major obstacles. "There are few things I could do as a KIPP leader that I can't do as a Spring Branch leader," said Witney. (One significant difference: firing low-performing teachers was far easier at KIPP.) Witney agrees that's not how charter leaders see traditional districts. They assume confines ranging from union contracts to mid-level school leaders resistant to change who would block meaningful reforms. Witney himself was surprised to discover otherwise. About the only thing he can't do is schedule a mid-summer teacher training exercise, a staple among the high-performing charters. But that can be made up with on-the-job professional development, says Witney.

The advantages that a traditional public school has are striking, says Witney, especially when it comes to school facilities. "We had a bond that passed in 2007 that allows the system to fund thirteen new schools and equip all our classrooms with technology all over the system." Charter leaders can only look at something like that and drool. Another advantage is being able to boost quality within the traditional neighborhood school system. No more open-enrollment-across-the-district charter policies that force parents to drive their students out of their neighborhood to find good schools, resulting in charter schools filled by students from multiple zip codes. "I think it's valuable to have kids connected to the community. Schools are an integral part of what creates connectedness. Pride keeps kids in school. In the charter world it's pragmatically hard to create a robust school life when kids are getting bused from all over the place. It's hard to stay for a football game."

What Spring Branch gets from its charter partners is how to translate culture and urgency into actual school policies. "We have started to take the KIPP school leadership program and infuse it into our system. We identify talent early and develop that talent so down the road we will have strong leadership at every level." And not just leadership within Spring Branch. "This system could easily produce six to ten superintendents in the next five years." What KIPP and YES Prep get from Spring Branch is a chance to reach thousands more students who were struggling in traditional schools. That was the goal of Rocketship, reaching one million students by the year 2030. Should SKY-like partnerships multiply, all the high-performing charters have a vehicle that could make those dreams come true.

I asked Witney what surprised him most about the switch. He laughed and answered, "When I tell people that I moved from KIPP to a traditional system, people from traditional systems listen to me more than they ever did before. Because now I'm one of them. Now, when we get into debates and they say charters do this and that, I say no they don't, or maybe the bad ones do, but let's talk about what's possible for you and your school."

To research this book I spent a year-and-a-half visiting schools around the country. My gut instinct from those travels: keep an eye on Spring Branch; this design has legs.

WHERE'S THE TIPPING POINT?

September 2013: Denver, Colorado

When I asked Don Shalvey, the cofounder of Aspire Public Schools and one of the wise men of the high-performing charter school movement, where I should visit to see the future of charter schools he pointed to Denver. While there I saw what Shalvey and the rest of his team from the Gates Foundation wanted me to see. Clearly, the compact between Denver Public Schools and local high-performing charters such as STRIVE Preparatory Schools and DSST Public Schools (Denver School of Science and Technology) is not only one of the nation's most compelling collaborations but also one with the most measurable outcomes.

The Denver compact, inked in 2010, is considered a model for other cities. The goal is to meld the charters and Denver schools. Not only would there be more sharing—Denver charters would get access to DPS facilities and charter schools would take on more special education students—but also more collaborating, such as using a unified school enrollment system for charters and district schools. On the date I visited, all sides appeared to be happy with the compact. Since 2010, DPS had opened twenty-one new charter schools, most of them scoring well on the Denver School Performance Framework. Three of Denver's highest-performing schools—DSST, STRIVE, and KIPP—had opened a combined eleven new schools, with a combined enrollment growing from 2,343 in 2010 to 6,100 in 2014. The unified enrollment system was working, and centers for highest-need special education students had opened in several charter schools.

Also striking was the shared program at Cole Middle School, with DSST occupying part of the building with a program that starts with sixth-graders and will build into a high school. Cole's history has been troubled enough to draw national attention. "Cole has tried every turnaround strategy there is," conceded principal Julie Murgel. Her school, now renamed Cole Arts & Science Academy, endured several reform efforts, then got shuttered by the state, and then got reopened as a KIPP school. But after two years, KIPP walked away—a rare defeat for KIPP—declaring they couldn't find the right principal to make it work. At Cole today, the energy seemed very positive, with DSST and Cole sharing lessons learned (as seen in Houston's Spring Branch School). Plus, some Cole students get the chance to enroll in DSST without going through the lottery. Considering the agonizing history here at Cole, that's like winning the lottery.

And yet, what struck me about the Denver compact were not those success stories but rather its long-shot effort, the attempt to improve traditional Denver public schools with peer-to-peer meetings between teachers and school leaders of charters and regular schools. It's called Compact Blue, and I arrived on a day when teachers and principals met for the first time at a charter school to observe one another during a professional development day. After watching Compact Blue for a morning and interviewing several educators from both sides of the fence I found myself asking, where's the tipping point? Where in that relationship is the point where the struggling school actually improves by adopting a few, many, or all of the practices that proved to be winners at the successful charters. Where is that line? Half? Three-quarters? Never?

STRIVE PREP-WESTWOOD

I get lucky when entering a classroom and right away meet two teachers who are perfect for telling the Compact Blue story, Kristie Burke, a seventh-grade reading teacher at STRIVE, and Kerrie McCormick, a sixth-grade language arts teacher at Henry World School, a district-run school. The schools are located in the same area of Denver, about a twelve-minute drive apart. Henry's immediate neighborhood is higher income than the neighborhood around Westwood, but looking at the student population, the two schools pretty much look alike: 90 percent or above low-income minority students, mostly Latinos. Beyond that, however, the schools might as well be Venus and Mars. STRIVE Westwood was a Blue Distinguished school in 2010 and 2011 (Colorado color codes its school by achievement levels). In 2010 it ranked first in the state for academic growth. In 2012 and 2013 it was ranked green: meets expectations. When I visited, the school had a waiting list of 150 students. Henry, by contrast, bounces between the lower-level colors, but currently is rated orange—just one color away from the dreaded red. Waiting lists are not an issue for Henry.

When I came across the two teachers, they were sitting together going over the just-received test score data broken down by the Illuminate data system used at STRIVE. McCormick watched in amazement as Burke downloaded a rich profile of where her students were either succeeding or faltering. "This is our second year with this software and it's been truly helpful," said Burke. "I can not only see if my students have passed or failed, I can see specifics and break them down into what standards they are mastering, where they need more help. We break it down further into reading and writing standards, fiction and nonfiction. So it really helps me focus and direct where my next six weeks of instruction will be. Looking at this data I see that my students nailed poetry but really struggled with nonfiction."

This was McCormick's first exposure to true data-driven instruction, a staple at the high-performing charters. It was dizzying to watch. At Henry, teachers get student data at the beginning, middle, and end of the school year. Even then, it's not fresh (Burke was seeing days-old data results). "To be able to go into the computer and see my students by skill level, all neatly lined up with bar and pie graphs—that would be so valuable." In theory, McCormick could do that herself, but it would take days. "Because of the time I have to spend on planning and grading, that's unrealistic."

In the next session McCormick was equally amazed as she watched a dozen STRIVE teachers sitting in a circle with laptops tuned into the same software, so the entire group followed together with constantly refreshed inputs as they discussed individual students. For the moment, forget about the fancy data sharing. What was striking to McCormick and the other Henry teachers were two things they never experience at Henry. First, the group leader for STRIVE declared at the beginning that only instruction-related comments were to be spoken about individual students. Not a word about behavior or hardships from their personal life. And if the student was struggling, the conversation has to focus on solutions. What had one teacher experienced with this student that would help the others? At Henry, discussions of individuals often started and ended with concerns about behavior problems. The second walkaway lesson from the Henry staff was that as many as a dozen STRIVE teachers knew an individual student. At Henry, far fewer teachers knew the same student.

Also present that day as observers were Henry's school leaders, principal Dackri Davis and assistant principal Yamile Reina-Ayadi. Not all Denver schools wanted anything to do with charter schools. It's so unfair to compare, say traditional educators. Parents have to apply to STRIVE; there are waiting lists at all their schools. Denver schools have to take any kid who walks in the door, regardless of how their parents value education or don't. But for the most part, Davis and Reina-Ayadi appear to have put those resentments on hold. Here was a school, STRIVE Westwood, educating the same kinds of kids in roughly the same neighborhood and coming out blue and green, while Henry struggled between yellow and orange. What was STRIVE doing that Henry could learn from?

The answer the principals came away with that day was the same answer McCormick came up with in the first few minutes: data-driven instruction. "We're trying to get there," said Reina-Ayadi. But listening to the two discuss the individual pieces required to "get there," including the fact that STRIVE teachers wrote their own tests, enjoyed a near-immediate turnaround, and had an exacting system for laying out results by students, complete with graphs and bars, it didn't sound like Henry was on the cusp. At the end of that professional development day, STRIVE teachers left with a military-like plan for what they needed to do with each class, each student, to win more academic gains. At Henry, there is no such plan.

More challenges arose in follow-up phone calls with Burke and McCormick. Even if Henry were able to achieve STRIVE's quick-turnaround testing, would that do any good if the school culture suffered? Any visitor to a high-performing charter knows that a school's success rises or sinks on establishing a culture. That means the first week of school is spent on seemingly odd issues such as how to walk from class to class imitating a blowfish—checks puffed out so talking is not possible—and hands neatly folded. Culture means learning how to talk about others only in positive ways, how to lock eyeballs on the student answering a question. It means hundreds of other nitpicky things you can't even imagine until you read *Teach Like a Champion*. STRIVE has it; Henry doesn't. McCormick understands the importance of establishing classroom culture; she devotes the first week of school to establishing the right culture in her classroom.

But her district leaders place the emphasis on fast instructional pacing, allowing little time for culture building. If there's no shared culture building there's no shared schoolwide culture, which limits the impact of what McCormick does in her class.

So where's the tipping point with Henry? The schools have another four days of "structured" meetings, but based on my observations it would be a stretch to assume that Henry will start looking like STRIVE as a result of these peer-to-peer meetings. But I could be wrong, which makes Compact Blue intriguing. What if the tipping point turns out to be lower than I assume it to be?

THE TENNESSEE LAUNCH

January 2014: Nashville, Tennessee

Rocketship breaks ground on a new school in the Dickerson Pike corridor in North Nashville. The school will have capacity for more than six hundred students and is one of eight elementary schools Rocketship hopes to open here. The school, which will open in the 2014–2015 school year, will be the first Rocketship school to serve a predominantly African American student population. Rocketship also has plans to open schools in Memphis.

CONCLUSION

Anyone who thinks urban schools haven't changed much as a result of high-performing charter schools spreading their influence needs to look again. Let's start with my hometown, Washington, DC. Five years ago you could sift through a month's worth of *Washington Posts* and find almost no reporting about charter schools. It was all about Michelle Rhee and the District of Columbia Public Schools. Pick up a copy of the *Post* today and you'll see stories speculating about whether DC schools can stand up to the competition from the fast-improving, fast-expanding charter schools. And you will see stories about DC political leaders offering up closed school buildings to charters. Before, those offers just didn't happen. This is a direct result of parents voting with their feet, moving quickly to charter schools, which now educate 44 percent of the city's students, growing faster than the traditional district. When that happens, attitudes among political leaders, those with the power to offer up facilities, change. At that point, they are talking about schools where their nieces and nephews attend. Or their own children.

Suddenly, DC chancellor Kaya Henderson is talking like a charter leader, proposing to send her teachers out for home visits, a strategy used by most top charter schools. She wants to form a compact with the high-performing Achievement Prep Public Charter School in the city's impoverished Eighth Ward. Henderson wants it all, including chartering authority of her own. "I sit here at this table and people tell me that charters are eating my lunch," said Henderson as she testified before the DC Council, referring to the greater freedom nonunionized charters have. "Why can't I have the authority to do that too?"[1]

And when looking around the country at cities experiencing major education changes driven by high-performing charters, DC would barely make a top-ten list. If you want to see revolutionary changes taking place, look at Memphis, New Orleans, or my personal favorite as a prototype for change, Spring Branch, Texas. If I had to pick a sleeper city where within a decade charter schools will become major players in the local education scene I'd pick San Antonio. Only a few years ago, the top-performing charters were limited to the "name" national charter groups such as KIPP. Not anymore. In Denver, STRIVE Preparatory Schools and Denver Science and Technology Public Schools are as good as anything you will find on the national scene. At some point, they may head national. Ever heard of Uplift Education? In the 2013–2014 school year they were educating 9,700 students in twenty-eight schools in the Dallas–Fort Worth area. Ever heard of Brooke Charter Schools in Massachusetts? Their three K–8 schools now serving 1,100 students will quickly grow to 1,500 students. Their all-minority, almost all-poor students turn in state test scores that are often comparable to suburban schools. They want to add a fourth K–8 school and a high school to accept all their middle schoolers. The only thing that's holding them back is a state cap on charter school students.

The keys behind this quickening are threefold. The first two are good charters learning how to learn from one another and former TFAers looking for new opportunities. That describes Brooke: cofounder Jon Clark was a TFA teacher in New Orleans who then taught at Boston Collegiate, a top charter in Boston. When launching Brooke he and the founding team were able to draw on lessons learned from Boston's Roxbury Prep, one of the earliest high-performing charter schools in the country. When he wanted to learn the best back-office operations in the nation he went to Chicago's Noble Network of Charter Schools. When he wanted to see how the best writing program in the country worked he visited Achievement First schools. "We steal from one another," said Clark, "realizing that's how people get better."

The third leg behind this quickening is school choice. I'm not talking about vouchers, which have proven to be an unhelpful distraction in the school reform movement. If a reform doesn't generate great schools then what's the point? I'm talking about really simple choice: the choice to attend another public school, including a public charter school. That's all it takes. Once you have that choice, and you mix some great schools into the mix, as we've seen in Washington, DC, positive change starts happening quickly. Once granted school choice, parents will not easily give it up. And once unions, superintendents, and school boards lose the power to force parents to send their children to zoned schools, regardless of quality, the game is over. Maybe not right away; there are lots of ways to fight back and delay. But eventually, a new game begins.

But wait, aren't charters currently losing a "pushback" war waged against them? True, the anti-school-reform movement has considerable momentum. In New York, there's support for Mayor Bill de Blasio's call to force at least some charters colocated in traditional public schools to start paying rent.[2] He even called out Eva Moskowitz by name, whose Success Academy charters committed the ultimate political sin of acing the new, tough New York tests based on Common Core standards and thus making other schools look bad. In San Jose, the pushback against Rocketship schools is gaining strength. The Stop Rocketship Now! website has become one-stop-shopping for any teachers union, superintendent, or school board anywhere in the country looking for ways to stop Rocketship. School-reform critic Diane Ravitch sells thousands of books and commands huge audiences, and school reformers are limited to earnest op-ed pages. Ravitch has directly attacked Rocketship. From her blog: "The Rocketship charter chain is known for replacing teachers with computers, relying on Teach For America to cut costs and eliminating the arts to have more time for test prep. The chain is backed by the rich and powerful California corporate charter industry and is opening more test prep charters across the country." All true; the pushback has momentum. But again, parents will not easily give up a newly granted right to shop around for schools. Eventually that shop around—if combined with a mix of other reforms such as clear standards, accurate outcome data for parents, a means for closing low-performing schools, and replicating high-performing schools—leads to better schooling options. In places such as Milwaukee, where reformers tried to rely solely on school choice, that process may take twenty years. In Memphis, where better schools got folded into the mix, I'm guessing we'll see real gains in twenty months.

The driver is school choice. Given the choice of a school that's clearly a better performer, will parents from the cluster of Milwaukee elementary schools that surround Southside Prep, the new Rocketship school, move their children for academic reasons? Already, enough of those parents chose Rocketship to put three hundred children into Southside Prep by the end of its first week. If Rocketship's experience in San Jose is a predictor of what will happen in Milwaukee and beyond, by year two Southside Prep will be full and by year three it will have a sizable waiting list. That assumes

Southside Prep turns out student achievement results that are clearly better than the neighboring schools (a safe bet, based on the low test scores at those schools). Parents don't move their children from schools that are doing right by their kids.

My hunch is parents will make that move, and I'm not the only one predicting this outcome. There's a reason why anti-Rocketship posters got plastered on streetlight posts and bridge overpasses—a campaign overseen by a member of the Milwaukee school board and fleshed out with Milwaukee teachers. Everyone connected with traditional Milwaukee Public Schools, from the union to the school board, senses what is likely to play out there in the coming years. They see Rocketship "taking" their students, which is an odd way of viewing it. Whose students are they?

That draining of those neighboring Milwaukee public schools doesn't have to happen. Again, parents don't move their kids from schools that meet their needs. Change is risky, especially when it comes to your child's school. Parents only take that chance when they conclude their child's future is compromised. That's a high threshold. But if the movement out of traditional neighborhood schools and into Rocketship-like charters picks up momentum, an unexpected force kicks in—political leaders reconsidering their long-held positions on charter schools, as seen in the dramatic changes in Washington, DC. It happened in Boston as well. When political opposition fades and charter schools get facilities the question of whether great charter schools can "scale" becomes silly. Of course they can; look at New Orleans.

The political power of parental choice is one of six reasons why I predict the Fibonacci sequence will come true in the coming years as the top charter school operators, including Rocketship, learn to expand quickly.[3] Following are some other reasons.

Charters are pioneering blended learning.

Online learning matched to teacher-led instruction, the core of "blended learning," is coming your way. Actually, it has probably already arrived, regardless of the type of school your children attend. Just one small aspect of blended learning makes its expansion inevitable: blended learning returns learning authority to the students, who have an active role in guiding it. Blended learning gives kids "agency," a power to make choices.[4] Just the opposite of the much-criticized factory school model believed to have been reinforced by No Child Left Behind.

The blended learning movement has been greatly shaped by the best charters such as Rocketship, Summit Public Schools, KIPP, and Navigator Schools. Thanks to their pioneering work, almost any school can undertake blended learning. It has become a formula: you set aside one room in the school; buy thirty Chromebooks; license some mix of, let's say, ST Math, DreamBox, Achieve3000, or i-Ready; draw up a rotational model that gives each student forty-five minutes of online learning; and good things are likely to happen.

But that's just the beginning of the story. Those same charters now lead the way into version 2.0 of blended learning, in which educators use flexible models in combined classrooms with all the laptops in the classroom. No more isolated computer labs; everything is under the direction of the teacher. And the software they are pioneering this time isn't just adaptive learning. "We know DreamBox is effective with our kids," said Smith, "but we also know that it is not always tightly aligned with what our teachers are teaching at that moment of time." Blended learning pioneers such as Rocketship are now looking for the best "assignable" software. If a particular student is working on single-digit addition, teachers want to assign software to target that precise skill. Who's making learning software that's adaptable and assignable? That's the new Holy Grail of blended learning. The version 1.0 of blended learning works just fine; version 2.0 is likely to work a lot better. And my hunch is that, once again, the high-performing charters will chart that path for all schools.

Positive change generates more positive change.

In theory, if you set out to dramatically reduce the nation's achievement gap you have to tackle the system at every level. But that's not how the Pareto principle works. Instead, you look for the crucial 20 percent element that drives the 80 percent. To Danner, elementary schools should be the drivers. Build enough of them in one place you will essentially flood the system with "overqualified" elementary school graduates. When that flood reaches a third of any middle school's incoming student population, the middle school will be forced to change its academic expectations—for the better. And so on for high school.

All this sounds like wishful thinking, but in the San Jose area you can already see it happening. Rocketship graduates may not add up to anywhere near a third of any middle school in the county, but making up for that are the politically empowered Rocketship parents, low-income Latino parents taught how to lobby for better schools. That base of inspired Rocketship parents was a factor in the nationally acclaimed Summit Public Schools deciding to expand in San Jose rather than other spots in Silicon Valley. And a cadre of Rocketship parents was directly responsible for bringing Alpha Public (charter) Schools into San Jose.[5] Rocketship's success inspired other charters in the area. Gilroy Prep (Navigator Schools), which pulled together lessons learned from Rocketship and other high-performing schools, posted breath-taking test scores its first and second years, outdoing Rocketship.

The best disruptive innovations are coming from charters.

In 2011 I visited Doug Lemov's True North Troy Preparatory in Troy, New York. Every teacher I observed used a personalized version of Lemov's "taxonomy," which are teaching techniques Lemov documented while observing the best teachers at high-performing charter schools.

While at True North I spent most of the time in the classroom of Lauren Catlett, who was teaching fifth-grade writing. For seventy minutes I watched and took notes as Catlett went through her paces. It started with the "threshold" greeting (technique 41), a three-step process in which Catlett greets each incoming student individually with a firm handshake, then establishes eye contact, and then says "good morning." It ended with "exit tickets" (technique 20) in which students demonstrate whether they truly understood the lesson of the day.

Whatever Lemov and the True North teachers were doing there appeared to work with their students, who had a higher poverty rate (95 percent) than the nearby traditional schools. The year before every single sixth-grader scored at proficient or advanced in math; two-thirds scored that high in reading and writing skills.

The point of this story, however, is not about True North or Lemov. The point is that most of the teachers buying Lemov's book were not charter school teachers but rather traditional teachers hungry for techniques that would help them succeed with low-income minority students arriving in their classrooms with academic skills lagging well behind grade level. This is teacher-to-teacher change, the kind of change that matters.

Top charter CMOs are picking up their replication speed.

IDEA Public Schools was founded in Donna, Texas, in 1998, by two Teach For America corps members who started an afterschool program in the schools where they were working. Their first charter opened in a church basement there in 2000 and enrolled one hundred students. By 2006 they ran six schools serving about two thousand students in the Rio Grande Valley. The next goal was to open twenty schools by 2012, a goal they overshot by four schools. For the 2013–2014 school year, IDEA will have thirty schools, and the IDEA 2017 plan calls for fifty-six schools serving forty thousand students with campuses in the Rio Grande Valley, Austin, and San Antonio. In San Antonio, IDEA plans to add four campuses a year for the next four years. That growth rate, about 25 percent a year, has been achieved while keeping its "exemplary" state accountability rating, the highest level possible. The IDEA leaders say they are on track for the 2018 goal of producing 1,625 low-income college graduates, making IDEA the biggest single source of low-income graduates in the state. The long-term goal at IDEA is to become the nation's largest single source of low-income college graduates, a mark they hope to reach between 2040 and 2050.

Uncommon Schools, a charter organization I view as the best in the nation, started in 2005 with 570 students. By the 2013 school year, that grew to thirty-eight schools and close to ten thousand students. In 2014 that will grow to forty-two schools and twelve thousand students. Projected growth by 2018: forty-six schools and eighteen thousand students.

In New York City, the first Success Academy Charter School opened in Harlem in 2006 with 165 kindergartners and first-graders. By 2008 three more schools opened, serving one thousand students. Success Academies continued to replicate; by 2010 they enrolled 2,500 students. By 2012 there were fourteen Success Academies across New York, serving 4,600 students in grades K–7. Currently, Success operates eighteen elementary schools and four middle schools, with almost seven thousand students enrolled. In August 2014, Success will open its first high school in addition to six more elementary schools and three middle schools, bringing the total number of schools to thirty-two in Manhattan, the Bronx, Brooklyn, and Queens. The goal is to operate one hundred schools in New York by the end of the decade.

KIPP, the charter school group Danner thought would be limited in its ability to grow based on his experience getting a KIPP school started in Nashville, has proven to be the fastest growing of all the high-performing charters. In 2014, KIPP will educate fifty thousand students in 141 schools. Over recent years, KIPP has grown at a rate of fifteen schools a year. Current projection: in the 2015–2016 school year there will be about sixty-four thousand KIPPsters at 171 schools.

And at Aspire Public Schools, which similar to Rocketship is expanding outside of California (see "Fibonacci Charters Summoned to Memphis"), the five-year growth plan places them with forty-five schools serving 18,320 students in the 2017–2018 school year, up from thirty-seven schools in 2013. Aspire is an example of what many high-performing charter could do if they shed their risk-averse habits. You won't find Aspire sticking to the safe path of building schools grade by grade. Said chief executive officer James Wilcox, "If we did that it would be thirteen years before we sent kids to college. To us, that would be another lost generation."

Not only does Aspire swallow entire schools in Oakland and Los Angeles—and now Hanley in Memphis—most of their schools turn out to be success stories. In Oakland, Aspire took over a district school performing so poorly that nearly all the families had fled. Today, Berkley Maynard Academy is a bustling K–8 school with 580 students who turn in impressive test scores. In Los Angeles, the district handed Aspire a new building to be run as a traditional boundary school. Today, the K–6 Aspire Tate Academy has 950 students split into three schools. The risk taking doesn't seem to hurt Aspire's reputation: in 2013 Aspire was California's highest-performing district that serves low-income students.

Is this replication pacing fast enough to make a massive difference in reducing learning gaps? No. Most leaders of high-performing charter groups remain cautious with their expansion plans—far too cautious, from my perspective. Aspire is not the only high-performing charter group capable of taking over entire schools in Memphis. But there are other developments playing out that will enable all the high performers, not just the boldest of the bunch, to extend their reach.

Powerful forces are about to propel the growth of these charters.

For years, traditional school leaders have mostly ignored or fended off charter schools, including the high performers. But in cities such as

Denver and Memphis that's changing fast. The powerful force? Mayors, governors, and school leaders starting to shun the simplistic debate that has propelled charter critics such as Diane Ravitch to fame and instead settling on the more practical question: how do we offer great schools? That's a powerful force. In fall 2013, Spring Branch's Duncan Klussmann seemed like an outlier of a superintendent. What kind of school leader actually invites high-performing charters into their schools? But when I looked elsewhere in the country there was more movement than I imagined, and not just with the Gates Foundation compact cities. In San Francisco, where several years ago Rocketship got frozen out, KIPP just opened a high school colocated inside a traditional San Francisco high school, the first new charter approved by the district in years. The ribbon cutting in August 2013 turned into a who's who event that drew Facebook founder Mark Zuckerberg as a guest speaker. In the audience were San Francisco mayor Ed Lee and schools' superintendent Richard Carranza.

Nobody was more amazed at the political turnaround than KIPP CEO Richard Barth. If anyone had told him even a year and a half earlier that San Francisco Unified would allow KIPP into a district building on a six-to-one board vote—and then see both the mayor and schools' superintendent show up for the ribbon cutting—he never would have believed them. That dramatic mind-set shift in San Francisco, says Barth, is one that he sees spreading as more school and political leaders ignore the toxic education debates and ask that simple question: how do we offer great schools? That's what Spring Branch superintendent Duncan Klussmann found himself asking after visiting two high-performing charters: how can I import the great classroom culture and sense of urgency that I saw at YES Prep and KIPP? Klussmann's answer: invite them in. The moment that question gets asked by more school superintendents is the moment the Fibonacci scenario becomes real.

That scenario isn't inevitable. Top charter leaders will have to shed their nervousness about fast expansion. "Far too many CMOs are ridiculously timid when it comes to growth, compared to leading organizations in other industries," said charter expert Bryan Hassel from Public Impact. Hassel is right. Rocketship may have slowed down a bit in 2013, but their expansion plans make other top charter groups look like turtles. And more superintendents such as Klussmann will have to step forward and make bold decisions that favor students over bureaucracy. It's not inevitable, but it can happen. And it should happen.

Notes

1. Emma Brown, "Gray Officials Object to Major Elements of Catania's Education Plan," *Washington Post* (July 2, 2013).
2. The far less successful traditional schools colocated with Moskowitz's charters would continue to enjoy free rent.
3. My focus on charter schools as a manifestation of parental choice, rather than voucher schools, is not an oversight. I see little evidence that voucher programs create high-quality schools.
4. Heather Staker, "Give Students Back Their Agency," Clayton Christensen Institute blog (September 3, 2013).
5. In 2013 Alpha students scored an 828 on the California API. Alpha, which uses blended learning, is seeking approval to open a second school in 2014.

ACKNOWLEDGMENTS

I have to start with Rocketship founders John Danner and Preston Smith. Long ago when they agreed to allow me full access (with no editorial input) they could not have foreseen that 2013 would prove to be a challenging year for them. Most high-performing charter groups have years like that, from which valuable lessons are learned and applied successfully in follow-on years. I just happened to show up for their lessons-learned year. Building and replicating schools that succeed with students who for decades have been failed by traditional schools is not easy. There will be turbulence. Despite that, they never limited access or refused to discuss sensitive issues. That's to their credit. Kristoffer Haines, who oversees national expansion for Rocketship, was a steady and fair-minded guide for me as I ventured into Rocketship's expansion cities.

This kind of reporting, which required multiple trips to multiple cities, is not possible without supplemental funding. The first to contribute was the Eli and Edythe Broad Foundation, followed quickly by the Kauffman Foundation. Later, the Fisher Fund and a private contributor (my ninety-six-year-old father, Blanton Whitmire, who reads every word I write and offers great advice) helped out as well. As a result, I never had to trim back my reporting and never had to transcribe interviews. That meant everything. None of the funders asked for editorial oversight.

Publisher Jossey-Bass and agent Howard Yoon, both of whom saw me through the Michelle Rhee book, *The Bee Eater,* backed me again with *On the Rocketship.* The entire Jossey-Bass team, including my editor Kate Gagnon, knows how to make a book a better read. Transcribers Samuel Beck and Sasha Flamm did quality work at amazing speed. I know they got weary of hearing my voice. My wife, ABC News producer Robin Gradison, carefully read several versions, and our daughters, Morgan and Tyler, lent moral support, as they have with previous books. And a nod to Steven Brill, whose *Class Warfare*[1] inspired my datelined book organization.

Education technology–charter school experts Brian Greenberg and Bryan Hassel generously offered to evaluate my rough draft, which resulted in several improvements. Joe Williams from Democrats for Education Reform was another valuable advisor. Other important outside guidance came from charter school pioneer Don Shalvey, who encouraged me to observe the district-charter collaboration in Denver. Another highlight was sharing a great Memphis BBQ lunch with charter school legend Chris Barbic. Who knew that such a thing as barbeque spaghetti even existed?

NOTE

1. *Class Warfare: Inside the Fight to Fix America's School* (New York: Simon & Schuster, 2011).

ABOUT THE AUTHOR

Richard Whitmire, a veteran newspaper reporter and former editorial writer at *USA Today,* is the author of *The Bee Eater: Michelle Rhee Takes on the Nation's Worst School District.* He is also author of *Why Boys Fail: Saving Our Sons from an Education System That's Leaving Them Behind* and coauthor of *The Achievable Dream: College Board Lessons on Creating Great Schools.* Whitmire is a former president of the National Education Writers Association.

EPILOGUE

April 2014: Arlington, Virginia

A year ago, when Preston Smith first heard that test scores dipped (see "Rumor Just In: Rocketship Falls through the Ice") he vowed that if he couldn't turn things around he would resign. "I'm in this for Rocketship and the kids to be successful and, you know, if we're not doing it then I'm going to be out." It appears there will be no need for Smith to offer up his resignation. If 2013 was the lessons-learned school year, then 2014 became the solutions-applied year. Not only did Rocketship adopt common reading and math programs but also Smith started off the school year personally managing most of the Rocketship principals. The huge distraction of the year before—which grades do we combine?—fell away as the schools settled on combining only fourth and fifth grades. Rocketship teachers, says Smith, got a lot better at focusing on small-group instruction, which was one of the main points of the model change. All those improvements, says Smith—"and a return to focusing on instruction and our Rocketeers and families"—explain why internal testing shows the schools bouncing back from previous-year dips.

To monitor student progress, Rocketship uses the NWEA tests and then translates those scores into California API results, a test in which a high-poverty school scoring above 800 is considered a success. (Hitting 900 is considered newsworthy.) That way, Rocketship knows how Milwaukee students are doing compared to the California students. Rocketship Mateo Sheedy, the flagship school, may not make it back to the low 900s this year, but is on track to hit the high 800s, says Smith. Most of the other schools will be in the mid-800s, he predicts. And the just-opened school in San Jose, Spark Academy, is on track to come close to hitting 900. Rocketship Alma Academy could end up with scores as high as 890, says Smith. Not everything has gone smoothly with the principals, says Smith. Rocketship Mosaic experienced a mid-year principal turnover.

Rocketship is set to open its first school in Nashville in August 2014, with an African American population as high as 70 percent, which is a first for Rocketship. Unlike in Milwaukee, where Rocketship faced enrollment challenges, this school met its goals by early spring. A second Nashville school might follow shortly, possibly a "restart" school in which Rocketship would take over an existing school. A restart was debated in San Jose (see "Setting Up Rocketship to Fail?") but dropped. "I'd love to do it. We start multi-grade schools already," said Smith, referring to Rocketship's practice of launching schools with multiple grades, rather than adding one grade at a time, a hallmark of many charters.

At the beginning of the year, students at Rocketship's Milwaukee school, Southside Prep, tested well below any of the first-year launches in California, but students appear to be on a track to break 800, says Smith. It helped that the school opened underenrolled, giving teachers more opportunities to focus on getting students up to speed. Next year, the school should increase in size from 300 to 450, says Smith. The Rocketship board green lighted the second Milwaukee school, which is set to open in August 2015, in an African American neighborhood.

Two Rocketship schools could open in Texas in 2015, one in San Antonio, the other in Dallas (odds favor opening just one). In San Antonio, Rocketship has considerable foundation backing and some momentum. In Dallas, Rocketship has a startup school leader wanting to return to her hometown, the principal at Alma, Sharon Kim (see "How Many Sharon Kims Are out There?"). Although Rocketship got rejected by the state last year, Rocketship leadership seems more confident about their chances this year. This time, they know how to answer the question about whether Rocketship practices bilingual education. Rocketship has a full-time staffer on the ground in Texas, Jarrad Toussant, who until recently was working on school reform issues in Newark.

Officially, the Tamien school site in San Jose is not dead, but it has all the appearances of going nowhere. Said Smith, "At this point it would be incredibly challenging for us to place a school there." The irony of the Tamien site: those fighting a Rocketship school at Tamien insisted that what they really wanted was a middle school. Suddenly, that possibility arrived when San Jose Unified proposed placing Downtown College Prep, the oldest charter in the county, on the Washington Elementary site, which has more than enough space to accommodate the school. It looked like a go until the same faction at Washington that blocked Rocketship whipped up opposition to Downtown College Prep. The Washington teachers just weren't comfortable cohabitating with a charter school. In hindsight, the fight was more about charters than a middle school.

That anti-charter sentiment appears to be building in Santa Clara County, especially among superintendents unhappy with the county board approving Rocketship charters to be placed within their district. In March a judge ruled that the county board could not override local zoning to pave the way for schools. And another lawsuit, brought for several county school districts, seeks to rescind the approval of the twenty charters.

In a fight that became both bitter and highly publicized, Rocketship ended up withdrawing its application to open a school in the Morgan Hill School District. That fight, led by the Morgan Hill superintendent who said he had a better plan for dealing with the poor outcomes for the low-income Latino students there, appears to have further weakened the ability of the county board to act as a champion for charters. Add it all up, and it's obvious that Rocketship's plan to build out to become a sizable district of its own serving high-poverty students is going nowhere fast. At the same time, most of the districts opposing Rocketship have yet to create schools that dramatically improve the outcomes for those students. The stasis in Santa Clara County appears to be a clear lose-lose for those families.

In Memphis, Aspire appears to be on track for remaking Hanley Elementary into a successful school. At the beginning of the year, only 3 percent of the students read at grade level; by late February that rose to 25 percent. Aspire's Allison Leslie is sticking by her original goal there (which is double the gains expected by the Achievement School District): 38 percent proficient in math, 26 percent proficient in reading.

In November 2013, school-reform candidates swept the school board races in Denver, meaning rapid changes will continue there. In February, the Beyond Averages report from the Donnell-Kay Foundation concluded that improvements in Denver Public Schools were due mostly to the controversial practice of closing low-performing schools and opening new charter schools.

In Washington, DC, a Rocketship school will open in August 2015 in a unique partnership with AppleTree Early Learning, a well-established,

very successful charter group that runs preschools.[1] AppleTree will oversee
the preschool serving three- and four-year-olds; Rocketship will pick it up
in kindergarten. The school is in Ward 8, Washington's highest-poverty
ward. Rocketship plans to open eight schools in DC by 2019. The DC
school plans to open with 440 students (including the preschoolers) and
eventually expand to more than 700.

NOTE

1. I profile AppleTree in "The Achievable Dream: College Board Lessons
   on Creating Great Schools," with co-author Gaston Caperton,
   College Board, 2012.

INDEX